ERP Systems for Manufacturing Supply Chains

ERP Systems for Manufacturing Supply Chains

Applications, Configuration, and Performance

By Odd Jøran Sagegg and Erlend Alfnes

CRC Press
Taylor & Francis Group
Boca Raton London New York

CRC Press is an imprint of the
Taylor & Francis Group, an **informa** business

AN AUERBACH BOOK

CRC Press
Taylor & Francis Group
6000 Broken Sound Parkway NW, Suite 300
Boca Raton, FL 33487-2742

First issued in paperback 2022

ISBN 13: 978-1-03-247476-2 (pbk)
ISBN 13: 978-1-138-58744-1 (hbk)
ISBN 13: 978-1-00-301593-2 (ebk)

DOI: 10.1201/9781003015932

Visit the Taylor & Francis Web site at
http://www.taylorandfrancis.com

and the CRC Press Web site at
http://www.crcpress.com

Contents

Preface

This book was initiated in connection with a course on ERP systems at the Norwegian University of Science and Technology (NTNU) in Trondheim, Norway. This class was aimed toward master students who were focusing on subjects like manufacturing management, engineering, industrial economics, information technology, and similar areas that would benefit from knowing how ERP applications behave in a manufacturing supply chain.

We realized that only a few of the students would have a career that directly builds on ERP applications in manufacturing supply chains (e.g., an ERP consultant or a programmer). The majority would likely be utilizing ERP as a process owner within a manufacturing supply chain area, as a business manager, or in other business roles where they must understand how ERP works in manufacturing supply chains in order to make qualified decisions. Since the students would probably work with different ERP packages when they graduated from the university, our teaching had to be general enough to be valid for all or most ERP packages on the market today. This led us to focus on the core functionality of ERP systems for manufacturing supply chains, as well as provide a broad picture of how these applications could be applied to increase the performance of a manufacturing supply chain.

In this book, we aim to present what one should expect to find at the core of all ERP systems for manufacturing supply chains and how this core can be applied in an enterprise's manufacturing supply chain. In their basic form, all ERP packages are quite similar in supporting manufacturing supply chains and the basic principle of how all ERP packages work within the manufacturing supply chain area is relatively simple to learn. So even if the user is not aware of this, familiarity with a specific ERP package for the manufacturing supply chain would mean they know a lot about the basic functions in all other ERP packages as well.

The book is for readers who are new to ERP applications, as well as users of ERP systems, business managers, and ERP professionals who seek an introduction to how the performance of a manufacturing supply chain can increase by using such a software application. We hope that this book provides an understanding of ERP systems for the manufacturing supply chain and will help the reader realize the potential of these applications.

Acknowledgments

This book could not have been written without inputs from colleagues and customers through more than 20 years of working with ERP implementations through consultancy organizations like CGI, Cap Gemini, SINTEF, Intentia, and iStone. There are more than hundred individuals who should be acknowledged, and due to the risk of forgetting someone, we have found it best to express general gratitude to all the insights and knowledge that we have received throughout the years. We want to convey thanks to the people working at the ERP-software corporations as well, since they are always open to share insight on their products; both when writing this book and through other projects throughout the years.

We express our gratitude also to the Department of Mechanical and Industrial Engineering at Norwegian University of Science and Technology (NTNU), for giving us the opportunity to formulate the course "ERP and PLM-systems" that led to this book. A special thanks to the students Clara Patek, Runa Lunde Tobro, and Nina Grøsvik Ådnanes who helped us complete the compendium that finally grew into this book. Our thanks to Swapnil Bhalla as well for an early review of the book and for coming up with the name "OptiStream" for the company discussed in this book.

We also thank our editor John Wyzalek and the team at Taylor & Francis Group/ CRC Press for their patience with our continuous delays of the manuscript and for being a great team that are easy to work with.

Writing this book took more time than we first imagined, especially when simultaneously working full time with consulting and research in the manufacturing and business software area. This means that ERP systems and their impact on manufacturing supply chains have been continuously on our mind during this process. We therefore send our deepest appreciation for the understanding our family and friends have shown for the nighttime, weekends, vacations that were used in writing this book.

About the Authors

Dr. Odd Jøran Sagegg has served as an advisor in the implementation of ERP systems in manufacturing and supply chain since 1998. He has undergraduate and post graduate degrees in mechanical engineering and production management, and in 2004 he was awarded a Ph.D. on application of ERP systems in manufacturing organizations. Dr. Sagegg has been involved in more than hundred ERP implementations in the manufacturing supply chain area, ranging from basic rollouts in small organizations to large international ERP programs.

Dr. Erlend Alfnes is associate professor in Production Management at the Norwegian University of Science and Technology. He works with industry on new ways of improving manufacturing planning and control processes supported by ERP systems. Dr. Alfnes has 15 years' experience as a leader of research projects within production management and has been granted 20 research projects. His research and teaching interests are in the areas of manufacturing strategy, lean planning and control, and ERP systems.

Chapter 1

Introduction

Learning Objectives

This book provides insight into the core architecture, modules, and process support of enterprise resource planning (ERP) systems used within a manufacturing supply chain. The book introduces the building blocks of the ERP system for manufacturing supply chain and their use in achieving increased manufacturing supply chain performance. After reading this chapter, you will be able to:

- Understand the basics of this book and Manufacturing Supply Chains
- Recognize terminology used in ERP-software
- Get an introduction to the case descriptions

1.1 What the Book Is All About

A manufacturing enterprise can be small or large, ranging from the most basic manufacturing organizations consisting of a single manufacturing facility to multi-billion businesses with multiple companies, each having several physical facilities to serve their customers. An illustration of a normal enterprise structure of such a manufacturing organization is shown in Figure 1.1.

Figure 1.1 outlines an example of a relatively simple manufacturing group's enterprise structure. In this example the group consists of a single parent company (Company X) with several subsidiaries. The parent company of a manufacturing group is often a holding company, and no supply chain activities are performed at this company. A manufacturing group may have multiple of non-operational companies in their enterprise structure, but we will not explore

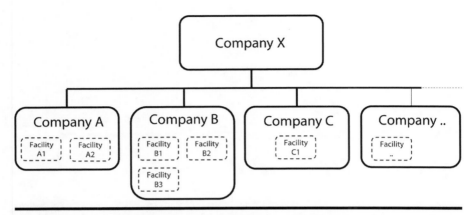

Figure 1.1   Example enterprise structure of a manufacturing group.

this further in this book and rather focus our discussions toward the supply chain activities. The operations are usually performed in subsidiary companies (e.g., company "A", "B", "C", etc. in the figure), that may consist of one or several physical facilities where the manufacturing and supply chain activities are performed.

In its simplest form, a manufacturing enterprise may consist of a single company with a single manufacturing facility. Larger manufacturing enterprises may have several operating companies, where each of these companies may include multiple facilities scattered around different geographical locations. Some of these facilities may be manufacturing facilities where products are manufactured, while other facilities may be distribution facilities for storing and distributing products and materials as they flow throughout the organization. To add to this complexity, each facility can hold several warehouses, meaning that there may be a vast number of places within a manufacturing enterprise where a specific item can be stored and managed.

1.1.1 About Manufacturing Supply Chains

Manufacturing supply chains are formed as items flow among the different facilities within the manufacturing enterprise. Manufacturing supply chains are networks of facilities, possibly owned by different companies, that are involved in creating and moving products to increase the value for the end customer. Each member of the supply chain receives products from a supplier, add value to it, and send it to the next member of the chain. Supply chains vary in complexity and ownership. A supply chain can consist of a single facility with local distribution centers and suppliers, or it can be a dispersed network operating on a worldwide basis with multiple

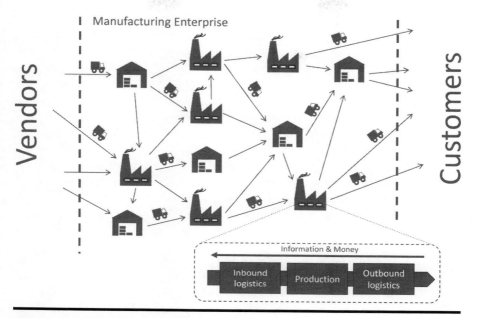

Figure 1.2   Manufacturing supply chains.

units that cooperate. The focus of this book is multi-facility manufacturing supply chains that operate within manufacturing enterprise consisting of a single or several operational companies.

Figure 1.2 shows that manufacturing and distribution facilities act like nodes in a network of the manufacturing supply chains within the enterprise. Each of these manufacturing facilities consists of inbound logistics, production, and outbound logistics as their major value-creating elements.

Inbound logistics refers to all the activities that involve obtaining items from a supplier, including ordering and reception of goods, and activities such as transportation, goods return, inventory control, and warehousing before the item is used. The production refers to activities that are involved in the process of physically altering the product. Fabrication, assembly, internal logistics, and inspections are important activities. Outbound logistics includes the activities associated with delivering finished products from the production line to customers. Important activities include order management, customer service, order processing, warehousing, inventory control, delivery scheduling, transportation and logistics, and packaging and materials.

While materials flow through these value-adding elements toward the customers, demand information goes in the opposite direction. The money also flows opposite the direction of the materials, to compensate vendors and other contributors for their goods and services. To add to the complexity of this network, each of these manufacturing facilities can be configured to follow different manufacturing strategies. These strategies include:

- Make-to-stock (MTS) – Items are produced and put into the stock within the facility before the customer order is received. The sales and delivery to the customers are thereby done toward these stored items.
- Assemble-to-order (ATO) – A product is assembled for each sales order. Components are produced and/or purchased in forehand, but the assembly does not start before a sales order is received from the customer.
- Configure-to-order (CTO) – Similar to ATO, but here the customer is given the option to configure variants of the assembled product. A simple example here is the configuration of colors and other options specified by a customer before buying a car. The car is then assembled using standard parts according to each customer's exact configuration.
- Make-to-order (MTO) – Under an MTO strategy the whole production process is not started before a customer order is received. The product is usually made by a combination of standard and custom parts to meet customer's specific requirements in a cost-effective manner.
- Engineer-to-order (ETO) – The ETO strategy suggests that the whole product is engineered toward the customer's specifications. An ETO process has often elements of source-to-order (STO), since engineered products often consist of complex parts that must be sourced from other parties within and outside the manufacturing supply chain.

Controlling the material flow through these networks of facilities can be a difficult task. Most manufacturing enterprises of today make use of information systems to manage their manufacturing supply chains, and within the core of these software tools lie one or several ERP applications.

1.2 How This Book Is Organized

This book is structured in three parts.

The first part consists of Chapters 1 and 2 and introduces the book and the concepts of ERP systems for manufacturing supply chains. This part provides the reader with the ideas behind this book, and an overview of the basics of manufacturing supply chains and ERP systems.

The second part consists of Chapters 3 to 7 and provides an overview of the core ERP modules that can be used as building blocks to support manufacturing supply chains. In each chapter, the basic information structure of the module is discussed. Before we go into the functionality and the general process support of the application. Case descriptions will be used for each module to illustrate how these parts of an ERP system can be applied in a real-life manufacturing enterprise.

The third and last part consists of Chapters 8 and 9 and describes how the ERP modules outlined in the previous chapters can be configured to support manufacturing supply chains. Chapter 9 describes how the ERP system is set up to support the manufacturing supply chain within single manufacturing facility. This provides insight in how the ERP system is used in the smallest of manufacturing enterprises, as well as laying a foundation to expand this view toward a manufacturing organization. Chapter 10 touches into ERP strategies for larger manufacturing enterprises and discusses how the ERP systems can be used to support a complete manufacturing supply chain across different facilities and/or companies.

1.3 About Terminology Used in ERP Software

Throughout the book we will discuss various data and functionalities found in different ERP-software packages. The different ERP systems on the market today use in a large extent the same terminology and naming for describing specific functions and data units in the software. For example, commonly known terms like "customers" and "customer order process" are recognizable and valid terms across a multiple of ERP packages. But the ERP packages have been made by different teams and people, and often for different markets in different time periods. Therefore, the terminology may not always be used consistently between the ERP packages.

In this book, we have used as many "generic" and descriptive terms as possible to make these valid for as many ERP systems as possible. This means that some of the terms we have chosen may differ from the terms used in some ERP packages. For example, we have selected the term "item" to describe an article, product, material, component, etc. that are purchased, stored, produced, or sold by a company, while, for example, the ERP-system Microsoft Dynamics 365 Supply Chain Management uses the term "released products" for describing the same thing. On the other hand, the ERP-system SAP S/4HANA uses the term "material" for practically the same purpose.

To make this book as relevant to as many systems as possible, we have pursued to use terminology that we have found to correspond with most ERP applications on the market, and if we have been in doubt, we have chosen the term that we think is most relevant for describing the function.

To illustrate this terminology problem for describing things across different ERP-application packages, in Table 1.1 we have linked some examples of important general terms used in this book and the corresponding terms used in two commonly used ERP applications, namely, Microsoft Dynamics 365 Supply Chain Management and SAP S/4HANA.

Table 1.1 illustrates that the terms we have chosen in our general descriptions in this book do often, but not always, correspond with the terms used in both Microsoft Dynamics 365 Supply Chain Management and/or SAP S/4HANA. Some of these can be connected to the architecture of the individual ERP package; for example, what we name as "warehouse" corresponds best with the function "storage location", and not "warehouses" in SAP S/4HANA. This is because SAP S/4HANA has a clearer separation between the inventory and warehouse functions than most other ERP applications on the market which usually groups these two functions together.

Our goal is to provide the reader with insight in the basics of how all ERP systems for manufacturing supply chains works, and therefore, we have tried to use our general terminology as much as possible. We have made effort to be as clear as possible and highlight any naming issues when discussing functionalities in specific ERP systems, so that the functions can be recognized in as many ERP software packages for manufacturing supply chains as possible.

Table 1.1 Examples of General Terms Used in This Book Versus Terminology Microsoft Dynamics 365 Supply Chain Management and SAP S/4HANA

ERP terms used in this Book	Corresponding term used in Microsoft Dynamics 365 Supply Chain Management	Corresponding term used in SAP S/4HANA	Comment
General ledger	General ledger	General ledger	Contains all financial accounts in order to represent a company's financial statement
Fixed assets	Fixed assets	Fixed assets	Assets owned by a company for permanent ownership and use
Accounts payable	Accounts payable	Accounts payable	An overview of all financial transactions for each vendor relationship
Accounts receivable	Accounts receivable	Accounts receivable	An overview of all financial transactions for each customer relationship
Items	Released products	Materials	General term for a manufactured or purchased part, a product, material, subassembly, or even a service
Inventory transaction	Inventory transactions	Inventory records	An information record of an event on an item in a warehouse

Table 1.1 *(Continued)* **Examples of General Terms Used in This Book Versus Terminology Microsoft Dynamics 365 Supply Chain Management and SAP S/4HANA**

ERP terms used in this Book	Corresponding term used in Microsoft Dynamics 365 Supply Chain Management	Corresponding term used in SAP S/4HANA	Comment
Facility	Site	Plant	A physical location within a company where its building and equipment are located
Warehouse	Warehouse	Storage location	A building or place where items are stored
Warehouse structure	Inventory breakdown	Warehouse structure	If you do not use the warehouse management system, the storage location is the lowest level of inventory management in the system
Transfer orders	Transfer order	Stock transport order	Used when transferring items between facilities in a company
Vendor	Vendor	Vendor ([a]Business Partner)	A person or a company that delivers goods or services.
Purchase order	Purchase order	Purchase order	A document that authorizes a purchase transaction
Customers	Customers	Customers ([b]Business Partner)	A person or a company that buys goods or services.
Sales order	Sales order	Sales order	A document that authorizes a sales transaction
Bill-of-material (or "BOM")	BOM	Material BOM	A list of items and their quantities required to produce a product
Route	Route	Routing	Routing defines the sequences of activities performed at the work center

(Continued)

Table 1.1 *(Continued)* **Examples of General Terms Used in This Book Versus Terminology Microsoft Dynamics 365 Supply Chain Management and SAP S/4HANA**

ERP terms used in this Book	Corresponding term used in Microsoft Dynamics 365 Supply Chain Management	Corresponding term used in SAP S/4HANA	Comment
Operation	Operation	Operations	Operations are used in routes to define the sequence of work that are necessary to produce a product. Operations are connected to one or a group for work centers
Work center	Work center	Work center	Described as a unit that performs the production, like a machine or a group of machines
Production order	Production order	Production order	A document that authorizes a purchase transaction
Planning polices	Coverage code	MRP type	Describes how the item should be planned
Item forecasts	(Demand) Forecasts	Materials forecast	A prediction of future sales
Master planning	Master planning	Material requirements planning	The process and calculations the system does in order to create a master plan
Master plan	Planned orders	MRP list	The master plan in ERP systems; holds all the planned orders made by the master planning run
Planned orders	Planned orders	Planned orders	Orders that are part of master plan, that can be released into production, purchase and distribution orders

[a] Vendors are managed through business partner in SAP S/4HANA.
[b] Customers are managed through business partner in SAP S/4HANA.

1.4 About the Case Descriptions

Throughout this book we will use case descriptions to illustrate the relation between the descriptions of the ERP systems and their real-life applications. The manufacturing enterprise is named "OptiStream" and they are using Microsoft Dynamics 365 Supply Chain Management as their ERP platform. OptiStream is an imaginary enterprise, but case descriptions are based on real-life companies. These real-life cases are collected from more than hundred different manufacturing enterprises using various ERP applications and are then adjusted and put together to form a uniform and complete end-to-end description of how OptiStream is using their ERP system. So, the way that OptiStream is using their ERP system is not far from how real-world manufacturing enterprises are using their ERP applications.

The case descriptions are done toward a specific ERP application (Microsoft Dynamics 365 Supply Chain Management). We have chosen to stick to one ERP package throughout the whole book to provide a unified picture throughout the case. However, the case descriptions in the book are kept on a general level, and we have fetched the case descriptions from enterprises using different ERP applications and benchmarked these toward a range of other well-known ERP applications, including SAP S/4HANA, Oracle E-business Suite, Infor M3, Infor LN, IFS Applications, among others. This is to provide descriptions that are valid for as many ERP packages as possible. By doing this, we have been aiming to create case descriptions that provide value for enterprises that use other ERP applications than Microsoft Dynamics 365 Supply Chain Management as well.

INTRODUCTION TO OPTISTREAM

OptiStream is a manufacturing enterprise delivering industrial pumps to the professional market. The enterprises consist of three facilities: Trondheim, Norway; Oslo, Norway; and Houston, Texas, United States.

OptiStream is a manufacturing enterprise with its core competence in manufacturing of advanced pumping solutions for industrial customers. They deliver industrial pumping systems from their factory in Trondheim, where they can perform a complete manufacturing process from machining of components, to the final mounting of the finished product. Nevertheless, they can't manufacture all parts themselves and some components must be purchased from vendors. The facilities in Oslo and Houston act mainly as sales offices, but they have their own local warehouses to ensure short delivery time and a good service level to their local markets.

OptiStream operates with three ways of delivering pumps to the market: stocked pumps that are delivered from stock; standard pumps that are made to order; special pumps that are individually engineered for each customer order.

The stocked pumps and the standard pumps are in practice the same types of products, using standard models, dimensions, and specifications. The stock pumps are the most popular pumps that are sold in high volumes from stock, while less popular models are only made when the company receives an actual customer order ("standard pumps"). Then they have the special pumps that are completely new products that require engineering (and sometimes special parts purchased from suppliers) before the manufacturing can start. All of the three facilities have stocked pumps in their local warehouses. The manufactured and engineered pumps are produced at the Trondheim facility in Norway, but can be ordered and delivered through the other two facilities as well.

1.5 Key Terms

- Introduction
- ERP systems
- Manufacturing supply chains
- Manufacturing strategies
- Make-to-stock (MTS)
- Assemble-to-order (ATO)
- Configure-to-order (CTO)
- Make-to-order (MTO)
- Engineer-to-order (ETO)
- ERP terms
- Case descriptions
- OptiStream

1.6 Chapter Summary

Through this book our aim is to provide insight in the ERP system's core modules and functions that can be used to support a manufacturing supply chain. This book will show how the ERP system can be applied to support a supply chain in the smallest of manufacturing organizations that only consist of a single manufacturing facility, as well as large enterprises where the manufacturing supply chain goes across multiple facilities and/or companies.

The book is structured in three parts. First, the concepts behind supply chain management and ERP systems will be introduced. Then the core ERP modules for manufacturing supply chains are presented followed by the applications of ERP system to achieve support in a manufacturing supply chain.

Case descriptions will be used throughout this book to illustrate how the descriptions can be applied in real-life environment. The case is described using an imaginary company using a single ERP application (Microsoft Dynamics 365 Supply Chain Management) to provide consistency of the case descriptions throughout the book. The case descriptions are built on real-life cases from manufacturing companies using various ERP applications, so they should be relevant for readers that are using other ERP packages as well.

Chapter 2

The Basics of ERP Systems for Manufacturing Supply Chains

Learning Objectives

After reading this chapter, you will be able to:

- Understand the basics of an ERP system
- Know the general functionality of an ERP system
- Name the modules of an ERP system for manufacturing supply chains
- Recognize the basic functionality for an ERP system for manufacturing supply chains
- Describe the core business processes supported by an ERP system for manufacturing supply chains

2.1 The ERP Solution

"ERP" is an acronym for "enterprise resource planning". This name does not give an accurate picture of the role these software applications plays in most manufacturing organizations today. The ERP system is less about planning resources, but rather seen as an application with a main purpose to integrate information and business processes between different areas and departments in an enterprise.

Roughly speaking it can be said that an ERP system consists of a database with a set of pre-built applications that works together to support core business processes within an enterprise. The ERP system is usually considered as the backbone of an enterprise's business software portfolio and usually interacts with various other business softwares to serve users and other actors. The ERP system and related applications form a complete solution to serve the stakeholders of an enterprise. Such a complete ERP solution is illustrated in Figure 2.1.

The big darker square in the middle of the figure is marking the ERP system, consisting of ERP-applications and ERP-database. The small square at the core of this ERP system is a database. A database can be described as a software component for structural storage of data. ERP database is normally organized in tables that again consist of fields of data that are sorted into columns and rows. For example, a table holding information on customers may have columns like customer number, customer name, delivery address, credit rates, etc. Each line in the table has a corresponding number of fields that describes the respective information for each customer.

The largest ERP databases may consist of more than hundred thousand tables, each holding waste information on things like customers, inventory transactions, price agreements, items, purchase orders, employees, financial balances, machine statuses, delivery terms, transport schedules, etc. Some of these tables may have hundreds of thousands, and sometimes millions of rows with various fields of information.

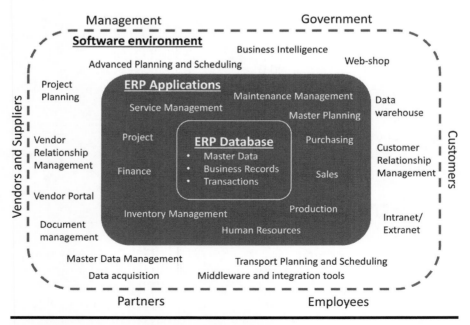

Figure 2.1   The components of an ERP solution.

The users access the data in the common database through different applications within the ERP system. An ERP system comes with many different applications that reads, writes, displays, and manages the data in the database. These pre-made applications use the ERP database to support different key areas within the company and help different users to enter and extract data from the database to support them in their daily work, and provide oversight of the status of the business. The applications of the ERP system work toward the same database and, thereby provide its users immediate access to the same data throughout the enterprise. The various applications are often grouped into modules according to what part of the business they support. Typically, there are modules for finance, sales, project management, production, etc., where the user can easily find the needed applications and functions that he or she needs to perform task connected to their business role in the company.

Businesses do often connect other applications to the ERP system for reading, writing, displaying, and/or processing the data in the ERP systems databases. These software packages do often have their own databases, that is, integrated ERP systems data to extend the functionality of the complete software solution. These other software packages may include tools for advanced planning and scheduling (APS), customer relationship management (CRM), master data management (MDM), Internet commerce platforms, and all sorts of thinkable and unthinkable software applications that may need interaction with the business transaction data in the ERP database. The ERP system and the related applications create a complete "ERP solution" that supports stakeholders like employees, customers, vendors, management, government, and external partners to use the ERP system and connected software to perform their daily business.

OPTISTREAM

OptiStream is using Microsoft Dynamics 365 Supply Chain Management as its ERP system. This is a cloud-based ERP system; this means that the ERP database and application is operated in the Cloud, and the users are accessing the application through a web browser. They are seeking to simplify their ERP solution as much as possible. This means that they are focusing to optimize the use of ERP systems to improve and integrate their core business processes, and are not seeking to exploit all the functionality that comes with this software that may only increase the complexity of the total solution. They use some third-party software to enhance the ERP functionality in some areas. Among others, they have been using the software application "Microsoft Power BI" as a reporting tool, since this tool comes integrated with Microsoft Dynamics 365 Supply Chain Management and in many areas outperform the reporting possibilities built in this ERP system.

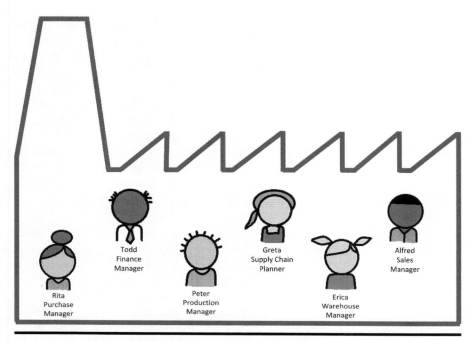

Figure 2.2   Roles at the Trondheim facility at OptiStream.

OptiStream has many different business units and stakeholders that use the ERP system and the connected software. The case descriptions will initially focus on manufacturing facility at Trondheim (what we refer to as "facility" in the book is named "site" in Microsoft Dynamics 365 Supply Chain Management). To illustrate how the ERP application affects the daily work at this facility, we will use personas of key personnel that are mostly involved in the use of the ERP system. The names of these people and their roles are shown in Figure 2.2.

The people in Figure 2.2 are:

- Peter (Production Manager) – Peter has the responsibility of the production department at OptiStream in Trondheim. He ensures that they always have the right resources and sufficient capacity to produce the pumps according to plan.
- Erica (Warehouse Manager) – Erica has the responsibility for the warehouses in the Trondheim facility. She must ensure that the warehouse personnel handle the inventor correctly to serve all the other departments with items so that the end customer orders can be delivered in time.

- Alfred (Sales Manager) – Alfred has the responsibility for sales in Trondheim. He is selling the products according to the company's guidelines and is actively working with the other departments to provide the correct goods to the customer to the agreed time.
- Rita (Purchasing Manager) – Rita must ensure that all contracts with vendors are up-to-date and that the purchasers acquire the correct raw materials, subcomponents, and other items in order to fulfill the overall supply plan at the Trondheim plant.
- Greta (Supply Chain Planner) – Greta's main responsibility is to coordinate all sales, production, purchases, and warehouse activities to optimize the flow of materials throughout OptiStream's supply chain. She is located at the Trondheim plant, but her responsibility embraces all companies and facilities in the group.
- Todd (Finance Manager) – Todd has the overall responsibility for the accounting and financial functions within OptiStream group. He ensures that the accounting rules and regulations are followed and that the group makes profit on their operations, both at the current date and in the long run.

OptiStream has chosen to implement the ERP-system Microsoft Dynamics 365 Supply Chain Management to help these people coordinate to fulfill their common goal of delivering the right product at the right time to the customers, while simultaneously making sure that the products are profitable. This need for an ERP system with a common database may be illustrated with a simple example showing how these different people handle the inventory in their warehouses:

- Rita, the purchase manager, buys items that go into inventory.
- Peter, in production, produces items that he adds to the inventory, simultaneously as his department consumes other items, like raw materials and components, from the same inventories.
- Erica, the warehouse manager, handles the inventory by moving inventory in and out of the warehouses, performing internal transfers within and between warehouses, conducts inventory counting's, and so on.
- Alfred, at the sale department, sells items that are delivered from the inventories.
- Greta, the supply chain planner, plans the flow of items throughout the inventories.
- Todd, in finance, accounts for the inventory.

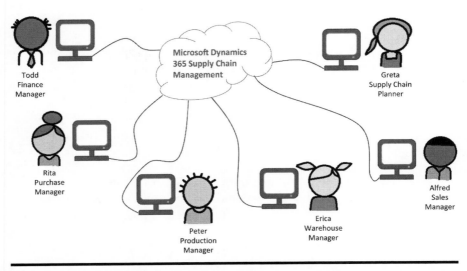

Figure 2.3 Cross-department interaction at OptiStream through an ERP system.

If the different departments at OptiStream above did use different software application with separate databases to keep track of the items in the inventory, the current on-hand information would be lost for the other parties as soon as anyone did anything on the inventory in their software application. In this case the users must continuously update the on-hand information of their system manually, or OptiStream will start to program complex software integrations between all individual applications.

Microsoft Dynamics 365 Supply Chain Management and other ERP systems solves this by the common database where all parts of the business are working toward the same data that is being updated for all parties as soon as anyone does anything in the system. Microsoft Dynamics 365 Supply Chain Management is a cloud-based software, and the users access the applications and the common database through a web browser on their computers as shown in Figure 2.3.

By using the ERP-system Microsoft Dynamics 365 Supply Chain Management, they can handle critical business tasks in their daily work through a single system without any need for transferring data between departments and application. Therefore, by using an ERP system OptiStream has eliminated the delay, errors, and cost for transferring business-critical information between stakeholders and applications in their enterprise.

2.2 ERP Data

The data stored in the ERP database can roughly be grouped into three categories:

- Master data – Data that hold static information of business-critical entities. The master data in an ERP database can take many forms; it is usual to find numbers or texts used to describe the business entity, such as item number or item descriptions, or parameters, like a marking in the item master that, for example, dictates that this item can be sold to customer. Master data are set once and used many times when the users are performing various tasks in the system. Examples on master data are information and parameters on vendors, such as address, price-lists, and delivery terms, or information on tax-rules like tax-groups, reporting calendars, and so on.
- Business records – Information that is entered by a user to perform a certain business function or process. The most recognizable business records in an ERP system are of different types of orders, but they can take other forms as well. Examples of business records may be a sales order, an inventory counting list, or a production order.
- System-generated transactions – Transactions automatically generated by software application when the users are working with business records. The ERP systems do typically generate two types of transactions: "inventory transactions" are used to execute and document all events on an on-hand item in stock. "Financial transactions" that updates and documents all events in financial accounting parts of the system. For example, a sales order may generate both inventory transactions and financial transactions when the sold items are shipped to the customer, since the physical on-hand of the item in stock must be reduced, simultaneously as the financial ledger is updated for deferred revenue.

The ERP system manages and uses this data to support and integrate the different functions within an enterprise. The ERP system uses the master data when creating business records, and both master data and information from business records is applied when transactions are being generated.

OPTISTREAM

Microsoft Dynamics 365 Supply Chain Management holds **master data** of all of OptiStream's employees, customers, vendors, warehouses, items, service items, production resources, and so on. Through their daily work the users utilize this master data when creating and/or managing **business records** like sales, purchase, and production orders, as well as warehouse journals. By processing these business records the ERP application generates **inventory transactions** that update the activities in the inventory, as well as **financial transactions** that update the ERP system's financial accounts.

2.3 ERP Modules

The ERP system integrates the business data seamlessly between all parts of the system through its common database. This creates an integrated software package where all applications are connected to each other and not naturally separated or broken into specific parts. For instance, a simple sale of an item in a sales application in the ERP application, will generate multiple system-generated financial and inventory transactions that affect the financial accounts, tax reporting, bank transaction, inventory levels, replenishment plans, shipment processes, warehouse movements, supply chain plans, management reporting, and another almost countless direct and indirect changes to the system and the organization.

Most ERP software vendors choose to group the applications into modules to make these easier to naming. These modules are more like a listing of similar functions in a menu than defined separation of the software code. For instance, all applications that are connected to a sales role may be put into a sales module menu, allowing the sales personnel access to a common menu where they may find all functions they need in their daily work, like adding customers, entering sales orders, printing sales statistics reports, confirming deliveries to the customers, and so on. The name of these modules, as well as the functions and applications they hold, may vary from system to system. The content and naming of the modules may even be changed by the developers between different versions and updates of the software. Nevertheless, most ERP systems have grouped the application in modules that are reflecting the core departments of the companies in target industries. For instance, an ERP system used for manufacturing or logistic centric enterprises may have modules to support areas like financial account, sales, production, project management, purchasing, HR, and so on.

OPTISTREAM

Microsoft Dynamics 365 Supply Chain Management has modules where functions are grouped according to their business function. These modules have been altered between the different versions and releases of the system throughout the years. The version of Microsoft Dynamics 365 Supply Chain Management at OptiStream contains more than 30 modules. The most important of these are as follows:

- General ledger
- Cash and bank management
- Fixed assets
- Accounts payable
- Accounts receivable
- Sales and marketing

- Procurement and sourcing
- Master planning
- Warehouse management
- Product information management
- Production control
- Cost accounting
- Budgeting
- Human resources
- Time and attendance
- Payroll
- Expense management
- Project management and accounting
- Service management
- Administration

All modules are structured in similar way in Microsoft Dynamics 365 Supply Chain Management. First are the applications where the users can perform the most common business task listed. Then comes applications for reporting and queries on the data that are relevant for the module, before applications for periodic jobs, parameters, and setup of the module. Figure 2.4 shows a screenshot of the modules in Microsoft Dynamics 365 Supply Chain Management (grey vertically banner to the left), with the procurement and sourcing module open.

OptiStream does not use all the modules that are available in Microsoft Dynamics 365 Supply Chain Management, but uses only the parts of the system that fits their needs. Most users at OptiStream rarely access the system through these modules, but they are using so-called "workspaces" to access the functions they need for performing daily tasks in the company. The modules are mostly used when they are seeking for new applications they rarely or never have used, or when setting up new functions in the application.

Figure 2.4   Modules in Microsoft Dynamics 365 Supply Chain Management.

2.4 ERP Systems for Manufacturing Supply Chains

ERP systems have continuously embraced more and more functionality throughout the years and do now include a large variety of modules and functionality for use in all kinds of industries and organizations. These industries include charity organizations, accounting firms, public organizations, car manufactures, house builders, and so on. This means that an enterprise rarely uses all of the functionality provided by the system, but only the parts that are necessary for them.

In this book we will focus on the ERP packages for manufacturing supply chains. Some core functions must be present in the software to make ERP system able to support a manufacturing supply chain. This functionality is rooted in the logical basis that these ERP applications grew from.

2.4.1 The Rise of Applications of ERP Systems in Manufacturing Supply Chains

The logic that the modern ERP applications for manufacturing supply chains are built upon has its roots from earliest days of using computerized tools in manufacturing enterprises. This growth of the ERP systems is outlined in Figure 2.5.

As Figure 2.5 shows, the seeds of ERP systems in manufacturing supply chains were laid in 1950s with some of the first computerized applications used in the industry, named bill-of-material processors (BOMPs). The core of these applications was bill-of-materials (BOMs), that can be described as lists of items (materials, components, subassemblies) that are required to create another item (end product). By knowing the requirements for the end products, the BOMP could easily calculate the gross requirements of all the items needed for production.

The BOMP applications were soon extended into what now is known as material requirement planning (MRP) systems. MRP extends the BOMP logic by adding things like the inventory stock levels and replenishment lead times into the gross-requirement calculations. By subtracting lead times from the projected on-hand inventory, and incoming replenishments from the gross requirements on all levels in the BOM, the MRP logic could calculate the future net requirements for the items needed in production. This made up a material schedule that suggested the point in time and the quantity for the replenishment of each item. The first MRP applications were put into use in mid-1960s, and this "MRP principle" is still

Figure 2.5   The evolution of ERP systems in manufacturing supply chains.

used as base for the planning methods in modern ERP systems for manufacturing supply chains of today.

The MRP applications were then enriched for finding capacity restrains production. This was done by adding elements like production routes and work centers in the applications. The production routes describe the production steps or "operations" that are required for producing an item, as well as the time each product need in each of these operations to be completed. Each operation was connected to a work center that again was connected to some resources with a preset capacity calendar where the work center's total availability is recorded. The MRP calculation could then use the information in the production routes to estimate the required capacity for all operations and compare this to the available capacity of the work centers. This planning logic was termed capacity resource planning (CRP).

If the capacity requirements calculated by the MRP/CRP run did not match the capacity available in the capacity calendars of the work centers, then the planner had to do some adjustments to the plan and do a new MRP/CRP calculation. This process of looping between checking the capacity of the work centers and adjusting MRP schedule would then repeat itself until the planner was satisfied with the schedule as well as the capacity utilizations in all work centers. This planning logic was named closed-loop MRP (CL-MRP), and was introduced in the 1970s.

These applications did grow further in functionality during the 1970s and efforts were put in to standardize the usage of software streamline and manufacturing organization. In the early 1980s Oliver Wight introduced a concept named manufacturing resource planning (MRPII). MRPII systemized the capabilities of the closed-loop MRP computer applications within a framework that involved activities that spanned from business planning to activities on the shop floor.

The term "ERP" was introduced by Gartner group in the 1990s. The base of an ERP system for manufacturing supply chains is undoubtable been inherited from the MRPII logic, but the functionality have grown. The MRPII application is mainly a planning tool for production, while an ERP application includes functions like financial accounting, sales order management, inventory management, purchasing order handling, and often other functions that are not connected to material handling. This had some implication on the planning methods provided by the system as well. The MRPII concept was focused toward production planning using forecast in a make-to-stock environment, did the new functions of the ERP system open for wider supply chain perspective and other planning methods as well like, for example, customer order driven production in a make-to-order environment.

The functionality of the ERP systems for manufacturing supply chains did grow significantly through the 1990s, embracing more and more functionally upon its core. From the mid-1990s, the ERP software vendors worked with utilization of the possibilities for electronic trade that followed through the growth of internet, adding support for things like internet portals, electronic trade capabilities, and integration frameworks for connecting vendors, customers, trading partners, and other external stakeholders seamlessly with the enterprise application. Some of the ERP systems did grow into larger ERP suites, where the most comprehensive systems do now have the potential to support most parts of a manufacturing enterprise in a single application package and can deliver a portfolio of additional business software that reaches far beyond what is traditionally associated with ERP software.

Today the ERP system for manufacturing supply chains is influenced with the possibilities of cloud computing. Putting the ERP system on a public cloud on the internet instead of installing the software in a private server room has opened the possibility connecting with other software which may break the monolithic nature of the large ERP suites. This has led to a trend of turning the focus of the ERP solution for manufacturing supply chain back toward its core, while integrating specialized (cloud) applications to extend these basic manufacturing supply chains functions toward other areas.

However, despite the later years growth of the ERP system and the strategies that follows, the core functionality of an ERP for manufacturing supply chain today is still a direct evolution that started with some of the earlier attempts to use electronic computers in the industry. This core logic of the manufacture supply chain functions remains untouched in the current ERP software applications on the market today, and due to the recent trend of cloud computing, how these basic parts on an ERP system can contribute to increased supply chain performance is even more valid today than it has been for years.

2.4.2 Core ERP Modules for Manufacturing Supply Chains

In this book we are adapting the following definition of an ERP system for manufacturing supply chain:

> *An ERP system for manufacturing supply chains is an out-of-the-box database application that through a central database supports the core business processes within at least the financial accounting, inventory, sales, production, purchase and master planning areas of a company*

This means we suggest that an ERP system for manufacturing supply chain must in minimum consist of modules for financial accounting, inventory management, purchase management, production management, purchase management, and master planning.

In a manufacturing supply chain, the information within an ERP system supports types of flows. First, it supports the flow of goods and services that goes through the company from the vendors toward the customers. Second, it supports the flow of money that goes from the customers toward the vendors.

In this book we will concentrate on the flow of goods and services in a manufacturing supply chain, and not the flow of money through the financial parts of the system. The reason for this is to simplify the descriptions, since we consider the financial accounting a more generic part of the ERP systems that has a indirect effect on the manufacturing supply chain performance. However, financial accounting is seamlessly integrated with parts that manage the material flow in an ERP system. We will, therefore, provide a brief introduction at the end of this chapter on how the financial module interact with the other modules in a manufacturing supply chain, without going into the details of the accounting parts.

This means that this book will focus on the parts of the ERP system that have a direct impact on the material flow of a supply chain, that includes following modules of an ERP system:

- Inventory management module
- Sales module
- Production module
- Purchasing module
- Master planning module

The modules listed above grasps the core functionality that supports the material flow in an ERP system for manufacturing supply chains. The naming and functions included in the modules may vary among the different ERP packages, but it is possible to find a similar pattern of the modules for manufacturing supply chains in as good as all ERP systems. Therefore, we suggest a generic model to illustrate the manufacturing supply chain functions in an ERP software packages.

Figure 2.6 shows the typical structure of modules found in an ERP system for manufacturing supply chains and how these parts relate to each other within a single company. The figure shows that in the base of the ERP modules of manufacturing supply chains we find the **inventory module.** This part of the application holds the master data regarding items, and keeps track of all the events in the warehouses through use of system-generated inventory transactions. The inventory module provides the other core modules for manufacturing supply chains with information on master data about items and item transactions. The inventory module has basic functionality for managing the inventory in the warehouses and in some ERP application the usage of transfer orders to movement of items between warehouses and facilities within the company.

An ERP application for manufacturing supply chain needs a **sales module**, that holds the customer master that holds all relevant information on customers and how they relate to the company. The sales module is using the customer master and item information from the inventory module to help the users to create and manage sales orders. These sales orders generate inventory transactions in the inventory management throughout the sales process until the items are issued and sent from the company's inventory.

In a manufacturing environment, the ERP system needs a **production module** as well. This model manages the transformation of inventory of items of raw material and components into items of finish products. Item information in the inventory management module is used to create production orders in the production

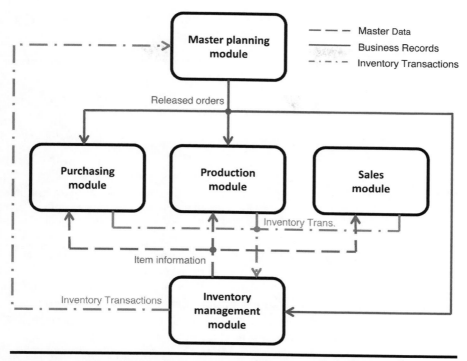

Figure 2.6   Core ERP modules for manufacturing supply chains.

module. And the production orders generate inventory transactions back on items in the inventory module as they are processed throughout the factory facility as materials, components, and finish goods. The production module shares the information concerning the work centers and production resources with the master planning module, in order to create consistency between the resource utilization between the master plan and the production floor.

The **purchasing module** holds the vendor master and uses data from these customers and item information from the inventory management module to create purchase orders. The purchase orders generate inventory transactions on the items in the inventory management module during the process from the items that are ordered from the vendors until they are received in the warehouse.

ERP systems in manufacturing supply chain do include a **master planning module** as well. This module runs a master plan calculation to create a master plan to coordinate the flow of materials throughout the manufacturing enterprise. The master planning module uses the inventory transactions from the inventory module to get an overview over all registered activities on the items in the inventor when running the master plan. Planned orders are released from this master plan that forms "real orders" in the other modules for physical execution.

In this way the ERP systems integrate the core module manufacturing supply chain into a single, interconnected application package.

OPTISTREAM

Greta, the supply chain planner, has invited some of OptiStream's largest trading partners to a meeting to discuss how they can improve the supply chain performance together. One of the topics in this meeting is how OptiStream is working with their ERP system. The trading partners do not use the same ERP system as OptiStream, and Greta is not familiar with their system. So, she is worried that they will not understand what she tries to explain, since the other persons in the meeting do not know anything about the Microsoft Dynamics 365 Supply Chain Management software either. Therefore, she tries to use the generic descriptions to establish a "common language" across the users of different ERP software. Her first step is to see what modules in Microsoft Dynamics 365 Supply Chain Management are used in what departments, in order to group the functions in simpler expressions that do not require the other party to have insight in this specific software package. The following bullet points reveal where Greta finds the functions of the generic modules for manufacturing supply chain listed in this chapter in Microsoft Dynamics 365 Supply Chain Management.

- The function described as the "inventory management module" is found in the "product information management" and the "inventory management" modules of Microsoft Dynamics 365 Supply Chain Management.
- The function described as the "sales module" is found in the "sales and marketing" module in Microsoft Dynamics 365 Supply Chain Management.
- The function described as the "production module" is found in the "production control" module in Microsoft Dynamics 365 Supply Chain Management.
- The function described as the "purchase module" is found in the "procurement and sourcing" module in Microsoft Dynamics 365 Supply Chain Management.
- The function described as the "master planning module" is found in the "master planning" module in Microsoft Dynamics 365 Supply Chain Management.

The bullet points show that Greta found a good, but not perfect correlation between generic modules in this book, and how the current modules in Microsoft Dynamics 365 Supply Chain Management are organized. The same goes for the attendees at her meeting; with high likelihood their ERP system modules will follow a pattern not far from the generic modules that are explained in this book. This means that by using the general modules for manufacturing supply chains as guidelines, she will in broad terms be able to present, communicate, and discuss how they are using their ERP system to support their manufacturing supply chains, even if the other attendees never have seen or used Microsoft Dynamics 365 Supply Chain Management before.

2.4.3 Business Processes Supported by an ERP-System for Manufacturing Supply Chain

As explained, most ERP systems arrange their modules according to their business functions. This means that each of these modules is made to support specific business processes within a company. The core processes supported by an ERP system for manufacturing supply chain are illustrated in Figure 2.7.

The figure shows how the ERP system provides support to the core business processes in a company.

The core process in the sales module is the sales order process. This process handles activities that happen from a sales order and are entered into the system until the items are picked from stock and sent to the customer, and the payment is received and registered in the financial modules.

The core process supported by the production module is the production order process. This process uses production orders to manage the activities in the production. The production order process includes production planning, picking the required raw materials and components, reporting the progress on the shop floor, and so on until the finish items are put into stock and the financial account is updated.

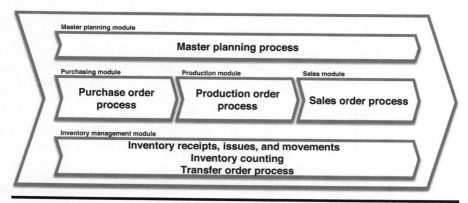

Figure 2.7   Core business processes supported by an ERP system for manufacturing supply chains.

The most important process in the purchase module is the purchase order process. The purchase order process starts with entering a purchase order and follows the purchase activities until the required items are put into the stock and the vendor is paid.

The inventory module supports the other core processes by handling the receipt and issues from the stock that are mainly made in connection with the sales, production, and purchase order processes. In addition, this module supports basic warehouse functions like the movement between warehouses and inventory counting. The inventory management module does often support a transfer order processes as well. The transfer order process supports the movement of items between warehouses sited in different facilities far from each other, and therefore must be transported by truck or similar means. Through issuing transfer orders, the company can manage the transportation and costs connected to the transfer, as well as triggering functions connected with the issue and receipts in the delivering and receiving warehouses.

The master planning module supports the planning process for the manufacturing supply chain. The function in this module uses the information from the other modules of a manufacturing supply chain and creates a master plan where the planner can release transfer, production, and purchase order to get the supply chain function organized and streamlined throughout the whole company.

2.5 Basic Functionality and Features in an ERP System for Manufacturing Supply Chain

The core modules for manufacturing supply chain give a complete picture of the core functionality of most ERP installations in a manufacturing environment. However, manufacturing companies utilize other more general functions that are used across the modules in an ERP system. The following chapter lists the most important of these functions. Some of these functions may be supported in various degrees in the different ERP packages. Simpler ERP software may miss some of these functions because they are made to support smaller organizations with less requirements for system support, while ERP packages for larger enterprises must have more functionality to be able to support all parts of a larger manufacturing enterprise.

2.5.1 Security Setup

The ERP data hold valuable information about the business and sometimes personal information of the employees within their human resources functions. The ERP system must therefore include security features that ensure that the users only get access to the parts of system they are authorized to access. An ERP-systems security module can be used to limit the different user's access to applications and functions roles at the enterprise. An administrator can typically connect a security role to a group of users according to their functions in the system. Modern ERP systems are often integrated to a single-sign function on allowing the users to access the enterprise's software using a single login with a username and password.

OPTISTREAM

All ERP users at OptiStream are registered in the security module in Microsoft Dynamics 365 Supply Chain Management. The users are connected to one or several roles that dictate what companies they can work with and the applications and functions they have access to in each company. Microsoft Dynamics 365 Supply Chain Management is a cloud-based application using the Microsoft's identification and access management service, meaning that when a user is logged on his or hers professional Microsoft account on their PC, they have secure access to the ERP application as well.

2.5.2 Language Management

An enterprise may have operations in many countries and other reason for that is they have users that use different languages. Therefore, an ERP system must be able to handle many languages through the same application, even if users work with the same information. The ERP systems allow users to set their preferred language on menus, screens, help-text, reports, and other texts that come with the applications from the software, while the master data in the database usually remain in the language that was used when the data was initially created. The master data in the database are most unique for each company; this means that each company can choose to enter data in their local language when implementing the system. However, some enterprises may require that a companywide language is used in all, or a selected set of master data to achieve standardization and ease trade and sharing of information throughout the companies in the group.

A company may have customers, vendors, and other trading partners sited in other countries, and that for other reasons use different languages. Most ERP systems support different languages on external documents like order confirmations and invoices and may even have possibilities to set different descriptions for each trading partner on certain master data, for example, "customers item description" on items.

OPTISTREAM

Since OptiStream has companies in both Norway and United States, most employees prefer using one of these languages when using IT applications. Microsoft Dynamics 365 Supply Chain Management supports a wide range of different languages, and the preferred language can be selected by each user. However, this language choice only affects menu items, field descriptions, help texts, and other text that are provided in the standard system. The information that they enter in the database like item names, customer groups, payment terms, etc. will be in large degree unique for each company and in the language that the data originally was keyed in to. Therefore, to avoid inconsistency in the data and opening the possibility for people to work across any part of the enterprise, they have chosen to use US English as their main language in the ERP application throughout the enterprise.

However, Microsoft Dynamics 365 Supply Chain Management supports that the company can enter external texts in several languages, so that customers and vendors can choose the language they prefer on their documents from OptiStream. Most information on the documents to customers, vendors, and other external parties will be in their local language.

2.5.3 *Personalization of User Interfaces*

The ERP system comes with a whole range of functions to meet the requirements for all kinds of businesses and enterprises. This means that the users of an ERP system may be exposed to a lot of information, fields, and functions that they may never use, while on the other hand functions, they need in their daily work, may not be easily accessible in the standard setup of the ERP application.

The modules of the ERP systems may help resolving this problem to some degree since they group the functionality of the application according to their business function. But still there are a lot of functions in these modules that a user does not need to perform in their daily work, and it is inefficient to search every time in a module for a specific function that is frequently used by the user. Therefore, most modern ERP systems come with some kind of screens and ways to present the most common functions each role in an enterprise need to complete their daily task. In these screens the users find the most functions that they need from the standard software package, simultaneously they can add functions or do other changes that will be stored to their profile to get the screen tailored to their personal preference.

OPTISTREAM

Most users at OptiStream access the applications and functions they need in Microsoft Dynamics 365 Supply Chain Management through a user interface "Workspaces". An example of such a workspace is shown in Figure 2.8.

This figure shows the workspace for purchase preparation. Through this screen Rita and the others at the purchasing department can get an overview of activities connected to the creation of purchase orders. In the middle of

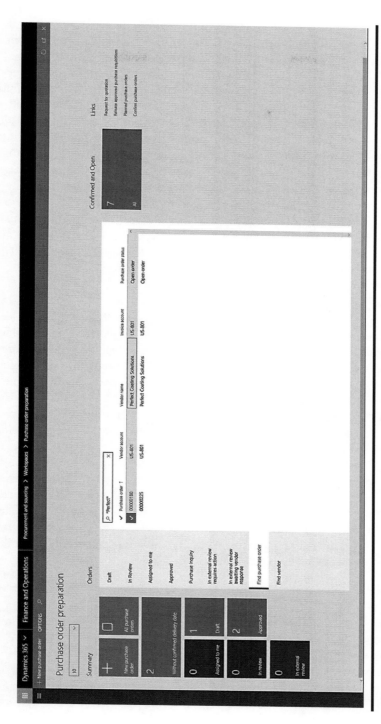

Figure 2.8 Workspace in Microsoft Dynamics 365 Supply Chain Management.

the screen the user gets list according to the state of their purchase orders, like who are in draft, in review, assigned to the user, approved, etc. On both side of screen there are "tiles" showing similar statuses, and the user can "click on" to jump the correct application in Microsoft Dynamics 365 Supply Chain Management. The user can add new tiles according to their individual needs. On the far right there are links to other applications in Microsoft Dynamics 365 Supply Chain Management that may have relevance for preparation of purchase orders. Microsoft Dynamics 365 Supply Chain Management comes with a lot of workplaces tailored to different work tasks and the user can change this workspace according to his or her preferences.

The users at OptiStream do not perform work in the workspaces but use them more as a menu to get overview over the work task ahead and to easy access to the correct application in the ERP application. For example, if Rita clicks on a purchase order in a workspace, Microsoft Dynamics 365 Supply Chain Management opens the purchase order application where she can process the orders further.

2.5.4 Number Sequences

Number sequences is an important feature in all ERP systems in order to identify the different information in the system. All basic data such as items, customers, and vendors get a unique number that identifies them throughout the system so that there are no conflicts between data entries in the system. The same goes for business records, such as purchase orders or counting journals, financial vouchers, and inventory, etc. Each of these gets a separate number sequence that identifies the separate records from each other. These sequences are often of great importance for the users since they represent a unique identification, both for the software application and the user. Some parts of the application may have legal requirements to how number sequences are used and structured, for example, certain financial postings. The ERP system more usually refers to, for example, item numbers or customer numbers than item names or customer names. The ERP system must, therefore, have a strong system for number series throughout the system to separate the individual transactions and data units in system, and simultaneously meet the individual requirements for each instance.

OPTISTREAM

OptiStream uses number series on Microsoft Dynamics 365 Supply Chain Management for various important business information. The number series ensures a unique identifier for all events in the system and makes OptiStream able to separate customer, vendors, items, orders, inventory transactions, and other data entities in a consistent manner. There is a little less than 10,000 different number series in OptiStream's ERP system,

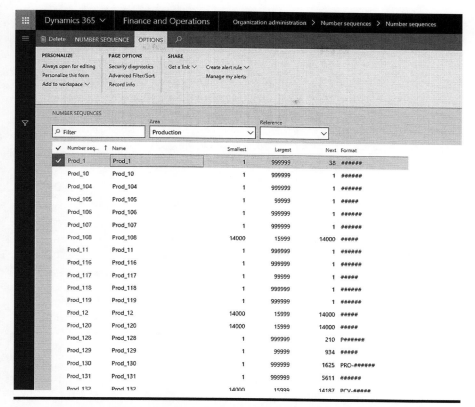

Figure 2.9 Number sequences in Microsoft Dynamics 365 Supply Chain Management.

wherein many of them are mandatory for the operation of the system. Figure 2.9 shows a small selection of the configuration screen showing some of these number sequences.

2.5.5 Enterprise Breakdown

The basic business organizational unit of an enterprise is a company. A company is a legal unit that in principle needs a separate set of data to record a legal business transaction. ERP systems targeted toward smaller enterprises may only have support of a single company for each installation of the software, while larger ERP systems support having several companies in the same software solution. If several companies are using the same system database, the data from the companies are separated logically in the tables within the database; so the different organizations act like independent business units, where the user is logged into the company they are employed in and only see the data that are valid for the company they are logged in to.

The companies in a group can be organized in certain ways. For example, some companies may be a subsidiary of other companies in the group, and/or the different companies can be clustered into divisions or business units. If an enterprise uses separate ERP systems for each company, this enterprise structure is handled independent of the ERP applications. However, if there are several companies in the same ERP application, there are usually functions to define an enterprise structure within the application in order to handle things like group financial reporting and other cross-enterprise activities.

OPTISTREAM

Microsoft Dynamics 365 Supply Chain Management solution is targeted toward larger organizations and do therefore support several companies in the same instance and database. OptiStream has set up three companies in their Microsoft Dynamics 365 Supply Chain Management solution. This setup is illustrated in Figure 2.10. One company covers the Norwegian part of their operation, and the second covers the US business. The last company is the group holding company that is used for tasks like financial consolidation and group reporting. The users can only see the data for the company they are logged in to, and only a few people at OptiStream have access to all companies in the system.

Most information is unique for each company. Nevertheless, some information can be shared across companies, and Microsoft Dynamics 365 Supply Chain Management has functionality to increase the interactions between the companies in certain areas. This includes things like a global address book holding addresses to business partners across the group; intercompany master planning; functions for automate intercompany trade; and a common item master where needed items can be released into each company (the global item master is named "products", and item master in each company is named "released products" in Microsoft Dynamics 365 Supply Chain Management). They use Microsoft Dynamics 365 Supply

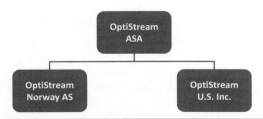

Figure 2.10   Enterprise structure at OptiStream ASA.

Chain Management to consolidate the financial accounts of the Norwegian and US company into the books of holding company to create a consolidated financial statement for the whole group.

2.5.6 *Master Data Management*

MDM involves the process of collecting and managing critical master data across different systems and business functions. The ERP system is a source of many of these data, and some ERP vendors have built some functionality for MDM into their applications. These functions may include searching, tracking, and resolving issues concerning redundant data, as well as elimination of duplicate data in the database. MDM functions of an ERP system can also include abilities to share and update master data, such as items, customers, and vendors across companies that are using the same installation of an ERP application.

The MDM functionality of an ERP system is limited to managing the data within the ERP applications and do usually not extend beyond the borders of the installed ERP system. This means that the master data functions in an ERP system do not account for external data that are registered in related applications such as a "CRM application" or a "Web-shop solution". If the enterprise has complex requirements around master data, they could consider buying a separate MDM software package that helps them automate and maintain master data across the ERP systems and other business applications.

Some of the most important questions concerning management of master data in an ERP system cannot always be resolved through use of software functionality exclusively. This can easily be illustrated through an example. Let's say that an enterprise in the food industry has two companies for processing and packaging of chicken eggs. These two companies do trade with each other if one of them has shortages while the other has excess of eggs on stock.

Let's say that one of these companies uses a single item and item number in the ERP system for all kinds of eggs. They have been able to do this simplification of the information management since they always sell and deliver the eggs according to the total weight of the shipment. The other company sells egg per piece and they have four separate item numbers for eggs in the item master of the ERP solution; each for each size of the egg (small, medium, large, extra large). In this way they can sell and set the pricing of larger egg's different from the price of the smaller eggs.

This bias between how these two companies have arranged the master data on chicken eggs can problematize the internal trade between these business units. For instance, if the first company use the item "eggs" to order an certain number of kilograms of eggs from the other company, the people that receive the order at the other company must first choose if they should register this order toward the item "Eggs-S", "Eggs", "Eggs-L", and/or "Eggs-XL", and then calculate the right number of eggs according to the requested weight. This is cumbersome when people are handling the trading process between the companies, and it may be very difficult to automatize.

This is a simplified example, but it illustrates that master data goes beyond the usage of information systems and can affect an enterprise's performance in high degree. Good MDM do, therefore, involve that the two companies should agree on how chicken eggs should be traded within the group in addition to how they must be structured in the ERP systems.

A common way used by many enterprises to organize the management of master data in the ERP system, is to restrict the users access to enter and change certain master data in the system, for them to establish routines for how master data should be created and maintained in the group. If a user needs to, for example, register a new item in the item master of their company, he or she must contact the group's master data responsible that checks if the items already exists and resolves any other potential issues before the item is registered in the system.

2.5.7 External and Internal Documents

All trade requires some output of documents, either in electronic form or as a physical printout. The ERP system must have capabilities to generate documents to communicate with external partners, as well as documents for internal communication. These documents can be order confirmations, delivery notifications, invoices blankets, printout of picking lists, and so on.

ERP systems can generate these documents and send them to a printer for physical printout. Alternatively, the system can generate electronic versions of the documents, like PDF documents that can be attached to an e-mail and sent directly to the receiving part. In most ERP systems the users can do some alterations of the documents layout, like adding and subtracting fields, adding text as well as adjusting the language of the document according to the language used at receiving part. However, in most systems the possibility for altering the content and design of the documents is limited, and modifications of the ERP system's programming code are often required if the users have special requirements to the layout.

Nowadays enterprises use less and less paper printouts and/or electronic versions of these physical print to communicate with the outside world. The trading information is transmitted directly between the ERP systems without the need for a human operator to read the documents, until the orders are registered in the receiving system. This communication happens often through standards for electronic messaging like "EDI messages" and similar formats. Some ERP systems generate these electronic messages by using some of the same functions as the system uses for generating the "physical" trading document. But instead for a document, the ERP system creates an output file that again is being processed further in a broker software to an output file that is readable to the software on the receiving end. Most ERP systems come with integration frameworks and "application programming interfaces" (APIs) to ease the electronic communication with external parties, but a part of the trade will probably always use documents that are readable for humans.

OPTISTREAM

OptiStream communicates trading documents mainly through e-mail to most external parties. They have set up Microsoft Dynamics 365 Supply Chain Management to automatically generate e-mails with the trading document as a PDF attachment in an event that should trigger a document to the customer. One example of this is when Alfred confirms a sales order to a customer in Microsoft Dynamics 365 Supply Chain Management, the ERP automatically generates an e-mail with the confirmation document as a PDF attachment and sends it to the customer. An example of this confirmation document is show in Figure 2.11. However, OptiStream sees that the need for generating documents from the ERP system is reduced, since the trade is getting more and more fully automated electronically. They are already using EDI messages toward their largest trading partners, and all the document exchange between the Norwegian and U.S. operation have been eliminated by the intercompany trade functions of Microsoft Dynamics 365 Supply Chain Management.

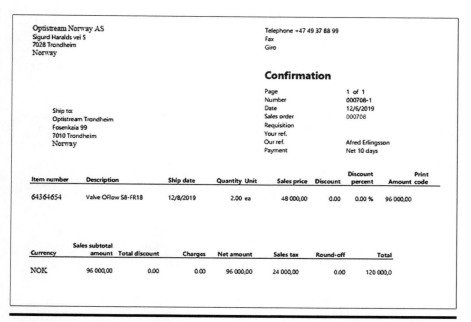

Figure 2.11   Order confirmation document from Microsoft Dynamics 365 Supply Chain Management.

2.5.8 Reporting Tools

ERP systems have built-in report generators for generating, viewing, and print-ing various reports on the status of the enterprise. This can be all kinds of reports showing things like the current on-hand, production cost, sales statistics, financial statements, and similar.

Most ERP packages come with a series of pre-made reports. These reports are often static with relatively limited possibilities for the user to change content and layout of these. This means that if a company has requirements for reports that go beyond the reports that are in the standard package, they either need to develop a custom report or generate the report using an external reporting tool. Some systems have built reports generators enabling user's bigger freedom to create their own reports in the ERP system, or alternatively extracting data to tools like Microsoft Excel.

Nowadays, the reports in the ERP systems are getting more and more exchanges with external reporting tools, like "business intelligence applications" (BI applica-tions). In order to use such tools, a portion of the ERP data is extracted to data warehouse, where the external tool can reach the data. The advantage of such a solution is that the database in the data warehouse is simpler and therefore easier for a user to find the correct data when he or she creates a new report in the BI applica-tion. In addition, the data warehouse can be populated with data from many differ-ent applications, so that the reports can be combined with information from other sources beside the ERP system. The main drawback is that the data warehouse is usually updated with data in timely manner, like every evening, so the users must use the reporting possibilities in the ERP system if they need an exact overview of the current situation.

OPTISTREAM

Microsoft Dynamics 365 Supply Chain Management has more than 200 pre-built reports. OptiStream uses only a few of these reports in its daily work because it has started to use the business intelligence tool Microsoft Power BI to cover their reporting needs. Microsoft Power BI is integrated in Microsoft Dynamics 365 application that has made many of the old reports obsolete. By using BI tool the users at OptiStream can tailor their own workspaces on the PC screen with their own performance indicators and graphical overview need if the standard reports in the ERP system do not fit their exact needs.

However, OptiStream still generates some reports directly from the ERP system since this is the fastest and most accessible for some of the users. For instance, Peter in production uses the capacity reservation report in Microsoft Dynamics 365 Supply Chain Management almost every day. An example of this report is shown in

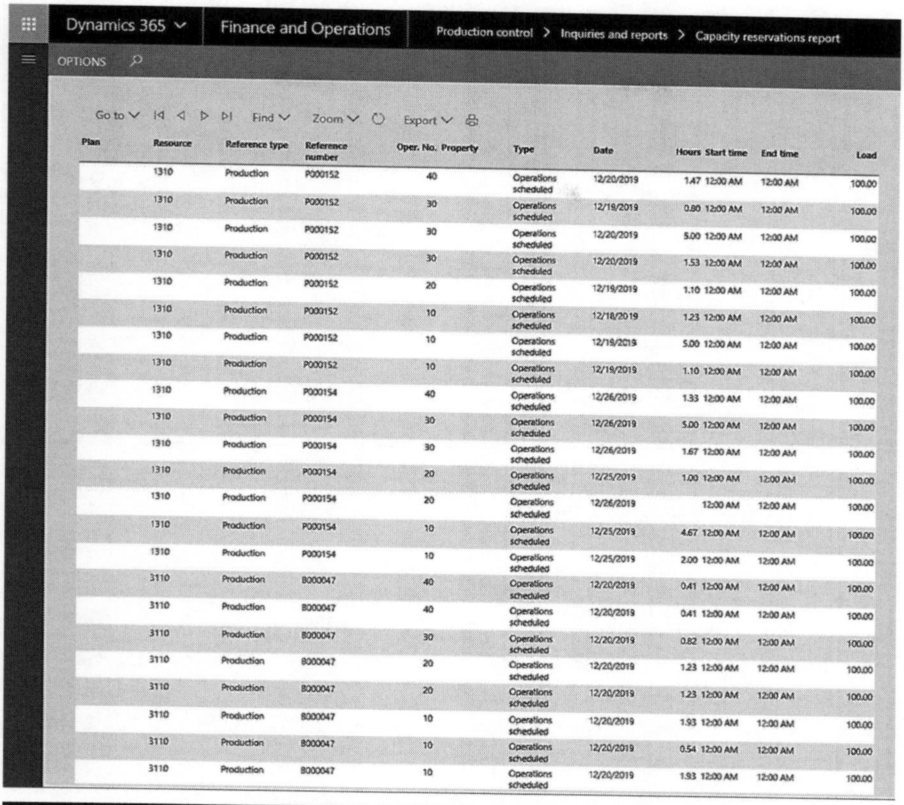

Plan	Resource	Reference type	Reference number	Oper. No.	Property	Type	Date	Hours	Start time	End time	Load
	1310	Production	P000152	40		Operations scheduled	12/20/2019	1.47	12:00 AM	12:00 AM	100.00
	1310	Production	P000152	30		Operations scheduled	12/19/2019	0.80	12:00 AM	12:00 AM	100.00
	1310	Production	P000152	30		Operations scheduled	12/20/2019	5.00	12:00 AM	12:00 AM	100.00
	1310	Production	P000152	30		Operations scheduled	12/20/2019	1.53	12:00 AM	12:00 AM	100.00
	1310	Production	P000152	20		Operations scheduled	12/19/2019	1.10	12:00 AM	12:00 AM	100.00
	1310	Production	P000152	10		Operations scheduled	12/18/2019	1.23	12:00 AM	12:00 AM	100.00
	1310	Production	P000152	10		Operations scheduled	12/19/2019	5.00	12:00 AM	12:00 AM	100.00
	1310	Production	P000152	10		Operations scheduled	12/19/2019	1.10	12:00 AM	12:00 AM	100.00
	1310	Production	P000154	40		Operations scheduled	12/26/2019	1.33	12:00 AM	12:00 AM	100.00
	1310	Production	P000154	30		Operations scheduled	12/26/2019	5.00	12:00 AM	12:00 AM	100.00
	1310	Production	P000154	30		Operations scheduled	12/26/2019	1.67	12:00 AM	12:00 AM	100.00
	1310	Production	P000154	20		Operations scheduled	12/25/2019	1.00	12:00 AM	12:00 AM	100.00
	1310	Production	P000154	20		Operations scheduled	12/26/2019		12:00 AM	12:00 AM	100.00
	1310	Production	P000154	10		Operations scheduled	12/25/2019	4.67	12:00 AM	12:00 AM	100.00
	1310	Production	P000154	10		Operations scheduled	12/25/2019	2.00	12:00 AM	12:00 AM	100.00
	3110	Production	B000047	40		Operations scheduled	12/20/2019	0.41	12:00 AM	12:00 AM	100.00
	3110	Production	B000047	40		Operations scheduled	12/20/2019	0.41	12:00 AM	12:00 AM	100.00
	3110	Production	B000047	30		Operations scheduled	12/20/2019	0.82	12:00 AM	12:00 AM	100.00
	3110	Production	B000047	20		Operations scheduled	12/20/2019	1.23	12:00 AM	12:00 AM	100.00
	3110	Production	B000047	20		Operations scheduled	12/20/2019	1.23	12:00 AM	12:00 AM	100.00
	3110	Production	B000047	10		Operations scheduled	12/20/2019	1.93	12:00 AM	12:00 AM	100.00
	3110	Production	B000047	10		Operations scheduled	12/20/2019	0.54	12:00 AM	12:00 AM	100.00
	3110	Production	B000047	10		Operations scheduled	12/20/2019	1.93	12:00 AM	12:00 AM	100.00

Figure 2.12 Capacity reservation report in Microsoft Dynamics 365 Supply Chain Management.

Figure 2.12. First, he generates the report on the screen in Microsoft Dynamics 365 Supply Chain Management where he scans down all the listed capacity on the resources/work centers from his PC screen to get an impression at the capacity situation. If he finds some abnormalities, he prints the reports and brings this paper report to the shop floor to share with his team.

2.6 Financial Accounting in an ERP System for Manufacturing Supply Chain

As stated in the previous chapter; an ERP system for manufacturing supply chain, includes modules for finance, inventory, sales, production, purchase, and master planning. This book will concentrate on the logistics part of these functions,

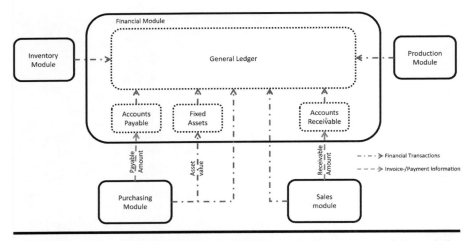

Figure 2.13 The integration between the financial accounting module and the core modules for manufacturing supply chain.

and will not focus on the financial accounting capabilities of an ERP system. Anyway, financial accounting is an important and integrated part in any ERP installation that must be considered even when focusing on the material flow. Following discussion will provide a brief introduction to the financial accounting on an ERP system and how this relates to the other modules of an ERP system for manufacturing supply chain.

Figure 2.13 illustrates the most important interaction points between the financial module and the modules of manufacturing supply chains.

Figure 2.13 outlines the basic principle behind the interactions between the core modules for manufacturing supply chains and the accounting parts of the ERP system. The financial module consists of a general ledger that holds all the financial accounts for keeping track of the company's assets, liabilities, equities, revenues, and expenses.

The financial accounts in general ledger is structured through a chart of account, that can be described as organized listing of all the accounts to help the company organize their financial statements and accounting work. In an ERP system, each company is a legal unit and has their own general ledger that operates independently from the general ledgers of the other companies in the group. However, the same setup of the accounts ("chart of accounts") can be used across different companies in an enterprise so that the general ledgers are structured in the same manner throughout the group. Some ERP systems have functionality for sharing the chart of accounts between companies and automatic conciliation of several general ledgers of subsidiaries into the accounts of a parent company.

Each economic event at a company will create a financial voucher that triggers financial transactions in the affected general ledger accounts. This also includes all events that happen in the purchase, production, sales, and inventory management module, that have economic impact in the enterprise. For instance, a sale to a customer will create financial voucher that creates financial transactions in the accounts for inventory valuation, revenue, outstanding tax, and so on.

Each transaction toward the accounts in the general ledger in an ERP system may be marked with one or several financial dimensions. The financial dimension is mainly used for reporting and tracing the financial events. How many and which financial dimension should be used, and how they want to follow up their financial status is up to each enterprise. For instance, a company that wants to trance the cost of their research and development efforts may create a financial dimension for the "R&D" cost center. All financial transactions that involve costs or incomes concerning research and development can then be marked with this dimension so that these costs can be refound and reported on in the general ledger. In the same manner as for the chart of accounts, some ERP packages with multi-company support allow sharing of financial dimensions between companies to ease consolidated accounting and financial reporting throughout the enterprise.

The general ledger uses subledgers to keep track of the details of accounting in certain areas. The sum of the details in the subledgers is transferred to the general ledger. In this way, the general ledger provides an updated overview, simultaneously as it is held in a manageable size.

The subledgers that interacts most with the core modules for manufacturing supply chain, is the accounts receivable and the accounts payable. The accounts receivable is connected to the sales module and keeps track of the balance of money between the company and each customer that are made through sales, but not yet paid for. The accounts payable is the other way around; this subledger accounts for the money outstanding to the vendors made by purchases done through the purchase module and other sources, but where the payments are not yet processed. The accounts receivable and the accounts payable, accounts for the outstanding amounts until the payment is settled and the amount is posted in the general ledger.

Some ERP systems have connection between the purchase module and the fixed assets subledger as well. The fixed asset subledger handles all the financial details on a company's fixed assets, like the value and depreciation machines, furniture, buildings, and so on. The fixed asset module and purchase module are usually integrated by the item (e.g., purchase of machines or office furniture) that can be bought via a purchase order and then transferred to fixed asset module, to be further accounted in this part of the ERP application.

Besides for the integrated general ledger, the finance module takes care of other accounting functions as well. Some of these functions are as follows.

- Tax accounting, reporting, and payments.
- Payments and invoice settlement. Part of the accounts receivable and payable sub-module to manage the payments from customers as well as payment to vendors.

- Bank management with electronic payment to automate the remittance of payments to vendors and ingoing payments from customers.
- Manual voucher payments to account for economic transactions that have been done without using the ERP system.
- Debtor reminder management. Functions to generate and follow payment reminders.
- Currency management. Management and conversions between different currencies used by the enterprise.
- Accruals. Possibilities to post revenues and/or expenses over a period
- Financial statements and other financial reporting.
- Accounting periods and periods close. Setup and management of accounting periods and functions to support closing the financial books on period ends.
- Intercompany accounting and intercompany consolidation. If the enterprise involves several companies, some ERP systems have support for managing accounting across each of these as well as functionality to consolidate the different charts of accounts into a group-wide financial statement.

Most ERP systems support cost accounting as well. Cost accounting enables managers to study cost connected with activities in the enterprise for making better business decisions. The cost accounting is usually not a part of the financial module of an ERP system but handled in separate module or in the modules where the cost appears. We will touch this subject when discussing the inventory value methods in the inventory management module.

Even if we will not discuss in details of financial accounting in a manufacturing supply chain, it is important to have in mind that the financial module is not a separate module that is working independently from the other modules in an ERP-system. The financial module is more a way of grouping applications for financial accounting together that again are seamlessly integrated with the other functions of an ERP system for manufacturing supply chains.

2.7 Additional Business Software Applications

An ERP system for manufacturing management, and especially the ER suites made for larger enterprises, can include much more functionalities that go far beyond the core functionalities that we can cover in this book. In many cases the best and most economical solution to use as much as possible of the provided functionality of the ERP system, is to have as much processes support as possible through a single and integrated software package.

However, there are areas where an ERP system for manufacturing supply chain is missing functionality or do only provide some basic functionality that cannot compete with a specialized software package. Therefore, many enterprises chose to use add-on software to strengthen and expand their total business software solution beyond core functions for manufacturing supply chains.

Another reason enterprises want to use a third-party software in relation to their ERP system is the possibility to increase the flexibility of the solution. By using additional software packages in relation to their ERP system, the solution can better absorb changes since doing alterations in one area may not affect other in same way that was supported by one software package.

Further, by using specialized software in areas where the ERP system has limited or no support, the enterprise can get to meet functional gaps in their ERP solution without the need for extra programming. For example, an enterprise working in the fashion industry may have gaps between their requirements and the functionality of the warehouse management module of their ERP system. In such case they may purchase a separate warehouse management system (WMS) tailored for the fashion industry and integrate this to the ERP system to meet the requirements through use of standard software packages.

This means that in some cases, it may make sense to buy and integrate an add-on application that extends or completes the functionality of the ERP system. These add-on applications may sometimes be developed by the same software vendor that delivers the ERP systems as a part of their "ERP suite" or the applications may be made by a third-party software developer. The most commonly found of these add-on software packages in a manufacturing supply chain are summarized below.

- Customer relationship management (CRM) systems – Software packages that manages customer relationships. These software packages handle all relations an enterprise has with its customers, and provide extended support within areas like sales, marketing, and customer service.
- Supplier relationship management (SRM) and eXtended relationship management (XRM) systems – An evolution in the applications and functionality of the CRM system toward suppliers (SRM) and various other parties within and outside an enterprise (XRM).
- Manufacturing execution systems (MES) – Software that supports the processes on the production shop floor. These applications provide deep support in things like production scheduling, work center sequencing and optimization, resource allocation, tooling management, production data collection, labor management, production performance analysis, and so on.
- Shop floor data collection (SFDC) systems – These software packages are focused on collecting data on the production floor. The SFDC systems can be understood as a simpler version of the MES applications that are well suited for companies that do not need work center scheduling and other advanced production functionality.
- Invoice automation systems – Solutions for data capture and automatization of the process connected to management of inbound invoices.

- Warehouse management systems (WMS) – Advanced software for managing warehouses. Includes deep functionality in areas like warehouse planning, staffing, monitoring, and optimization.
- Quality management systems (QMS) – It is a formalized system of documents, procedures, manuals, etc. to ensure quality within an organization's core business processes. The QMS system is usually built on standards such as the ISO 9000 family.
- Transport management and scheduling (TMS) systems – Tools for transport planning and scheduling. Can be used in connection with both inbound and outbound logistics. Included among other functions like freight audit and payment, advanced shipping management, and transportation routing.
- Advanced planning and scheduling (APS) – Do typically extend the master planning functionality within the ERP system with functions like advanced forecasting, quantitative optimization routines, and supply chain network planning.
- Master data management (MDM) systems – Used for the management of master data. These applications are often used to manage master data across several applications, and business units.
- Product lifecycle management (PLM) – Involves collection and storage of all data related to product through its lifetime.
- Data warehouse and business intelligence (BI) tools – The ERP data are often drawn out in external data warehouse for further analyses and reporting through a business intelligence tool, for example, "Microsoft Power IB" or "Tableau". These tools provide improved visualization, analyses, and distribution of business-critical information.
- Enterprise content management (ECM) systems – Tools used to handle structured and unstructured information like documents, files drawings, and e-mails. These applications manage the information through its lifecycle from it is created, until it is delivered, archived, or deleted. ECM tools are often used in connection to ERP system to handle unstructured information in connection to business transactions like files with technical drawings for use in a production order process; e-mail communications with a customer in a sales order process; or external notes in connection to a purchase process.
- Middleware and integration tools – Software applications to ease integration sharing between software applications. Involves extraction of the data from the source application, and then the transformation and orchestrating of the data until it is released into the correct receiving application.
- Product information management (PIM) – Used to manage all information on products, like product descriptions, data, and pictures. These software applications are often used in connection to electronic commerce for providing production information to ecommerce sites and similar.
- Web portals – The ERP system can interact with all kinds of web tools. This can be ecommerce portals for business-to-business (B2B) or business-to-consumer (B2C) trade. Web portals do also include enterprise portals where information

from several sources is gathered in order to be accessed by internal and external users. ERP system can be used in relation to enterprises portals, for example, letting employees and external workers easy access for things like time-sheet reporting or entering purchase requisitions without logging into the ERP application.

These software packages listed above are just a fraction of the software that may be used in relation to an ERP system. Enterprises do usually choose to make automatically integrations to the ERP system to these applications to ensure that both applications are updated with as little manual work as possible. Figure 2.14 shows where one can find the mentioned supply chain in the supply chain, and roughly where they integrate with the processes supported by ERP system for manufacturing supply chains.

Figure 2.14 shows that applications like SRM, invoice automation, and B2B portals are usually integrated toward the purchasing side of the ERP application. MES and SFDC applications can be used to extend the production module, while the ASP software is used against the master planning functions of the ERP system. A WMS package can be used to strengthen the inventory management module if the enterprise finds the warehousing functions of the ERP system insufficient for their use. On the sales side, applications like CRM and B2B/B2C are integrated toward the sales module. The PIM systems may be used throughout the system, but these applications are mainly integrated toward the sales parts of the ERP system, since these applications are often used to produce information and pictures for publishing on sales websites. BI, ECM, Middleware, QMS, and web-portals are more general applications that are used and integrated with several parts of an ERP system for manufacturing supply chain.

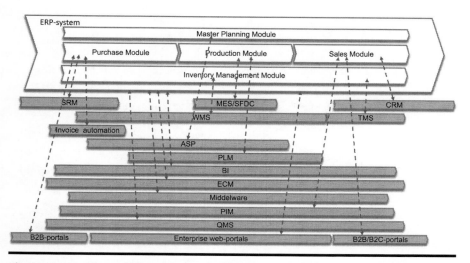

Figure 2.14 The relation between an ERP system for manufacturing supply chains and some additional software packages.

2.8 Key Terms

- Bill-of-material processor (BOMP)
- Material requirements planning (MRP)
- Closed-loop material requirements planning (CL-MPR)
- Manufacturing resource planning (MRPII)
- Enterprise resource planning (ERP)
- ERP systems for manufacturing supply chain
- Financial accounting module
- Inventory management module
- Purchase module
- Production module
- Sales module
- Master planning

2.9 Chapter Summary

In this chapter we have seen that ERP system is a database system consisting of many modules that may be used to support most areas within an enterprise. Some of these functions are made to support a manufacturing supply chain, and we proposed the following definition on an ERP system for manufacturing supply chain:

> An ERP system for manufacturing supply chains is an out-of-the-box database application that through a central database supports the core business processes within at least the finance, inventory, sales, production, purchase and master planning areas of a company.

We are focusing on the material flow in this book and do therefore define the inventory, sales, production, purchase, and master planning modules as the core modules on ERP systems for manufacturing supply chains. This chapter introduced some basic functions of these applications including security setup, language management, number sequences, and enterprise breakdown.

The core modules supply chains can be expanded with other module and add-on software to strengthen software support within the manufacturing enterprise. Some of the most common of this add-on software was mentioned in this chapter.

Chapter 3

Inventory Management

Learning Objectives

After reading this chapter, you will be able to:

- Describe the basic data components found in the inventory management module
- Recognize key features and functionalities supported by the inventory management module
- Provide an overview of the main work processes supported by an inventory management module
- Understand the most important features and modules that relate to inventory management module

3.1 The Inventory Management Module

The inventory accounts for all on-hand quantities an enterprise needs to perform its business. The inventory may hold a broad variety of items like finish goods and other sales products, materials and components used as input in production, semi-finish goods, spare parts, and other types of items that many been used within the company. The main task of the inventory management function is to account for the inventory; this means that the inventory management module in an ERP system is all about the storage and management of a company's items.

The main activities of a manufacturing supply chain involve to sell, purchase, produce, and plan items throughout the organization, and these activities depend upon the item information from the inventory management module. This means that the ERP system for manufacturing supply chain is built for the management of item, whereas the inventory management module is the core of any ERP system for manufacturing supply chain.

3.2 Key Data in the Inventory Management Module

An inventory management module holds vast amounts of functionality and data to fulfill any requirement different enterprises may have for managing their inventories. The possibilities of the inventory functions may vary between different ERP software packages, but some basic components are found in most ERP packages. This core information components can be summarized as:

1. Master data connected to items
   - The item master contains a listing of all items that the company handles with their related data
2. Master data connected to warehouses and facilities
   - Information on the facilities and their connected warehouses held in the company. The smaller ERP packages on the market do only have support for warehouses, while more comprehensive ERP packages manage facilities as well
3. Functionality for managing business records for warehouse activates like inventory movements, counting, inventory transfers, as well as transfer orders.
   - Basic warehouse management functionally to maintain an updated inventory status in the system. This management involves functions like moving items within the warehouses, counting items on stock, as well as transferring items between different warehouses.
4. Inventory transactions
   - Inventory transactions are system-generated information units that hold information on all activities performed on the items within the different facilities and warehouses. All current and historical inventory information on an item can be found from its inventory transactions.

The Item master is the main master data component within the inventory management module. The item master holds data on all items that a manufacturing company can sell, produce, purchase, and otherwise trade or handle. Nonphysical commodities may also be defined as items in this item master database. Such intangible items will not influence the on-hand inventory in the system but can for instance be used for selling services in connection to other physical items, like transportation or installation of products at the customer site.

The item master data stores information about the items and their behavior throughout the system. The item master may hold hundreds of data components like parameters, functions, and other information on each single item. Examples of types of data found in the item master are:

- Various fields and descriptions for item identification like item number, item naming, item descriptions, item groups, and so on.
- Data describing how item should be managed in stock. Like if the item can be stored with a batch or serial number, what warehouse they can be stored, reservation rules, and how its inventory valuations should be managed.
- Information and parameters for how the items should be sold/purchased toward customers and vendors, including price lists, reservation rules, and delivery methods.
- Planning and ordering parameters, including safety stock levels, lead times, and planning methods.
- Parameters controlling how the financial postings in the general ledger in the finance module should happen and other cost accounting settings.

The facilities and warehouses are another key master data in the inventory management module. The main storing entity in an ERP system is the warehouses. A warehouse in an ERP system can be described as a place where item can be stored. This can be physical warehouse building or a part within a storage building, depending on how a company choose to define their warehouses in the system.

What we describe as facilities can be termed as "site", "plant", or by using other expressions in some ERP systems it is a geographical business location that includes one or several warehouses. For example, a company may have two facilities located in two different cities, each having their own set of warehouses.

The main purpose for having facilities in an ERP system is to identify what business resources and/or warehouses are grouped together and who are far from each other, so that these can be managed differently. Not all ERP systems have support for facilities and, therefore, only operate with warehouses even if the facilities are sited waist distances apart. Therefore, most things like management of transportation between warehouses far from each other are handled in other ways, or outside the ERP system.

The facilities/warehouses in many ways extend the enterprise breakdown described in Chapter 2. The enterprise breakdown typically breaks down the enterprise to separate companies, where each company is its own legal entity with separate master data. The inventory module continues the breakdown of each company into its facilities and warehouses.

The inventory module has functionality for managing the inventory within the warehouses. The functions are for light warehouse management like counting, transferring, and moving the inventory. Most ERP applications have warehouse management module with advanced functions for managing warehouses that build on the functions in the inventory management module. But we consider these as a part of the warehouse management modules of the ERP system and not one of the core modules of manufacturing supply chains.

Inventory transactions are the main transaction data found in the inventory management module. The item transactions hold information about the historical and ongoing events of the items within the warehouses. Every time a logistic event happens to an item (if the item is issued, sold, moved, picked, etc.), the system generates an inventory transaction for this event. In this way, the ERP system maintains control on the status of the inventory of each item, as well as the historical activities on these. The users seldom look at or work directly with the inventory transactions in most ERP systems, but they are used by the system to generate and display other key user information like, on-hand calculations, inventory statistic reports, and other functions where the current status and historical events of the inventory in the warehouses is needed.

An overview of the components of the inventory management module is shown in Figure 3.1.

This figure shows that the core of the inventory module consists of two interlinked units of master data on items and master data on the facilities and/or warehouses.

The information on items is often combined with the information on facilities/warehouses in an ERP system for manufacturing supply chain. For example, an item may require different safety stock levels in different warehouses, and, therefore, most ERP systems are able to hold a set safety stock data for each warehouse and item in the company. Different ERP systems may solve this in different ways, but on of the most common is to have separate item masters for each warehouse where warehouse unique item parameter and information can be set. How this is technically solved in each individual ERP system is not explained further in this book, but it must be noted that the item master and the inventory breakdown with facilities and warehouses are related to each other in one way or another in all ERP packages.

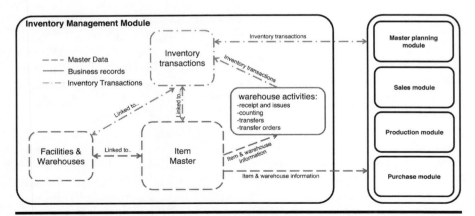

Figure 3.1   Basic data components in the inventory management module.

The items and facilities/warehouses are linked to the warehouse transactions as well. In principle all inventory events recorded in an ERP system be traced toward both an item and the facility/warehouse where the inventory transactions happened.

Figure 3.1 shows that the inventory management module has support for basic inventory management functions as well, like counting, moving, and transferring the items on stock between the warehouses and/or facilities. These functions use information from the items master and facilities/warehouses and generate new inventory transactions when they are processed.

The same pattern is found when creating and processing business records in other core modules of an ERP system for manufacturing supply chain. Master data from the items and facilities/warehouses are used when making the business record, and inventory transactions are generated when the business record is processed in the ERP system. For example, when creating a sales order, both the item and the warehouse must be registered on the order, so that system can fetch master data like item number, item time, price, lead time, delivery terms, etc. for delivering the item from that specific warehouse. This will also create an inventory transaction telling that the item is on an order and about to be shipped from this warehouse that again will change status and/or create new inventory transactions on item as the sales order is processed.

From these core components the ERP system can keep track on their items in their warehouses, as well as their historical movements. The inventory management module interacts with the other core modules of an ERP system for manufacturing supply chains and is cornerstone that the other module relies upon. All parts of the ERP systems have access to the data in the inventory management module. This means that all information that relates to items, warehouses, and inventory transactions is stored and maintained in one place for the whole ERP system.

OPTISTREAM

Figure 3.2 illustrates the enterprise breakdown in relation to inventory breakdown at OptiStream ASA.

As explained in Chapter 1, OptiStream consists of three companies. OptiStream ASA is the holding company at the enterprise and OptiStream Norway and OptiStream US are the two daughter companies.

The inventory breakdown at OptiStream Norway AS consists of two facilities; the first is in Trondheim where they perform their production, and act as a sales office toward the middle and north of Norway. In this facility they have registered a general warehouse, a production warehouse, and a finish goods warehouse in Microsoft Dynamics 365 Supply Chain Management. The second Norwegian facility is in Oslo that handles sales for the south and west of Norway. The US operations consist of a sales office in Huston. Both the sales office in Oslo and Houston has local sales warehouses so they can deliver standard pumps to their respective markets in short notice.

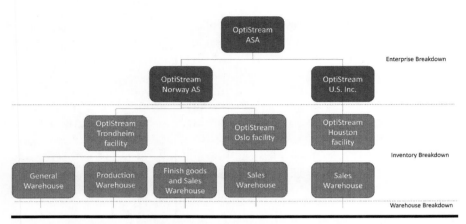

Figure 3.2   Enterprise structure and inventory breakdown at OptiStream ASA.

OptiStream has both companies in Microsoft Dynamics 365. Each company in Microsoft Dynamics 365 Supply Chain Management has their own set of data. But this ERP system has some functionality for sharing master data between the different companies in the group.

The item master for each company is named "released products" in Microsoft Dynamics 365 Supply Chain Management, but there is a function named "products", where information on items that should be registered in the item master for both companies can be entered and maintained. OptiStream uses this structure to distinguish between items that can be used in all companies in the group (global items) and items that are only used in one company in the group (local items). All global items in Microsoft Dynamics 365 Supply Chain Management are created and maintained by the supply chain manager, Greta, who is also assigned as responsible for the item master data within the group.

Greta registers all global items as a product and then releases them into the released "item database" of these companies as they are needed. All products, components, and raw materials are released into the Norwegian production company, while only the items that are sold in the US market are released into the sales company in Houston. Therefore, they use the same item number in the sales company in United States as in the Norwegian facilities, which helps in coordinating the sales and supply chain.

When Greta adds a new item in Microsoft Dynamics 365 Supply Chain Management, she must remember to add a storage dimension group. The storage group defines on what level Microsoft Dynamics 365 Supply Chain Management should account for the item's inventory. All items at OptiStream are stored using a site (Facility) and warehouse dimension. She can then add parameters to the item and review its inventory according to the level defined in the item's storage dimension group. Figure 3.3 shows

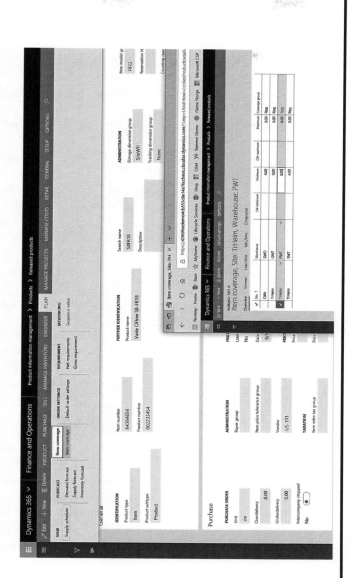

Figure 3.3 Setting of minimum stock on item in "released products" in Microsoft Dynamics 365 Supply Chain Management.

an item in the "released products" (item master) in the Norwegian company and the minimum stock she has entered for this item at each site and warehouse in the "item coverage" application.

When an unexpected stock shortage happens, Greta checks the item transactions on the item to see what has happened, and if possible, corrects the error to prevent it from happening again. The inventory transactions show all activities that have happened on the specific item, and what warehouse they have happened in according to the inventory dimensions. Figure 3.4 shows item transactions on an item in Microsoft Dynamics 365 Supply Chain Management.

3.3 Basic Features and Functionality

The number of features and functionality included in the inventory management module, and how these are executed in the software will of course vary in high degree between the ERP-software packages. But some functions are common for most ERP systems. The most important of these are discussed below.

3.3.1 Item Numbering

Each item in the ERP system item master is given a unique identifier to achieve a concise solution. While some enterprises choose to let the user set the item numbering for each new item, do others let item numbers be generated by the ERP system.

The dependence on the item numbers is strong in most ERP systems. This means that item numbers are used as the main key everywhere items are used in the system, like when adding an item to purchase order or seeking the on-hand of the item in the warehouses.

The item number can consist of both letters and numbers. The way item numbering is structured and handled in an ERP system is important because the users often know the items, and communicate around these, by only using the item numbering. ERP systems do normally assign unique item numbers sequences for each company. So, the item number "SP-110-28" in one company may be completely different product than item number "SP-110-28" in another company. This may lead to confusion and, therefore, large effort is put in understanding how the item numbers are structured in ERP systems. In most ERP systems, there is a possibility to add external parties item numbers to each item in the database, so that "customer's item number" or "vendor's item number" in external documents are such that the receiving part can find the items in their systems. The same goes for those using an industry standard for item numbering, like the International Article Number (EAN-codes). Most ERP systems have functions to connect such standard numbering to the items in the item master, to automate trade to parties that are using the same standard.

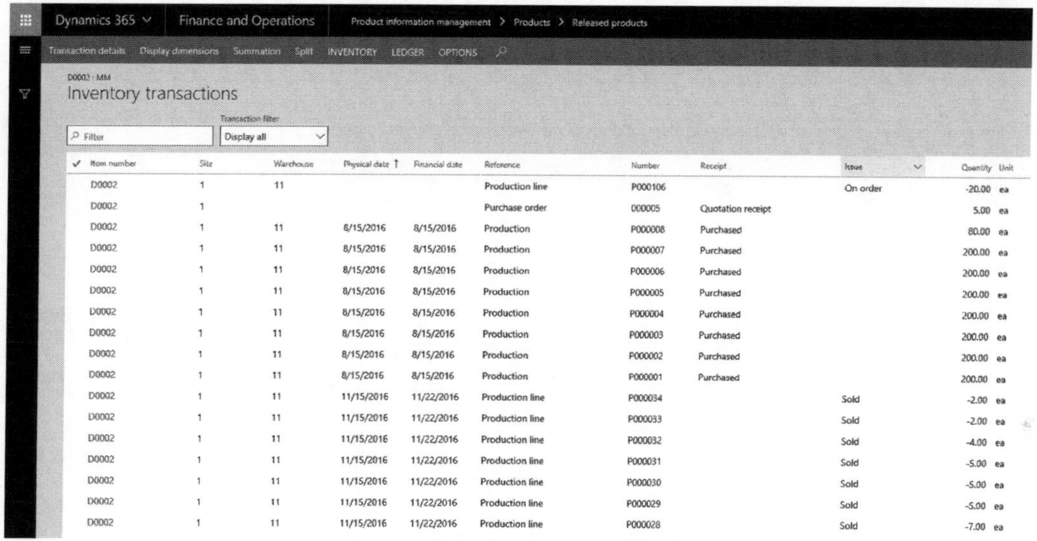

Figure 3.4 Inventory transactions in Microsoft Dynamics 365 Supply Chain Management.

Sometimes the companies put a logical structure in their item number to make it easier for the user to identify the item from the item number. This means that the company many put a fixed structure where the number in certain position describes the product in some way or another. For example, the item number of all sales products starts with 2xxxxxxx ("x" are random or sequential selected numbers), and all products within product group "Hydraulic" have 010 as their three next digits. So, all hydraulic sales items have an item number starting with: 2010xxxx. And so on.

This seems like a good strategy for making it easier, for example, people in department only need to key in "2010*" in the item number filed in the ERP system to see all relevant items when selling hydraulic equipment. But the item number is usually a part of the logical key in most ERP systems database and, therefore, may be very hard to change when it is first set. Meaning that putting logic in the item number may give great problem if company needs to change something in this logic. For instance, when restructuring product groups, when changing their product lines, or if they need to merge with another company that use another logic in their item numbering.

Therefore, modern ERP system has flexible user interface that allows using multiple fields when working with items. This makes the users less dependent of using item numbers with a built-in logic when working with the ERP system. This has enabled the company to rather use a sequentially selected item number that will make the whole ERP solution more flexible and future proof.

OPTISTREAM

When Greta adds new item in the product master in Microsoft Dynamics 365 Supply Chain Management, the item gets a global product number. This product number is generated from a running number sequence. When the item is released into each company in OptiStream, the item gets a company-specific item number that is used for identification within that specific company. An example of item numbering on an item in the "released products" (the item master) at the OptiStream Norway is shown in Figure 3.5.

The item numbering was a big topic some years ago when OptiStream did buy two companies that became the Oslo facility and OptiStream in the United States. Each of these companies had their own ERP system where they had defined their own item number sequences. When they merged their system into Microsoft Dynamics 365 Supply Chain Management, they could not agree on a common way of numbering the items. Therefore, the item numbering at OptiStream became a "mess" and they are now using a mix of item-numbering sequences from all three companies in their ERP solution that are close to impossible to restructure to a common standard.

Microsoft Dynamics 365 Supply Chain Management is flexible when it comes to using other fields when working with items in the system. One

Figure 3.5   Item numbering at OptiStream.

of these fields is "search name" on the item where OptiStream has put the product code. This field is used in the same manner as the item number in many cases, such as when searching for items, adding items to orders, and so on. But unlike the item number, the content of "search name" can easily be edited. Therefore, Greta does not use any logic in the product and item number of any new item she adds into the solution. She does only use a system-defined running number sequence for the item numbering, and rather use the "search name" and other fields on the item for describing the product. If more companies are coming into this solution, she will force them to use this logic instead of holding on to any old item-numbering structure. In this way she maintains an ERP solution that is more flexible to change and better suited for merging new companies into the solution as their business grows.

3.3.2 *Product Descriptions and Other Identifications*

Besides the item number an ERP system usually uses a lot of other fields for describing the items, like item groups, items descriptions, item texts, and possibilities for adding documents, technical sheets, pictures, and work instructions to the item. Some of the software packages have possibilities for setting attribute values on the different items. Such attributes can describe the products' technical or physical properties, helping the user to search and find the right product. Product attributes can also be used to provide technical description and other product information that, for example, can be used when publishing the item on an ecommerce website.

In recent years, the item and product information have become more important due to the increasing growth of electronic trade. Software tools for product information management (PIM) to manage item information such as product descriptions, pictures, and technical features have grown to accommodate all information needed to ease the publication of products on websites, print catalogs, and other ecommerce channels. Some ERP systems have some PIM functionality build within the standard application. But this functionality is usually quite limited, and companies do often choose to use a third-party PIM application in connection to the ERP solution to better support the product information.

3.3.3 Variant and Configuration Management

Another way of identifying items is by using variant or configuration codes. These codes do in many ways extend the item number. A simple version of variant codes is often used in the fashion industry where they specify the specific size or color of the item in inventory. For example, by storing a shirt (e.g., item number "1234") with configuration code for color (as "black") and a configuration code for size (such as "medium"), the ERP system can then maintain a single item in the item master, while managing for multiple variants on stock.

Configuration codes work in a similar way; however, these configurations codes may consist of several characters for describing a specific configuration of an item. This means that there may be almost an unlimited amount of configuration codes of one item. Let's use a car as an example. A car can have a large variety of options like color, types of sound system, engine types, fabric or leather interiors, etc. Instead of registering an item in the item master for each possible variant of the car, the enterprise can use a single item number for the car, combined with "product configuration" function. Using a "product configuration" the user can add the item number for the car on, for example, a sales order line, and he or she will then guide through different screens for selecting the options. When, finished the "configurator" in the ERP system will create a configuration code according to the choices that are made, as well as a specific bill-of-material (BOM) and production route (the production BOM and route will be explained later). Using this the specific configuration of the car is produced and registered in the inventory with the item number for the car and the special variant code. Use of configuration codes is usually in assemble-to-order environment where the assembly of various versions of a product is managed through a configuration process.

OPTISTREAM

OptiStream does not use variant or configuration codes today. But they are doing tests on a pump with configurable pumping capacity. This will ease the maintenance and reduce the number of items in the item master, since a single item can cover all variants with different pumping capacity for the otherwise similar pumps.

3.3.4 Units of Measure

All items can be stored, traded, and managed in different units of measure. For instance, the same item for copper wire may be purchased in kilograms, stored in the warehouse as rolls, and used in production in meters. An ERP system must, therefore, handle several units of measures for each item to support the item's flow throughout a facility. ERP systems do specify one base unit for measuring each item, whereas the other units are converted from. This base unit of measure is usually not possible to change after the item is put into use, and therefore, it is important to set this to the correct unit when the item is registered.

OPTISTREAM

Greta uses unit functions in Microsoft Dynamics 365 Supply Chain Management to register all units of measures used by the organization. An unlimited number of units of measures can be setup and connected to the different products. The unit conversion function describes the relations between units, such as 100 cm equals 1 m, etc.

The base unit of measure of an item is termed "inventory unit" in Microsoft Dynamics 365 Supply Chain Management. Greta sets this inventory unit each time she releases a new product. This "inventory unit" is set on the released products screen and cannot be changed after item transactions are generated toward the item in Microsoft Dynamics 365 Supply Chain Management. Therefore, it is important that if Greta is unsure on what inventory unit to choose for an item, she thinks of a unit she normally uses when counting this item in the warehouse, and then uses this unit of measure as the inventory unit for the product. After she has set the base unit of measure, she adds the other units on the item, like the sales unit and the purchasing unit. Since most conversion rates are already registered in the system she only needs to add this unit, and the conversion between units will be taken care of by the ERP application.

3.3.5 Inventory On-hand

Keeping track of the on-hand inventory is a basic, but very important function of an inventory management module. An item on-hand inventory value can be calculated by using item's transactions. The ERP system may use different methods or technologies in order to reduce the need to calculate all historical transactions on an item every time a user needs to know the on-hand inventory. This can be done by removing old transactions from the calculation and/or storing the on-hand inventory in an own, separate table in database that are refreshed when an inventory transaction is completed. However, to simplify our descriptions and to separate the general principles from the technical execution of the different ERP-software packages, we will in this book present that the on-hand inventory is always calculated from the inventory transactions.

OPTISTREAM

The users at OptiStream can find the inventory on-hand in various places in Microsoft Dynamics 365 Supply Chain Management, such as the on-hand screen. On the on-hand screen, Greta and the other users can find the inventory on-hand and another inventory information of an item. Microsoft Dynamics 365 Supply Chain Management uses storage and items' dimensions to allow the user to select the level at which the on-hand inventory should be displayed on the screen, such as per site, per warehouse, per batch number, and so on.

The on-hand screen can be reached from other places in the application as well, such as the sales order screen. This allows sales workers to view the inventory on-hand before promising sales on their sales items. Figure 3.6 shows an example of an on-hand screen of an item located at OptiStream Norway, where the on-hand inventories in both the Trondheim and Oslo facilities are listed.

3.3.6 Item Tracking

Item tracking in ERP systems involves finding all inventory transactions an item previously had directly or indirectly been involved in. Item tracking is especially important within quality management and tracing the source for quality issues upstream the supply chain.

A user can trace and follow all actions that have been performed on an item through its inventory transactions. But an item's inventory transactions do only describe what has happened to physical items that have the same item number, and not to a single product that, for example, has been delivered to a customer. Therefore, two concepts are especially important when it comes to item tracking in ERP system.

- Batch number – An identification for certain quantity of some items with the same item number
- Serial number – An identification for a single unit of an item

Most ERP systems support the use of batch and serial numbers. The usage of batch and serial numbers is required when tracing items for quality issues, since they can

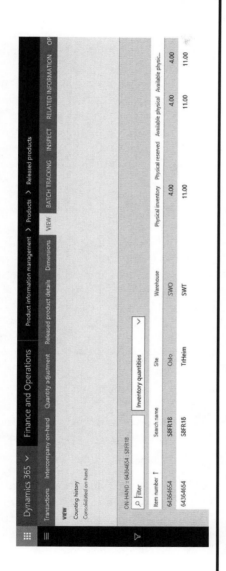

Figure 3.6 On-hand screen in Microsoft Dynamics 365 Supply Chain Management.

help pinpoint which units of the items are the sources of the quality problem. The disadvantage of using batch or serial numbers is that a user must register the batch or serial number every time he or she makes an entry toward the item in the system. For instance, when picking material for a production order, the worker who is picking must report back to the ERP system of what item number is picked as well as what is the serial or batch number of each picked item. This makes it less sensible to enable batch and serial numbers on all items, and use this only on item that requires this form of tracking.

Some ERP applications support lot number as well. Lot numbers are similar to batch number but are often connected to quality inspections in order to group items with the same test results. The lot number is normally used within the quality functions of the ERP system not used in tracing throughout the supply chain. On the other hand, items from a certain lot are transferred to the same batch numbers in order to make them traceable throughout the ERP system for manufacturing supply chain.

OPTISTREAM

Peter in production use batch and serial number to deal with quality issues in production. As a rule, they use batch numbers on critical components and high-volume products, whereas all high-value and engineered products are marked with a serial number. If the quality testing reveals a leakage in a pump caused by a material error in a rubber sealing, he will use the ERP system to find the other pumps that have used a sealing from the same batch of rubber sealing, in order to call in and change this sealing in all the affected pumps.

3.3.7 Reservation

Reserving items is important to keep track of what on-hand quantities are available and not that no other transactions can withdraw these from stock before the reserved transaction is processed.

The reservation process in an ERP system is usually trigged as an order in the system, like a sales order requesting sales products from stock, a production order that require components for production, or a transfer order for moving items from one facility to another. The reservation can either be triggered manually by a user or the ERP system can be set up for automatic reservation of the required items in stock immediately after the order is entered in system.

Reservation is critical to plan and promise future orders and other inventory movements. Most ERP systems have advanced functions for reserving goods. This can include reservation prioritizing rules, or "soft" versus "hard" reservation, where "soft reservation" only reserves an arbitrary unit of the item on stock, while "hard reservation" allocates a specific, often serialized, unit of the item in the warehouse.

OPTISTREAM

Microsoft Dynamics 365 Supply Chain Management is built to support both automatic and manual reservation of stock. The reserved quantity available for reservation will appear in the inventory on-hand screen, and users can access the reservation screen from many places in the system like from the sales order.

Alfred's sales team uses Microsoft Dynamics 365 Supply Chain Management to reserve all sales order lines for future deliveries of standard pumps sold from stock. In this way, they achieve control over the inventory on-hand that is available for new orders. The reservation is done manually by the sales representative in the Microsoft Dynamics 365 Supply Chain Management reservation screen as soon as the order is confirmed through the telephone. Sales order lines with manufactured and/or engineered products that do not have any finished goods available on stock when the order is entered, and are marked to be reserved automatically in the ERP system as soon as the production order is completed and the finish items are put into the finished stock.

Reservations toward a production orders are set up in the same manner. The needed materials and components that are on stock are reserved by Peter in production when the production order is entered while components that must be produced or purchased are marked against the production order and reserved as soon as they are available in the warehouse.

3.3.8 *Inventory Valuation*

Inventory valuation is connected to cost accounting and involves the estimation of the value of the items in stock. The inventory valuation is important for the connection between the logistics parts and financial accounting of an ERP for manufacturing supply chain. Each inventory transaction in the ERP system is associated with a cost that increases as the item flows through the manufacturing supply chain.

Let's say that an item that is used as a component in production is purchased for a certain price. To get a correct value of the on-hand inventory of this item, the ERP system adds an overhead cost to this purchase price and uses this as a value for the item in the warehouse. The purchase module updates the correct accounts in the general ledger with this purchase and change in inventory valuation.

Then, the item is used in production. The ERP uses the cost price of the item (and other items that are needed in this specific production order), as well as labor cost and overhead to find the cost price for the finish product. From the production order ERP system updates things like in inventory value and other postings in the general ledger in the finance accounting module.

Finally, when the produced item is sold the financial accounts are updated according to cost price of the end product and the enterprise can analyze their earnings by comparing the cost price and sales price of the product.

This is a simple example using a single product. Setting the inventory value of an item can be more difficult if there are a lot of item transactions with different cost prices that affects the on-hand stock. This is solved through what is known in ERP system as inventory valuation. Cost accounting in ERP systems is a large and complex area that is besides the focus of this book. But when configuring and using in an ERP system supply chain one should always consider the inventory valuation method to get the finical parts aligned with the material flow. The most commonly used inventory valuation methods used in ERP systems include:

- Weighted average costs – The ERP system uses an average cost of all units of an item on stock to set an inventory value.
- First-in-first-out (FIFO) – The ERP system assumes that the cost of the first transaction into the stock is same as the cost of the first issue of this item from stock.
- Last-in-first-out (LIFO) – The ERP system assumes that the cost of the last transaction into the stock is same as the cost of the first issue of this item from stock.
- Standard cost – A fixed unit cost is used for all inventory transactions on an item in a predetermined period.
- Actual cost – Every individual unit of an item on stock and their transaction cost is traced to find its valuation (often used in connection with serial numbers).

Most ERP systems can be set up to use all of these, or variants of all of these. What methods should be used are up to the cost accounting policies of the enterprise, and sometimes what method is best supported by the ERP system. However, there are some rules of thumb that can be used to guide the direction on what method should be used. Standard cost is often used in production environment to smooth out cost fluctuation from variances in production reporting. Weighted average, FIFO, and LIFO is often used in stable high-volume environment since it demands less work for setting up and managing the system. Actual cost, that gives the best cost estimate, is demanding that all items are managed individually, usually using serial number on each transaction, and is therefore mostly used in low-series manufacturing of high-value products, typically in a project engineering environment.

Inventory valuation is a key factor in ERP systems for manufacturing supply chains since this allows setting a price on each item and inventory transactions in the material flow that again is necessary in order to get the correct postings in the financial accounting module.

OPTISTREAM

The challenge of inventory valuation at OptiStream may best be illustrated through an example. OptiStream do sometimes buy the pump housing on certain pumps from another manufacturer. Let's say that on the first day, OptiStream buys two pump housing for 30 USD each, and puts these on stock. This means that that they now have two of these items on stock of the total value of 60 USD (to simplify we do not consider any overhead or other costs that may affect the cost price of the items). On the next day, OptiStream buys two new, identical, pump housings, but this time they manage to get each of them for 25 USD. The result is that they now have four pump housings adding the inventory value of 110 USD (= 30 USD × 2 + 25 USD × 2). On the third day, they sell one of these housings to another manufacturer.

What will be the value of the rest of the pump's housings on stock in Microsoft Dynamics 365 Supply Chain Management after the sale of this pump? OptiStream can use the ERP system to calculate this value in several ways:

- They can use the weighted average cost of all the pump housings on stock and subtract one. This will result in a remaining total inventory value of 82.5 USD (110 USD − 110 USD /4).
- They can use a FIFO (first-in-first-out) principle and assume that the first housing they put on stock is also first they did sell. This will result in a remaining inventory value of 80 USD (110 USD − 30 USD).
- They can use a LIFO (last-in-first-out) principle and assume that the last pump housing they put on stock is first they did sell. This will result in a remaining inventory value of 85 USD (110 USD − 25 USD).
- They can use a standard cost price on the pump housing of 30 USD independent of what they was purchased or sold for. This will result in a remaining inventory value of 90 USD (30 USD × 4 − 30 USD).
- They can track all handling of physical pump housings by, for example, using a serial number on each of them and get the real valuation of the warehouse. This may result in more complex and cumbersome solution since all units/housings must be registered individually in the system. The inventory cost after the sale will then be 80 or 85 USD (depending on whether the physical item sold had a purchase price of 30 USD or 25 USD).

This example indicates that OptiStream must decide what method of item costing they want to used in their system. The OptiStream has chosen to use the FIFO model on most of its products, components, and materials in Microsoft Dynamics 365 Supply Chain Management. Except for certain produced items where they use standard cost, so that keying errors, breakdowns, and other unforeseen events in the production do not affect the cost price of the item and thereby the inventory value and financial statements.

3.4 Key Inventory Management Processes

The inventory management module of an ERP system provides basic functions for managing the inventories. The inventory management module is often integrated with the warehousing module of an ERP system. However, the inventory management module does only provide basic support for managing the inventory. In this part, we will discuss the processes support that should be found in the inventory management module of all ERP systems for manufacturing supply chain.

3.4.1 Inventory Receipts and Issues

Inventory receipts and shipment transactions in and out of the warehouse are mostly done through sales, production, transfer, and purchase orders. The simplest of ERP systems only handle simple receipt and shipment transactions in connection to the individual order, while other ERP systems may support advanced inbound and outbound processes with functions like quality control, transportation management, and planning. However, in this book we will discuss these processes in connection with the modules that are managing the orders that are triggering the receipt and issues from the warehouses.

3.4.2 Inventory Counting

Things like erroneous or missing user entries and other unforeseen events may result in mismatch of the physical inventory levels in the warehouse with the inventory levels recorded in the ERP system. Therefore, an enterprise must periodically adjust the on-hand inventory in the ERP system so that they are matching the physical quantities on stock. Such a counting process can be a simple adjustment of the few on-hand items and/or locations in the warehouse, or it can be a larger routine involving a closedown of the warehouse and employing the whole warehouse workforce in a counting session.

ERP systems support different counting processes, but the basic inventory counting process does often follow a familiar pattern. Figure 3.7 shows an example of an ERP counting process. In order to illustrate the core process supported by the ERP system, the process in the figure uses physical paper print of counting lists, but

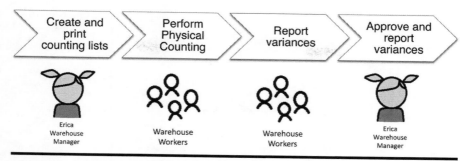

Figure 3.7   The inventory counting process.

mobile or handheld devices are used to speed up these actives in many enterprises. We have added some persons from the OptiStream case to illustrate a typical distribution of work across different roles in the process.

A simple counting process starts by creating a counting request and printing the counting lists. The system may generate counting lists based on principles such as periodic, cyclic, and zero-point counting. The warehouse personnel uses the counting list from the ERP system to execute the physical counting process and reports the variances between the inventory level in the ERP system and the physical inventory on the warehouse. The results of this counting are entered into the ERP system. The counting process ends by reporting and updating the variances in the ERP system.

OPTISTREAM

The warehouse department adjusts the on-hand quantities in Microsoft Dynamics 365 Supply Chain Management in two ways. First, they adjust minor gaps between the on-hand inventory in Microsoft Dynamics 365 Supply Chain Management and the physical on-hand inventory levels, whenever they find these. They report these directly on quantity adjustments on the on-hand screen in Microsoft Dynamics 365 Supply Chain Management.

Secondly, they have a major counting of their warehouses every year. Erica, the warehouse manager uses the counting journal functionality in Microsoft Dynamics 365 Supply Chain Management to organize this work.

Erica closes all activities in the warehouses during the counting process so that nobody takes items in or out of stock, to avoid errors in the printed counting lists. She starts this process by creating a new "counting journal" in Microsoft Dynamics 365 Supply Chain Management that contains all items in the warehouse. She does this by using a function in the ERP application that fills the journal with all selected items, as shown in Figure 3.8.

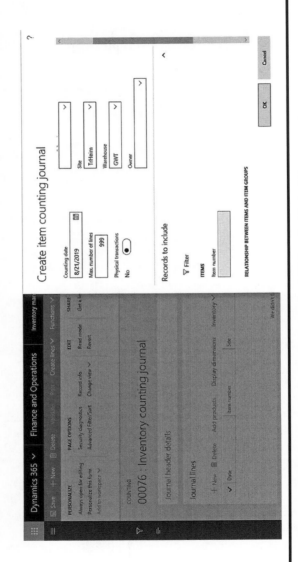

Figure 3.8   Creating a counting journal in Microsoft Dynamics 365 Supply Chain Management.

Then she prints the needed counting lists from this journal and hands these out to the warehouse personnel who starts counting the on-hand inventory using these lists.

Then Erica updates counting journal in Microsoft Dynamics 365 Supply Chain Management with the verified on-hand inventory values as soon as she receives the updated lists from the workers. When all counting journal lines have been updated, Erica posts the counting journal which updates the on-hand inventory in Microsoft Dynamics 365 Supply Chain Management.

3.4.3 Inventory Transfers

The movement of items between areas, locations, and other units within a warehouse or two warehouses that are in the same facility is an inventory activity that may be executed without using order in the ERP system. Nevertheless, the ERP system must trace the inventory transactions made from these activities in order to keep track of the goods stored within the warehouse. Figure 3.9 illustrates a typical inventory transfer process in an ERP system.

The figure shows an inventory transfer process using the basic functions of an inventory module. First, there is a request to transfer the items from one place to another, so that the persons that are going to do the transfer know what goods to transfer and where to move it. This request can either be triggered by a user or it can be generated by the ERP system, for example, filling up items in a production warehouse from a supplying warehouse. Next, someone must physically perform the transfer before the transfer is reported in ERP system and the on-hand inventories are updated in the application.

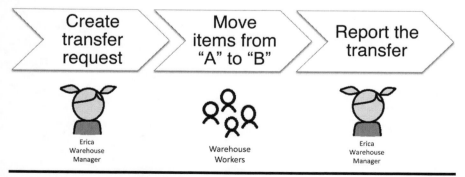

Figure 3.9   The inventory transfer process.

OPTISTREAM

OptiStream uses the built-in warehouse bar code scanner functionality of Microsoft Dynamics 365 Supply Chain Management to ease the entry of inventory transactions in the warehouse. If they, for some reason, do not have the possibility to use these scanners, Erica can use the transfer journal in Microsoft Dynamics 365 Supply Chain Management manually to report all transfers of items within the warehouses.

When transferring items, Erica creates a new journal and adds lists of the items and from/to the units the transfer is about to happen. These requested transfers appear in the bar-code scanners in the warehouse, where the warehouse workers perform the transfers. After the transfer is physically performed, the warehouse workers report this in his handheld device that posts the transfer journal in Microsoft Dynamics 365 Supply Chain Management and updates the inventory values in the warehouses.

3.4.4 The Transfer Order Process

A company may sometimes move goods between warehouses that are sited in facilities far from each other. These activities require more support from the ERP system than as simple warehouse transfer in order to manage logistics functions like the shipment, transportation, and receipts in the receiving warehouse. Many ERP systems have therefore a separate order type, which we have chosen to name "transfer orders", to handle these types of internal company distribution. Figure 3.10 illustrates a basic transfer order process.

The transfer order process starts with entering a transfer order in the ERP application. The order is either created manually or is released from a planned order generated from the ERP system's master plan (see chapter on master planning). Thereafter, the warehouse personnel uses the picking list and shipment functions in the ERP system to pick, pack, and ship the items from the sending warehouse.

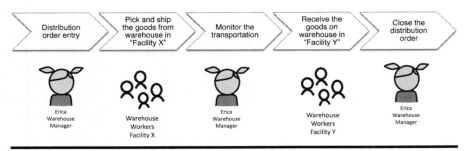

Figure 3.10   Transfer order process.

Since this is an internal transfer, the items never "leave" the company, and they remain a part of the company's on-hand inventory. Therefore, many of the ERP systems operate with "transportation warehouses" where the inventory of the items in transport on transfer orders is temporarily stored so they can be traced and accounted for.

When the transportation arrives at the receiving warehouse, the warehouse personnel receives items, puts them on stock, and reports this back toward the transfer order in the system. The transfer order is closed when the receiving warehouse reports all items as received and in stock.

OPTISTREAM

OptiStream Norway AS stores all finished goods from production in their sales warehouse in Trondheim. Afterwards they transfer required quantities to their sales warehouse in Oslo that lies approximately 500 km from the Trondheim facility. When the stock level is getting low for a certain item in Oslo, Erica the warehouse manager uses the master planning functions to create a new transfer order in Microsoft Dynamics 365 Supply Chain Management for refilling the Oslo warehouse from the Trondheim production facility.

Erica uses this transfer order to print a picking list in Trondheim and arrange the transportation. The warehouse workers pick the goods and register the picked goods for the order in Microsoft Dynamics 365 Supply Chain Management.

Erica posts the shipment when the goods are loaded in the truck and on their way to Trondheim. The transfer order is then marked as "in transit" and the ERP system takes the goods from stock of the sales warehouse in Trondheim and puts them on an "in-transit warehouse" in Microsoft Dynamics 365 Supply Chain Management.

The warehouse workers in Oslo post the receipt when the goods arrive at the destination. Microsoft Dynamics 365 Supply Chain Management do then move the items from the "in-transit warehouse" to the Oslo warehouse. The order is then completed, and Erica can control this and close the transfer.

3.5 Other Inventory Management Functionality

Most ERP systems have modules that extend the core functionality of the inventory management module. Some ERP systems have a lot of built-in functionality to strengthen the inventory management functions, while other ERP systems have less. In this section we will highlight and give a brief overview of some of the most common of these additional modules and functions.

3.5.1 Warehouse Management Module

As shown in this chapter, the inventory management module does only provide basic support for managing inventories. However, most ERP systems include more advanced functions for warehouse management. The warehouse management modules can be overlapping with the inventory management module. One way to separate these two parts of an ERP system is to say that inventory management module organizes each warehouse as a single unit, while a warehouse management module breaks the warehouses further down in different zones, locations, etc., and down into each picking location.

A warehouse management module builds on the basic functions of the inventory management module and expands these functions into within each warehouse as well. This expanded support can include things like pallet management, advance reservation routines, warehouse staffing management, barcode and labeling, support for handheld devices, and advanced picking methods (such as "wave picking" or "voice picking", etc.). More advanced ERP systems have functionality that matches some simpler "warehouse management systems" (WMS).

3.5.2 Shipment and Transportation

Advanced ERP systems have separate modules for shipment and transportation management. Simply speaking, a shipment management module in an ERP system involves the grouping of outbound deliveries from customer orders, transfer orders, and other sources into manageable shipments, and then pick, pack, and other ways handling these shipments according to the shipping routines within the warehouse. The shipment module may also include things like freight and transportation management, transport planning, as well as transport route optimization functionality. Many ERP systems have functions to manage inbound transportation as well. However, if an enterprise can consider using a transportation management system (TMS) in conjunction with the ERP application, they need to extend the shipment support of their total solution.

OPTISTREAM

By using the shipment functionality in Microsoft Dynamics 365 Supply Chain Management, Erica groups outbound orders into shipments. In this way, she can coordinate the picking, packing, and loading of all orders that are involved in the shipment until their transportation carrier arrives. Figure 3.11 shows a screenshot form a shipment in Microsoft Dynamics 365 Supply Chain Management.

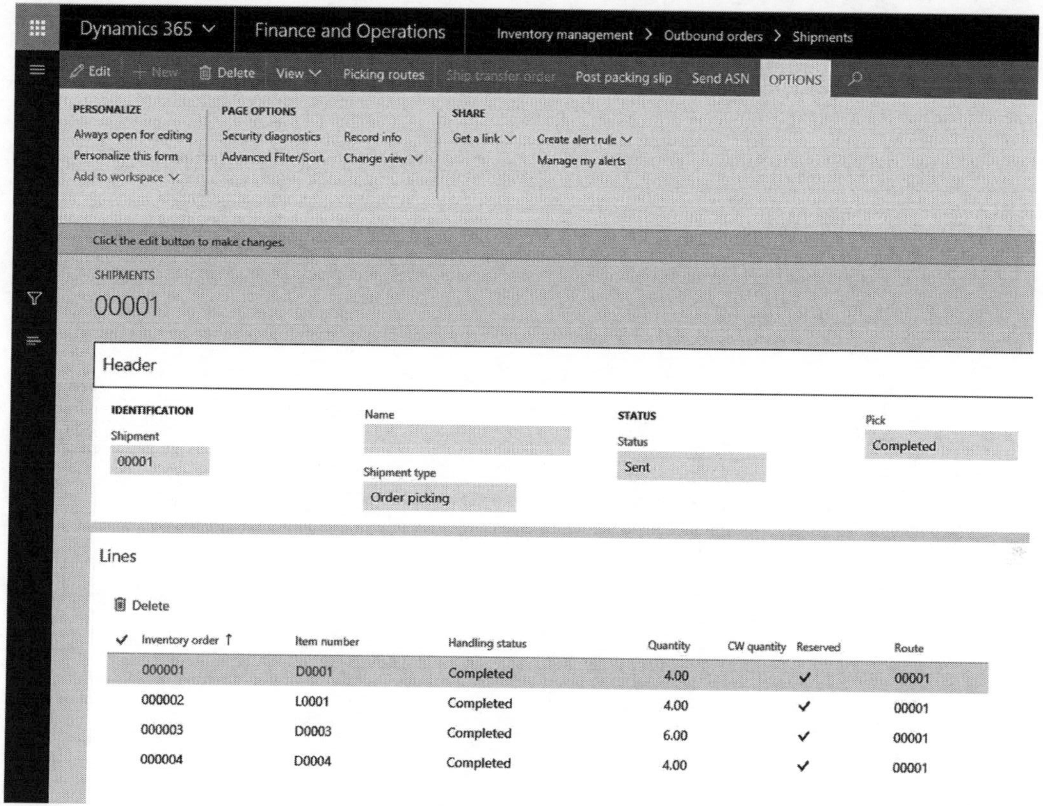

Figure 3.11 Shipment in Microsoft Dynamics 365 Supply Chain Management.

3.5.3 Quality Management

Most ERP systems support quality management in connection to the inventory management module. This module can be simple, for instance only allowing a portion of the stock to be locked for further processing until the quality control is performed. Some ERP applications open for setting up more advance quality management functions like quality testing with automatically sampling and result control. These tests are usually managed through quality orders that can be triggered in certain activities in a supply chain. For instance, when receiving goods from a vendor or finishing an item in production. When a quality order is started the items on the order are locked for processing in the inventory and/or moved to as specific quality testing warehouse. The users can then perform quality testing according to a quality criterion set in the parameters of the ERP systems quality management functions. If the item passes the quality test, its on-hand inventory can be unlocked or moved into the stock again. If the item fails the quality test, the on-hand inventory can be wrecked, returned, or stored according to how the ERP system is set up to handle these quantities.

The quality management functions are especially useful, and are often required in connection with batch and serial numbers since this functionality can identify the exact parts of on-hand items that are involved in the quality process.

The quality management functions of an ERP system may include nonconformity handling as well. Nonconformity handling in an ERP system usually involves a user that reports a nonconformity event related to item somewhere in the facilities supply chain. The nonconformity event process triggers corrective actions and other quality actions according to the setup of the system.

The main advantage of using quality management within an ERP system is that it is fully integrated with inventory transactions in the ERP system. All quality events can be traced and followed up as a part of the items movement in the ERP system. However, quality management in an ERP system is usually hard-linked to quality issues connected to items, and seldom coordinated with the quality standard like the ISO 9000 series. Therefore, some enterprises use a quality management system (QMS) in addition to the ERP system to ensure that quality standards are followed in all parts of their business.

3.6 Key Terms

- Item master
- Inventory movement
- Inventory transactions
- Transfer orders
- Storage units
- Transfer management

- On-hand
- Item tracking
- Reservation
- Inventory valuation
- Inventory counting
- Warehouse management
- Shipment and transportation
- Quality management

3.7 Chapter Summary

The main data elements for an inventory management module are the item master, facilities and warehouse master, and inventory transactions. The other modules for manufacturing supply chains are using the item information from the inventory management module to create orders and other business records, and then writing inventory transactions back to the inventory module as these are processed.

The inventory management module includes basic inventory management functions like inventory receipt and issues, counting, and transfers between warehouses in the same facility. Most ERP systems support transfer orders for transferring items between warehouses in different facilities as well.

An ERP system can support more advanced inventory and warehouse management functions through modules like warehouse management, shipment, and quality management. However, these are additional functions that extend the inventory management functions and are not found in the simplest of ERP systems for manufacturing supply chains.

Chapter 4

Purchase Module

Learning Objectives

After reading this chapter, you will be able to:

- Recognize the basic data structure of a purchase module
- Understand the key functionality of the purchase module
- Describe the purchase order process
- Describe functionalities related to purchase management found in an ERP system

4.1 The Purchase Module

Procurement is an important part of all manufacturing organizations, and the purchasing module is one of the most commonly used modules in any ERP installation. The purchasing processes supported by an ERP system for manufacturing supply chain mirrors what happens in the sale processes at vendor's facility. This means that the structure of the purchasing module relates to the sales module of an ERP system, and these modules acts as endpoints in the same trading process, even if different ERP packages are used on both the customer's and vendor's side. This indicates that the core processes of the the purchasing module have similarities in all ERP packages in order to reflect the sales processes of ERP packages at the sending side.

4.2 Key Data in the Purchase Module

The process of purchasing items in a manufacturing enterprise is centered around execution of purchase order. This is reflected in the ERP systems. Different ERP-software packages may have differences when it comes to purchasing functionality and possibilities, but the purchases module is built around vendor master and purchase orders. Therefore, the core information components found in a purchase module of an ERP system can be summarized as follows:

- Master data on vendors
  - A list of the company's vendors, with the connected data the company need to trade with these.
- Business records in form of purchase orders
  - A purchase order is made for each trade toward a vendor. These orders consist of a purchase order head that describes the vendor, delivery terms, delivery addresses, order status, mode of delivery, and other information that are valid for the whole order. The purchase order line describes what items are being ordered, number of items that are bought, their price, and other purchase-line specific information.

The vendor master holds all the vendor information that company needs to perform and follow up its purchasing activities. A vendor in the vendor master in an ERP system can be anyone that the company makes a payment to. This means the vendor master may not only hold information on trading partners for exchanging goods in the supply chain, but can also include information on vendors selling services as well, such as external consultants or insurance companies. In some enterprises even employees can be registered in the vendor master for making payments on things like travel expenses. The focus of the vendor master in an ERP-system manufacturing supply chains is on vendors that deliver items within their supply chain. The vendor master includes data like:

- Description of the vendors like vendor number, vendor name, language, vendor type and descriptions.
- Contact details for contacting and issuing purchasing orders to the correct person on the receiving end like addresses, contact persons, phone number, and e-mail addresses.
- Delivery terms for ensuring that vendors are sending the ordered items in the agreed manner like receipt addresses, freight terms, delivery methods, and packing terms.
- Information on the vendors price lists, discounts, and other trade agreements.
- Information used in statistic and follow-up of the vendor, for example, fields for statistic groupings and "ABC codes".
- Planning parameters used by the master planning functions of the ERP system. This information includes supply lead times.
- Information connected to the receipt of goods like receiving warehouse and if the vendor should trigger quality control functions in their warehouses.
- Vendor statuses, describing if the company can do trade with the vendors, or if the vendor is stopped, for example, because they have reached their credit limit.

■ Information connected to how the vendors should be handled in the financial parts of the ERP systems. Financial posting profiles, financial dimensions, and vendor's currency are examples of this information.

The other key data elements of the purchase module are the purchase orders. A purchase order consists of an order head and one or several order lines. The order head holds information about the vendor and overall descriptions of this specific delivery, like it's delivery address, the transportation method, delivery dates, and so on. The lines hold information about each item on the order, like what items should be purchased, how many items should be bought, and for what price. ERP systems use the information from the vendor master and the item information from item master in the inventory management module to populate the information on the purchase order. The purchase order generates inventory transactions toward the item and warehouse in the inventory management module when it is posted through a purchasing process. These inventory transactions keep track of the items from the time items are ordered, and the steps the items go through the whole purchasing process until they arrive and are placed into the warehouse.

Figure 4.1 summarizes the key components of a purchase module of an ERP system.

The figure gives a rough overview of the purchasing module of an ERP system. In its basic form it consists of two main data units, the vendor master and the purchase order. The vendor master is the main master data in the purchase module and the vendor data are used when creating a new sales order head. The sales order lines are mainly populated using item information from the inventory management module. The purchase order lines create inventory transactions that enable the ERP system to keep track of the purchasing processes.

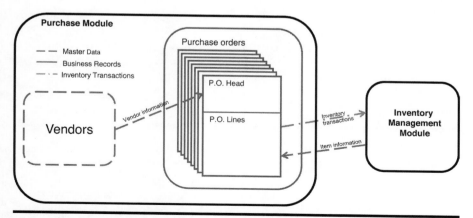

Figure 4.1   Basic data components in the purchase module.

OPTISTREAM

Rita, the purchasing manager, is about to make a purchase toward a new vendor that she has not used before. She registers the new vendor in the vendor master of Microsoft Dynamics 365 Supply Chain Management. In the vendor master, the vendor is given a vendor number, and information like name, addresses, payment terms, delivery terms, other information how the trade toward this vendor should be performed, and financial posted. She also updates the item master with the new items that the vendor can deliver.

The purchase orders are usually created through master planning process (the master planning will be described in Chapter 7), but in this case Rita wants to make the purchase order manually. She enters the "all purchase order" screen in Microsoft Dynamics 365 Supply Chain Management where all purchase orders are listed. Each purchase order consists of an order head and one or several order lines. Rita clicks on the button for creating a new order, and the new order screen appears. Then she selects the correct vendor from the vendor master in the vendor field that the systems fill in the fields with information for the vendor that she just added in the vendor master. She changes the warehouse and site (Facility) since this first order should be delivered directly to the warehouse in Oslo and not Trondheim as it normally should, and presses "OK" to create the order head.

Then she creates the order lines, one for each item that she will purchase on this order. She selects the right items from the item master, and the relevant item information she added in the master data is automatically fetched on order line. This information includes the purchase price, vendor's item number, and required shipment time calculated from the lead time on the item. She has created a new purchase order in Microsoft Dynamics 365 Supply Chain Management as shown in Figure 4.2.

If the basic data in the ERP system are maintained correctly, Rita do only need to fill a vendor number and required date on the order head, as well as the item number and wanted quantity on the order line when entering new manual purchase orders to this vendor in the future.

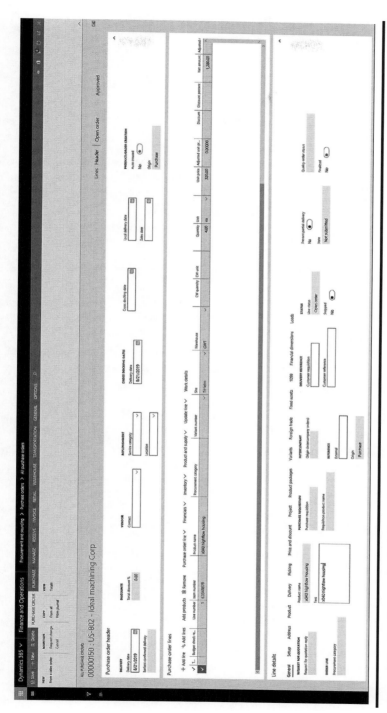

Figure 4.2 Purchase order in Microsoft Dynamics 365 Supply Chain Management.

4.3 Basic Functionality

Many of the purchasing functions are similar across the different ERP packages. This section introduces some basic functionalities one should expect to find in a purchase module of an ERP system for manufacturing supply chains.

4.3.1 Purchase Order Numbering

Like most things in an ERP system, the purchase orders are identified through a system-generated number sequence. The purchase order number is unique for each company, and each company can define their own unique number series to separate the purchase orders from other types of orders in the system. Some ERP systems allow for making different number series to different purchase order types. Most ERP packages have a number attached to each order line on the purchase order as well; this allows for an exact definition of a specific purchase that may be useful in many situations.

OPTISTREAM

Some purchase orders at OptiStream have up to hundred order lines and sometimes the same product is added in multiple order lines due to different requested delivery dates and receiving warehouses. The ERP system previously used at OptiStream did not have any numbering on the purchase order lines that sometimes could make it difficult for Rita to communicate with the vendors.

When transferring to Microsoft Dynamics 365 Supply Chain Management, OptiStream did get numbers on the purchase order lines. This means that Rita now can, for example, refer to "order 0003234 and line 4" when asking a vendor for a delivery of an ordered item, instead of using the item number, delivery date, and warehouse to find the correct purchase line on the order.

4.3.2 Purchase Order Types

Most ERP systems operate with different purchase order types to separate different types of purchase orders and how they should be processed in the application. Some ERP systems allow users to setup and define its own purchase order types, while other systems have predefined and fixed categorizations. A large range of order types exist; some examples are listed below.

- Normal purchase order – Used for normal orders
- Internal purchase order – Used for things like subcontracting or stock transfers between warehouses
- Frame agreements call-off – Purchase orders from connected frame agreement

- Rush order – Orders that should be processed before normal orders
- Dummy orders – Orders that are used for examples or testing
- Electronic orders – Orders that are communicated electronically, for example, through the internet or by EDI messages
- Subcontracting orders – Purchase order connected to a production order for doing subcontracting work
- Service orders – Purchase orders connected to a service module in the ERP system
- Project orders – Purchase orders connected to a project module in the ERP system
- Template orders – Temporary order that can be used as a template to request a specific price, receipt date, or other delivery terms
- Return orders – Orders that manage returns to vendors

As the list indicates, purchase order types can be tool separating the different types of purchases. This purchase order type information can be in a single field or spread over multiple fields on the purchase order. In some systems, the purchase order types are mainly used to separate between the orders that the application needs to treat differently, like for identifying subcontracting purchase orders where the application needs to post the purchase costs toward a production order. While in other applications they can also be used to provide information to the users of the application for how they should process and report on the orders as well, for example, a purchase order with order type "rush order", that is only used to inform the users that they need to process this order first.

A company can use the purchase order types in many ways, especially if they have an ERP system that opens for both adding user-defined order types and providing parameters for how these should be handled in the system. So, the orders of the users and the ERP system can be processed differently. Purchase order types can be used for statistical purposes as well, by using the order type to separate different purchase types in reports and status screen, for example, for measuring the delivery precision the different vendors have high-priority orders.

Therefore, depending on the possibility of the ERP application and how the company has chosen to set up the system, purchase order types can be an important part in the information handling of the purchase department, or it can be an minor function mainly used to solve functions within the application.

OPTISTREAM

Microsoft Dynamics 365 Supply Chain Management currently operates only with three fixed purchase order types. OptiStream uses them as follows:

- Journal order – Represents a template or a dummy purchase order that may be used for simulation reasons. It will not affect stock quantities or generate item transactions.

- Purchase order – Used for normal orders, when a vendor confirms an order.
- Returned order –For items that will be returned to the vendor.

Rita can choose the purchase order type when she makes a new purchase order as shown in Figure 4.3.

In their previous ERP system Rita could make her own order types, where she had made a separate order type for rush orders. Since Microsoft

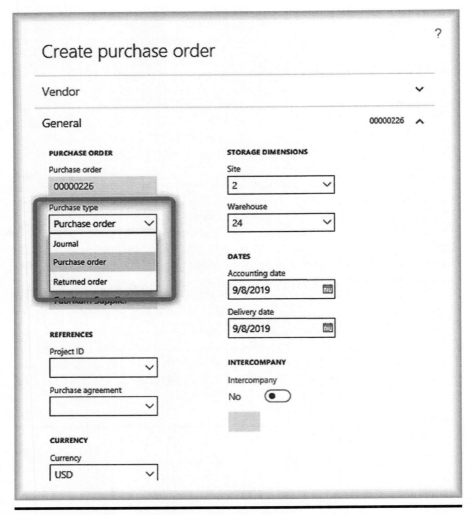

Figure 4.3 Purchase order types in Microsoft Dynamics 365 Supply Chain Management.

Dynamics 365 Supply Chain Management only operates fixed order types, she has no possibility to separate rush orders from other purchase orders in the ERP system. During the first time with Microsoft Dynamics 365 Supply Chain Management this did seem like a disadvantage compared with their old system and they did consider doing a modification in the system to get more purchase order types in the system.

But Rita and OptiStream did not choose this modification and did rather introduce an attitude in the purchasing department that all orders should be delivered on-time instead treating certain orders at the expense of others. This attitude has reduced the amount of rush orders. There are of course still some orders that are more important and must be worked with the vendors to get in time. But the amount of these orders has been reduced and can therefore be managed outside the system. All delays will be managed by the planning department that has the overview anyway, and any deviations must be handled manually in cooperation with the vendor.

Even if Rita still would have preferred to be able to create her own sales order types in Microsoft Dynamics 365 Supply Chain Management, she is glad that they have managed to change the way they are working instead of doing modifications to the standard ERP system.

4.3.3 Purchase Order Statuses

All purchase orders have a status that indicates how far it has gone in the purchasing process. Some ERP systems use number codes and others use text fields to describe the status of a purchase order. The statuses do usually indicate if the order is new, if it has been sent to the vendor, if the items on the order have arrived at the warehouse, if the vendor invoice been registered toward the order, and so on.

OPTISTREAM

Microsoft Dynamics 365 Supply Chain Management has several different status fields on the purchase orders where Rita and other users at OptiStream can find the status of their orders. The three most important of these are:

- Status – Holds the main status of the order. Statuses in this field are "open order", "received", "invoiced", or "canceled".
- Document status – Indicates what order documents have been submitted. Values in this field can be "none", "purchase inquiry", "purchase order", "product receipt" or "invoice".

- Approval status – Used for internal approval of the order so that it can be processed. Statuses are "draft", "in review", "rejected", "approved", "in external review" or "confirmed".

Rita and others in the purchase department uses these statuses daily to check the progress with the purchases. However, they wish that the "status" field also would incorporate the information from the "document status" in a single field, so they do not need to check two fields to see if an open order has not yet been sent to the vendor.

4.3.4 Purchase Pricing and Agreements

A company may define purchase prices for the items in an ERP system. The prices can be set for each vendor, forming vendor price lists that can be managed and updated to meet changing trade requirements. Most ERP systems have advanced functionality for purchase pricing like allowing the users to operate with different pricelist for different types of trades, discount and rebate management, setting time on prices, automatic price adjustments, and so on. When a user enters a new purchase order line, the system can use these predefined rules and suggest correct pricing accordingly on the order line. Most systems open for letting the users change or enter a missing purchase price directly on the purchase order lines, but the company can choose to lock the purchase price on the orders as well, forcing the user to use the price from a valid price list on the order.

Purchase pricing and agreements management can be a complex area where many ERP systems provide deep functionality. There exist third-party solutions for purchase price management that can operate in cooperation with the ERP system, if it is necessary to strengthen this area further.

OPTISTREAM

Rita has registered a base purchase price for all items in Microsoft Dynamics 365 Supply Chain Management, for ensuring that all items have a suggested purchase price if there are no pricelist register toward the item in the system. She negotiates prices with the vendors on timely basis and registers and adjusts all vendor pricelist in a function named "vendor trade agreements" in the system. The vendor trade agreements hold information on any line, multiline, and total discounts they may have with the vendor. When a purchase order is created in the system, Microsoft Dynamics 365 Supply Chain Management looks in the pricelist to see if there are any purchase prices registered for the particular vendor in the trade agreement; if not, the system suggests the base price on the order line.

4.3.5 *Delivery Time and Promising*

ERP systems hold lead times in the master data that can be used on orders to calculate the delivery time of a purchase order. The delivery lead timer is used by the master planning function to plan future purchases so that the items are delivered in time. In most systems, the vendors confirmed delivery time can be updated on the purchase order and/or orders line. This delivery time will then override the delivery time calculated from the lead times in the next master planning run.

OPTISTREAM

Rita has set purchase lead time on each item for each facility in Microsoft Dynamics 365 Supply Chain Management as shown in Figure 4.4.

Microsoft Dynamics 365 Supply Chain Management uses the purchase lead times when calculating the delivery time on the purchase order lines and in the master planning functions (the master planning module is discussed later in this book). If for some reason the vendor cannot meet the agreed delivery time on the whole or parts of the order, Rita updates the affected orders line with a new, confirmed delivery date. Microsoft Dynamics 365 Supply Chain Management will then use the confirmed delivery date on the purchase orders next time Greta runs master planning to account for the effect this change may have on OptiStream's overall master plan.

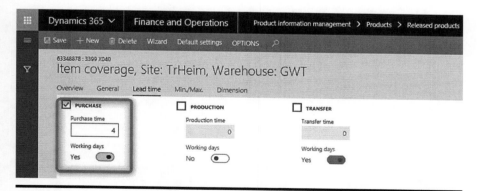

Figure 4.4   Setting purchase lead time on an item.

4.4 The Purchase Order Process

Most of the functions within a purchase order module are in some way or another connected to the purchase order process, and the purchase order process can be identified to the core business process within the purchase module in any ERP system. This process is illustrated in Figure 4.5.

The figure illustrates that the purchase order process starts by creating a new order in the ERP system. The purchase order can be created manually, or it can be released from planned order in master plan, triggered from a sales order, or similar functions.

After creating the purchase order, the next step is to send the ordering information to the vendor. ERP systems do usually support various ways of sending purchase orders. Users can manually print the order and send the physical document to the vendor, or they can use various forms for electronic communication like e-mail, a vendor web portal, electronic messaging, and so on.

When the vendor confirms the delivery, the purchase order in the ERP system is updated. If the vendor cannot deliver the order or not meet some of the wanted requests, such as the price, ordered quantity, the delivery date and/or other delivery terms, the buyer either agrees on the changes or cancels the order. The purchase order is then updated accordingly. The purchase order then gets a status in the ERP system that indicates it is confirmed (or canceled/closed).

In the next step the vendor ships the goods from his warehouses. It is possible to register on the purchase orders that the goods have been shipped from the vendor in many ERP systems, while in other ERP packages this is managed in a transportation module. We have, therefore, simplified the figure by excluding this step, since this is not a mandatory step and is not always used in real-life ERP implementations.

The receipt activities start when the goods arrive at the receiving company. This may be done in several steps depending on the possibilities in the ERP system. More basic ERP systems do only support a one-step receipt process where a user updates the purchase order manually when he or she gets a notice that the items have been received and put into stock. More advanced systems may support a multistep receipt process that also includes warehouse management functions that updates purchase order automatically as is it processed during the receipt process. These registrations can include the arrival of the goods at the warehouse, quality control routines, put

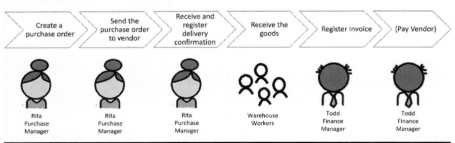

Figure 4.5 Purchase order process.

away in the warehouse, and so on. When the items are in stock, the purchase order gets a status that reveals that the order has been received in the warehouse.

When the company gets the invoice from the vendors, the invoice can be registered in the system and its amount and quantity is matched toward the order and the receipt. If the invoice is OK it will be included in the company account payable and this does normally concludes purchase order process in the ERP system. The finance department processes the vendors payments in the account payable module and updates the financial accounts.

OPTISTREAM

All new orders in Microsoft Dynamics 365 Supply Chain Management have the status "open order". The first step in the purchase order process at OptiStream is to send the purchase order to the customer. Rita does this by confirming the purchase order. Microsoft Dynamics 365 Supply Chain Management do then create an e-mail with a PDF of the purchase order, which Rita sends to the vendor. The order still has the status "open order", but it has got an approval status "confirmed".

The vendor sends a confirmed delivery date back to OptiStream if the he cannot deliver the order at the requested delivery date. Rita updates the field "confirmed delivery date" on the sales order lines to mark the change in delivery date. If the vendor needs to do any change on things like the quantity or pricing, she usually only updates the order line with the new information and sends a new confirmation to the vendor.

Erica, the warehouse manager uses a "workspace" named "purchase order receipt and follow-up", where she can get an overview and update an incoming purchase order. Such a workspace in Microsoft Dynamics 365 Supply Chain Management is shown in Figure 4.6.

When the goods arrive at the warehouse, Erica posts the receipt list on the purchase orders in Microsoft Dynamics 365 Supply Chain Management. The purchase order still has the status "open order", but the document status is changed to "receipt list". Rita and other users can then see on the purchase order that the goods have arrived at the warehouse but have not yet been put into stock.

Erica and the warehouse workers use a hand-held device when putting the items in the warehouse. When the items are put into the stock, the receipt is posted, and the purchase order gets status "received". The on-hand in the warehouse module is then updated with the new goods and the items are available for the other departments at OptiStream for further processing.

When the invoice arrives from the vendor, Todd in finance uses the invoice matching function in Microsoft Dynamics 365 Supply Chain Management to check if the invoice corresponds with the original purchase order as well as the number of items that Erica received in the warehouse.

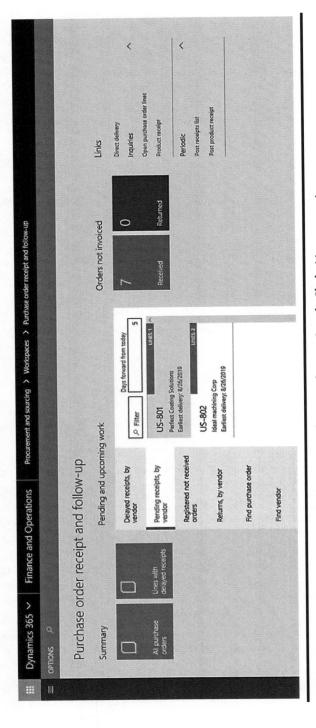

Figure 4.6 Purchase order workspace in Microsoft Dynamics 365 Supply Chain Management.

If the invoice is correct, he posts invoice that updates the status on the purchase order to "invoiced". This triggers the last financial transactions on the order and closes the purchase order. The payment to the vendor is now included the next time Todd is running a remittance process in Microsoft Dynamics 365 Supply Chain Management for paying this vendor.

4.5 Other Purchase Module Functionalities

Users can expect to find a lot of additional support for various purchasing activities within a purchase module. Here we will mention two functions that are present in almost all ERP packages for manufacturing supply chains.

4.5.1 Internal Purchase Requisitions

Many ERP systems have functions to support internal purchase requisitions. Requisitions are requests made by employees for purchase of equipment, services, and other supplies.

Normally, the requisitions are sent through an approval routine before it transforms approved requisitions into a purchase order for procurement of the required items or services. Ensure that no purchase is done before it has been approved by the right authorities at the enterprise.

OPTISTREAM

OptiStream uses the built-in requisition function in Microsoft Dynamics 365 Supply Chain Management that is available in the standard employee web portal. An employee can create a new requisition in the ERP system, which then uses a workflow routine to ensure that the requisition is approved by authorized employees. When the requisition is approved it is transformed into a purchase order that Rita and the others in the purchase department can process together with the other purchase orders.

4.5.2 Request for Quote (RFQ)

A company may sometimes need to issue a "request for quote" (RFQ) to several vendors to check if they are willing or able to deliver an order. The RFQ process in an ERP system for manufacturing supply chains normally starts by creating new RFQ-record toward the item. Then, the vendors are registered on this RFQ, so that the quotation documents can be generated and send to the correct parties. When the vendors respond the price, quantity, delivery date, and other information that may be of interest for the choice, are registered toward the vendors on the RFQ. When all the data are collected and one of the vendors is chosen, the ERP system automatically creates a purchase order toward this vendor, while the others get a rejection letter.

Some ERP systems support advanced functions for RFQ management, which includes options of releasing RFQs from master planning, advanced functionality for comparing offers from the vendors, integration to vendor internet sites for automatic response, and so on. However, the RFQ management in an ERP system for manufacturing supply chains is centered around trading items. If an enterprise wants, for example, to run a RFQ process on a larger project, they are probably better off to choose RFQ support from a project module in the ERP system or an external tool.

OPTISTREAM

OptiStream uses the RFQ in Microsoft Dynamics 365 Supply Chain Management for larger purchases. This functionality in Microsoft Dynamics 365 Supply Chain Management allows Rita in purchase to create a RFQ and send it to several vendors. After this, Rita registers and compares vendor replies before one is chosen and the quotation is transformed into a purchase order in Microsoft Dynamics 365 Supply Chain Management.

4.6 Key Terms

- Vendor master
- Purchase order
- Purchase order types
- Purchase order statuses
- Purchase pricing and agreements
- Delivery time and promising
- Purchase requisitions
- Request for quote

4.7 Chapter Summary

This chapter has shown that the basic data in a purchase module in an ERP system is the vendor master and purchase order. The basic functionality of a purchase module includes purchase order types, purchase order statuses, purchase pricing, and delivery time calculations.

The most important steps in the purchase order process are creating of the purchase order, sending the purchase order to the vendor, getting a confirmation from the vendor, receiving the goods, checking the invoice, and paying the vendor.

The purchase order module of an ERP system does usually hold other functions beside the core functionality; two of these are support for internal purchase requisition and request for quote.

Chapter 5

Sales Module

Learning Objectives

After reading this chapter, you will be able to:

- Understand the basic data structure of the sales order module
- Describe the key functionality of the sales order module
- Get an overview over the sales order process
- Describe relevant functionality in a sales order module

5.1 The Sales Module

The sales module supports the sales process and other customer activities in a company. Sales orders represent the trade with customers which, directly or indirectly, triggers other replenishment processes throughout the supply chain. A large portion of sale that is made around the world today ends up in a sales order in a sales module of an ERP system. This includes business-to-businesses trade of high-value goods, a small consumer purchase through a Web-store, or a sale from a point-of-sales device in a grocery store. The sales module is an essential part of an ERP solution, and one of the most commonly used ERP modules in a manufacturing supply chain.

5.2 Data in the Sales Module

The sales module of an ERP system for manufacturing supply chains consists of the data a company need to sell items toward its customers. The possibilities and functionality found in these modules may vary a lot between the different ERP applications. However, two basic types of data components that are always found across all ERP software packages are:

- Master data on customers
    - The customer master lists all customers and the needed information in order to make trade with these customers.
- Business records in form of sales orders
    - Orders are created for each sale toward a customer. The customer order consists of an order head and one or several order lines. The customer order head holds information on the customer and delivery information valid for the whole order, while each order line describes the items that customer has ordered as well as the quantity, price, and other sales line specific information.

The customer master is the key master data recorded in the sales order module. In the customer master, a company can list all the parties with whom they can trade items or services. A customer in the customer master is a legal entity such as a natural person or a company, and each customer should only be registered once in the customer master. If a customer is a company where multiple persons can order, the ERP system allows registering the company as a single customer, with several contact persons and delivery addresses attached to this account.

Some ERP systems may allow organizing relations hierarchies between customers. For instance, let's say a company is doing trade with a larger group consisting of a head office and several subsidiaries. The head office and each subsidiary is organized as a separate company/legal unit and therefore registered as separate customers in the customer master at this company. However, the subsidiaries are doing the trade of the physical goods while the payment processes are centralized at the head office at this group. The ERP system can then be set up so that the sales orders are made and registered toward the subsidiaries that also will receive the goods, while the invoices from the same sales orders are sent to the head office and the accounts receivable is registered toward this customer account in the customer master.

Often may customers in the customer master are also be registered as a vendor in the vendor master. This means that the same organization may be registered at two places in the ERP system, both in the customer master and the vendor master. Therefore, the customer master and the vendor master merged into a "trading partner master" in some ERP packages. Such "trading partner master" includes all vendors and customers and the needed information for doing sales and/or purchases from them. Even if there are advantages of collecting all trading partner in one register, this does not affect how the ERP system is used in a manufacturing supply chain.

Typical information found on the customers in an ERP system includes:

- Description of the customer like customer number, customer name, preferred language, customer type and descriptions.
- Contact details for contacting and issuing sales orders to the correct person on the receiving end like addresses, contact persons, phone number, and e-mail addresses.
- Delivery terms for ensuring that customers are sending the ordered items in the agreed manner like receipt addresses, freight terms, delivery methods, and packing terms.
- Information on the customer price lists, discounts, and other price information and agreements.
- Information used in statistic and follow-up of the customer, for example, statistic group and "ABC-codes".
- Sales lead times and other planning information used by the master planning functions of the ERP system.
- Information connected to the shipping of goods like delivering warehouse and carrier information.
- Customer statuses and credit rates describing if the company can do trade with the vendors, or if the vendor is stopped.
- Information connected to how the customer should be handled in the financial parts of the ERP systems. Financial posting profiles, financial dimensions, and customer currencies are examples of this information.

The management of the sales orders is the main function supported by a sales module in an ERP system. The sales order can be made manually by a user, or they can be automatically created through electronic communication with a trading partner like "EDI orders", a WEB shop, a point-of-sales device, or any other sales channels a manufacturing company may have access to.

The sales order consists of an order head and order lines. The order head describes the customer and the delivery terms for the order, like the customers address and their transportation methods. The lines describe the items that are to be sold and the sales price.

The sales orders are built for trading items, but sometimes a manufacturing company must sell a service in addition to the physical products. A way of dealing with this is to add an order line with a "service-item" for including things like transportation costs or installation of the products or other services that should be invoiced together with the ordered items. Most ERP systems have functionality for managing service-items that only affects the revenue from sales orders, and do not affect inventories. Using service-items on sales order lines is best suited for trading small-scale services and in connection to sale of

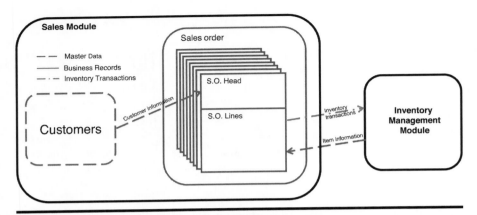

Figure 5.1   Basic data components in the sales module.

physical products, if the services are a major part of the business, the company should rather use another part of the ERP system, like a service module or a project module.

Figure 5.1 summarizes the basic components of a sales module of an ERP system. The figure illustrates that the fundamental data components in the sales module are the customer master and the sales orders. The former holds master data about the customers, while the latter holds business records for supporting the sales process. A sales order consists of a sales order header and a sales order line. The sales order header includes information about the customer and other key information of sale and delivery of the specific order. The sales order lines use item information from item master in the inventory management module and describe what items the customer is acquiring, the quantity, pricing, and, so on. The sales orders generate inventory transactions so that the other parts of the system are updated with the effects the sales process has on the inventory.

OPTISTREAM

OptiStream sell their products to other businesses that use the pumps in their own products and/or resells these to the consumer market. OptiStream seeks long-term relationship with their customers, and Alfred, the sales manager does not need to add a new customer in the customer master every day. But when he does, he creates a new customer account and adds things like customer group, contact addresses, contact persons, mode of delivery, country/language, sales prices list, and so on. Then he contacts Todd in finance that adds credit limits, bank accounts, currencies, financial posting profiles, and other information that the financial department needs to get the finance accounting to work on this customer in Microsoft Dynamics 365 Supply Chain Management.

The two sister companies OptiStream Norway and OptiStream US both are using the same Microsoft Dynamics 365 Supply Chain Management solution, but they are separate companies, and therefore, do not share the same customer master. This also implies that OptiStream US is registered as a customer in OptiStream Norway customer master, and consequentially OptiStream Norway is registered as a vendor in the vendor master at OptiStream US. In this way they can do trade together, in the same manner as they trade with other legal companies. However, parts of the trading process between these two OptiStream companies can be automated through the "intercompany functionality" of Microsoft Dynamics 365 Supply Chain Management. These possibilities will be explored later in this book.

Alfred can get an overview over the customer orders through the "all sales order" application. Here he can add new orders, or review and edit orders on ongoing sales. A sales order in Microsoft Dynamics 365 Supply Chain Management is shown in Figure 5.2.

All sales at OptiStream are recorded through a sales order. This includes sales of pumps, spare parts, and services. Services do only account for a very small fraction of the sales at OptiStream. But sometimes a customer may ask for a one-time service, like help with installing a pump in one of their products. In such cases Alfred uses an item, named "installation" with item type "service" on the sales order line. These "service items" do not affect the inventory in Microsoft Dynamics 365 Supply Chain Management but are only used to process sales of services in the system.

Today OptiStream is focusing toward mass production of pumps, and they leave most of the installation and other services to their resellers. If in the future OptiStream will start to expand their business toward the service market as well, they should rather start using the project and/or service modules of Microsoft Dynamics 365 Supply Chain Management that have functionality that are more focused for this type of sales processes.

5.3 Basic Functionality

The sales module requires some basic functionalities to support a sales order process. This section mentions the most important of these.

5.3.1 Sales Order Number

As for the purchase orders, the ERP system generates a unique number for all sales order registered in the system. These numbers can be used when referring to a specific order or when seeking after sales order in an ERP application. Order numbers are used in communication toward outside parties and are printed on all documents and included in all electronic communication toward the customers. The sales orders in an ERP system do usually have field where the customer's reference number can

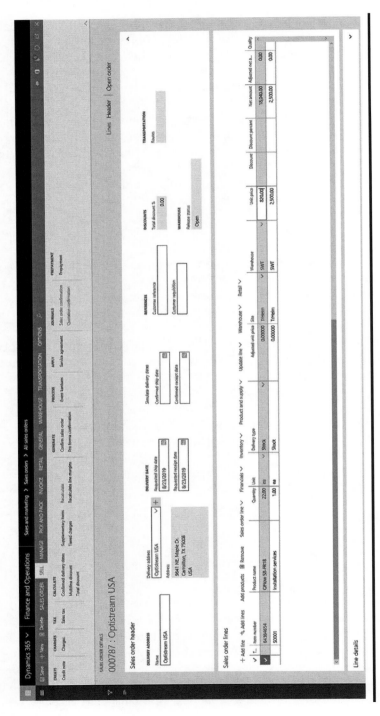

Figure 5.2 Sales order in Microsoft Dynamics 365 Supply Chain Management.

be entered. When doing business to business transactions in a manufacturing supply chain, this reference is usually set to be the customer's purchase order number so that orders in the ERP system of the two different parties can be inked together.

OPTISTREAM

All sales orders in Microsoft Dynamics 365 Supply Chain Management get a unique sales order number. Alfred and the others in the sales departments use these orders to find the exact sales order when, for example, getting questions from customers on a specific order. The sales order number is also used as a reference in the incoming and outgoing messages, when they are doing electronic trade with their customers.

5.3.2 Sales Order Type

Sales order type is used to define the different types of sales orders registered in an ERP system. The sales order type may be used to define how the ERP system and the users should process the order so that it can be used in search, reporting, and statistic functions.

As for purchase order types some ERP systems only come with a limited and fixed set of order types, while other ERP systems may allow the company to define an unlimited number of sales order types. Some of the sales order types that are found in ERP systems are listed below.

■ Normal sales orders – For selling goods and services
■ Return orders – For managing returned goods from the customer
■ Credit orders – For sending money back to customers for returned goods
■ Direct deliveries – For sending goods from a vendor directly to a customer
■ Rush orders – For fast deliveries, that should be prioritized before other orders
■ Intercompany orders – Orders used in sales toward other companies in the same group
■ Cash sales – Where a cash payment is received when the order is confirmed
■ Manufactured orders – Orders that are produced and not delivered from stock
■ Stock orders – Orders that should be picked from stock

The sales order type dictates how the ERP system manages the order process. In some ERP system the sales order type dictates things like the reservation sequences, the execution of the shipment process, master planning parameters, modes of delivery, and payment process. In other ERP packages the usage of the sales order type is more limited, and the users must typically check several fields on the sales order to find the same information that can be revealed through the sales order type of other ERP applications.

OPTISTREAM

Microsoft Dynamics 365 Supply Chain Management operates with a few, fixed order types. These order types include:

- Sales orders – For most types of sales
- Journal – For sales order templates
- Returned order – For returns from customers
- Item requirements – For consumption of item in projects

This means that Microsoft Dynamics 365 Supply Chain Management, and thereby OptiStream has only one order type ("sales order") on all "normal" sales to customers. OptiStream has therefore implemented routines for managing sales orders individually, like manually reserving items toward the sales orders; they do not use the term "rush orders" but handle any emergencies manually outside the system; they use the delivery warehouse to indicate if the order is for spare parts or a manufactured product; and so on. In this way, they can use one order type in Microsoft Dynamics 365 Supply Chain Management and manage the different types of sales processes in the system by using other fields, functions, and routines.

5.3.3 Sales Order Statuses

ERP system marks the sales orders with statuses according to how far it has gone in the sales process. The level of detail the order status reveals varies depending on the ERP system. For example, one system may have statuses on sales orders head that indicates if its order lines have reserved the goods in stock. In other systems, the user can only see if the order has been processed and must, for example, open a separate reservation application in the ERP system to see if any inventory reservations have been made toward the sales order. Anyway, all systems do have statuses to indicate how far a sale order has been processed, and the way the ERP application solves this affects how the users works with the system.

OPTISTREAM

Microsoft Dynamics 365 Supply Chain Management at OptiStream provides several statuses on the sales orders. Two of the most important statuses are:

- "Status" – The status field on the sales order holds the main status of the order. The statuses can be "open order", "delivered", "invoiced" or "canceled".
- "Document status" – Indicates the documents have been submitted from the order.

Alfred uses the status field to see which order is still open, received, invoiced, or canceled. However, he uses the document status if he needs to see the details of how far an open order has gone. For example, if the status field says, "open order", and the document status says, "confirmation", he knows that the order confirmation already has been sent to the customer. Hence, Alfred knows that OptiStream can deliver the order and the customer is informed on that. An example on the status field on a sales order in Microsoft Dynamics 365 Supply Chain Management is shown in the marking in Figure 5.3.

5.3.4 Sales Price and Sales Price Agreements

Sales pricing is an important topic in all companies that are a part of a manufacturing supply chain. Most ERP systems manage the sales prices through price list functionality. Price lists can be set on items or groups of items in combination with what customer or customer groups the pricelist should be valid for. The prices on the price list can be set in combination with other pricing dimensions as well. Like in what time period the price should be valid, for what sales quantity that triggers the price, and so on. The sales price lists and sales price functions include other functions as well, such as discounts, campaigns, supplementary items, commissioning, and bonuses. The ERP systems may have a whole range of different pricelists and pricing options for an item, to provide different prices to different customers with different deals and agreements.

The system can calculate and update the sales price automatically according to the valid price lists and other parameters. The ERP system can be configured to make the users unable to enter or change the prices on the sales order lines. Alternatively, the users may be allowed to overrule and adjust the item's sales price from price lists manually, all after the policy of the company and the parameter setup of the ERP system.

OPTISTREAM

Alfred manages the sales price lists through the "trade agreements" function in Microsoft Dynamics 365 Supply Chain Management. Through the trade agreements, Microsoft Dynamics 365 Supply Chain Management connects different sales prices and discounts for the items with different customers. Alfred negotiates the prices and other terms with the customers and makes sure that the "trade agreements" in Microsoft Dynamics 365 Supply Chain Management is updated. In this way the correct sales price is set by the ERP system every time a new sales order line is made in the system.

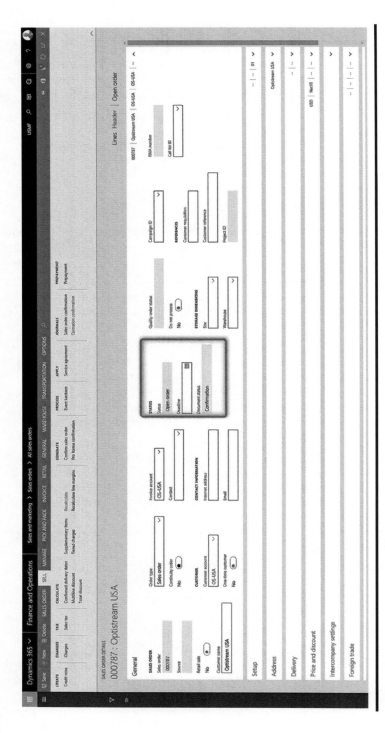

Figure 5.3 Status fields on sales order.

5.3.5 Order Promising

Order promising involves the process of setting the correct delivery date to the customer. In its simplest form, this may be a check if the desired items are available on stock, and/or where the ERP system uses a fixed lead time set in the master data to find the possible delivery dates.

Normally the ERP system holds more advanced methods for estimating delivery date for goods. The most common of these are:

■ Available-to-promise (ATP) – The ERP system estimates what can be promised to customers by calculating an item's future on-hand and balancing this toward planned receipts and issues.
■ Capable-to-promise (CTP) – Enhances the ATP calculation for manufactured items by including potential capacity shortages in production and the availability of subcomponents to find when an item can be delivered to the customer.

The way ATP, CTP, and similar calculations are executed can vary according to the needs of the specific company. The ERP systems use the item's inventory transactions to perform the ATP calculations. The inventory transactions hold information on all historical, planned, and open inventory event and can therefore be used to find the future on-hand and the ATP information. The CTP calculations are using calculations similar to the gross/net and capacity planning functions that will be discussed in later chapters, to find when the company can get the needed items and production capacity to deliver the products.

A basic ATP formula is: ATP = on-hand + supply − demand, where on-hand is available inventory or capacity, supply is planned and scheduled receipts, and demand is sales orders (forecasted demand is not included).

For example, let's find the ATP for an item "A" in "period 1". Using the inventory transactions on item "A", the following information can be found: The scheduled receipts are 130 pieces and inventory on-hand is 30 pieces that equals 160 in total supply for item A for period 1. To calculate the total availability to promise for period 1, all committed demand from the total supply is subtracted. Let's say that the total demand for item A in period 1 is 110 pieces where 70 comes from a forecast for and 40 from sales orders. Since the forecast is not considered committed demand, but the sales order is, the total committed demand is 40. Therefore, the ATP is 160 minus 40, or 120 pieces for item A in period 1.

The ATP, CTP, and similar order promising calculations require that the company is confident that the data in the ERP system is correct and always up-to-date in order to provide exact delivery dates.

OPTISTREAM

OptiStream normally operates with standard delivery times on all their products. When Alfred creates new sales order, Microsoft Dynamics 365 Supply Chain Management uses the lead times in the master data to set a delivery date on the sales order lines. Alfred only performs an ATP if there are shortages on a stocked product that should be on-hand in the sales warehouse and, therefore, cannot be delivered to the customer in a right way. In this way the customer gets information when they can expect the delivery of the items.

The ATP calculation for a sales order line in Microsoft Dynamics 365 Supply Chain Management is shown in Figure 5.4. This ATP application displays the available quantity that can be delivered each day ahead for the item, allowing Alfred to find when is the delivery date, and update the order with this information.

5.4 The Sales Order Process

The sales order process is also termed the "order-to-cash" process. Figure 5.5 illustrates a normal sales process supported by an ERP system.

Entering the sales order is the first activity in the sales order process. This involves creating a sales order header, which holds information about the customer and the order's overall delivery terms. The sales order lines give information about the desired items, the quantity of items, their pricing as well as their individual delivery terms. A sales clerk may enter the sales order directly into the system, or the sales order can come from other sources such as an internet site or an electronic ordering standard such as web-service or EDI messages.

Then an order confirmation is sent to the customer to verify and document agreed sales terms, price, delivery time, and other order-specific details. This is can be also be performed through electronic means of communication such as an EDI-message, or alternatively, the customer receives an e-mail or a printout of the sales order confirmation.

The next step is to pick the goods from stock. This normally starts by printing a picking list from the ERP system. The picking policy of the company and the possibilities of the warehousing capabilities of ERP system dictate the structure of the picking processes. However, the most basic picking routine found in all ERP systems for manufacturing supply chains is that one sales order triggers one picking list. The warehouse workers pick and pack the goods and report the picked quantities back into the ERP system. Data collection tools, such as handheld devices and/or radio frequency identification (RFID) of items, can reduce the management of the picking lists and help workers to handle the picking lists in the ERP system in a more efficient manner.

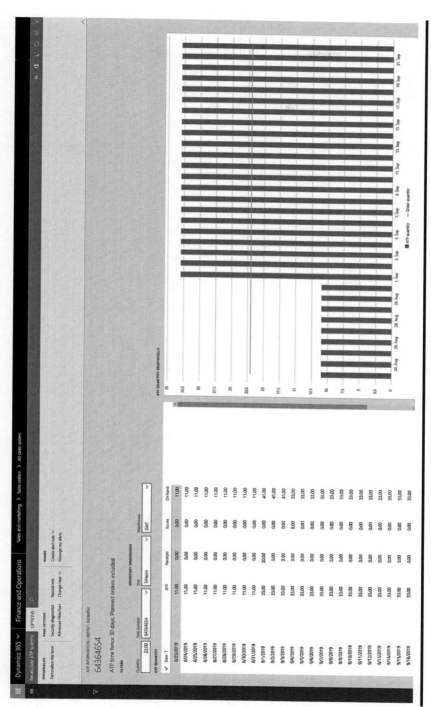

Figure 5.4 ATP check in Microsoft Dynamics 365 Supply Chain Management.

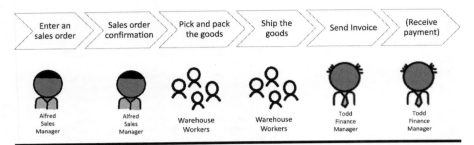

Figure 5.5 Sales order process.

After the goods have been picked and packed, the next step is to ship these to the customer. This involves printing of a packing slip from the sales order in the ERP system. A simple printing of a packing slip is the minimum outbound support one should expect from an ERP system for manufacturing supply chains. Advanced ERP systems have deep support for outbound shipment and transportation management that can include things like the freight management, advanced loading functions, and route planning. The items are removed from the on-hand inventory levels in the ERP system as soon as item is reported as shipped.

Printing and sending the invoice to the customer do normally ends the sales order. This also includes economic postings in the financial modules of the ERP system where the management of the payment takes place in later phases. The payment from the customer can then be managed from in the account receivable in the financial parts of the ERP system.

OPTISTREAM

Alfred and the rest of the sales department at OptiStream continuously work with the sales module. They have two types of sales personnel: travelling sales representatives and in-house sales representatives. The travelling sales representatives access the sales module and enter the sales orders at the customer site through a mobile app. The in-house sales representatives communicate with customers through e-mail and telephone and enter the sales order through the desktop interface of Microsoft Dynamics 365 Supply Chain Management.

OptiStream has established a business-to-business web portal where customers can enter and follow up their orders. The customer portal is integrated with their ERP system, so any order a customer enters in the customer portal will automatically create a sales order in the sales module. This portal is then updated as it goes through the sales process at OptiStream. They try to direct the customer to enter the orders in the customer portal. But still a large portion of their customers continues to use telephone or e-mail for the ordering process, where Alfred or someone in his sales team must run sales process manually.

For their largest customer they have established electronic messages ("EDI messages") that communicates directly with the customer's ERP systems. This allows orders to be made and updated automatically between the two organizations without any need for manual information handling.

The sales order process at OptiStream is similar despite the order is created and updated automatically or manually by a user. Alfred can follow up and manages his orders through a workspace named "sales processing and inquiry" in Microsoft Dynamics 365 Supply Chain Management.

Figure 5.6 shows the workspace Alfred is using when creating new sales orders manually. He clicks on the function for new order, enters the customer account, checks the data, and adjusts a delivery date. After all necessary details have been entered, he presses "OK" and a new sales order head is created. The new order will have an "open order" status.

After a new sales order has been created, Alfred enters the sales order lines, where he selects applicable item(s) and the ordered quantity in each line. He checks if the other data on the order line seems correct like the price, site (facility), warehouse, serial numbers, etc. If he finds some errors, he usually updates the master data of the customer and/or item as well, so the information is corrected on future orders.

When the order lines are complete Alfred confirms and prints the sales order. Most customers accept an order confirmation on e-mail. So, Alfred has set up Microsoft Dynamics 365 Supply Chain Management to automatically send an e-mail with the order confirmation attached that he sends to the customer.

For sales order created automatically through the website, EDI or intercompany orders the order entry; delivery date check and confirmation are done automatically by the system without any processing by a user. This is of course more efficient and less costly but requires that all data involved in the process is correct and updated in Microsoft Dynamics 365 Supply Chain Management.

After the sales order confirmation, the next step is to pick and pack the items for the delivery. Erica in the warehouse prints the picking list. Previously, this was a physical paper printout that was handed out to the warehouse personnel that are doing the picking, but nowadays OptiStream uses a handheld device on the warehouse where the workers can access the picking list and report these without any use of physical pen or paper.

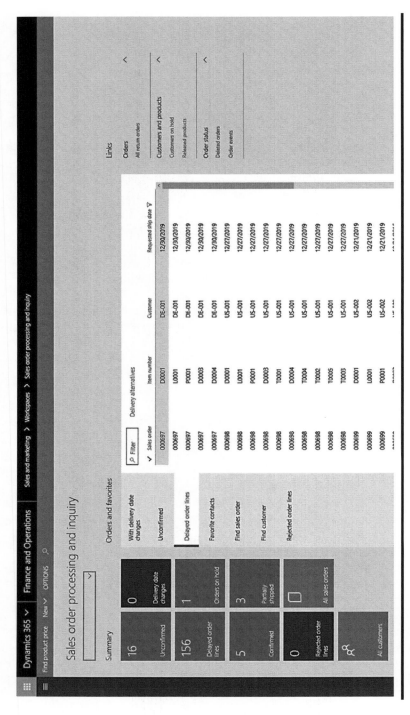

Figure 5.6 Workspace "sales order processing and inquiry".

The warehouse personnel uses the picking list generated from the sales order to pick required items. The workers report what is picked on their handheld devices that update Microsoft Dynamics 365 Supply Chain Management so that on-hand inventory values are up-to-date. If necessary, Erica can go into picking list in Microsoft Dynamics 365 Supply Chain Management to do any manual adjustments or post any picking manually directly in the system.

After picking the goods must be packed and shipped. This is reported in Microsoft Dynamics 365 Supply Chain Management by posting and printing the packing slip. The printout of the packing slip and other related documents such as shipping labels and products data safety sheet are printed from systems and used in the shipment process. Microsoft Dynamics 365 Supply Chain Management registers the goods as issued from the stock when the packing slip is posted. The sales order status is now "delivered".

The final step in the sales order process is posting of the invoice. This is done in a periodically manner where Todd in the Finance department runs a job in Microsoft Dynamics 365 Supply Chain Management that prints and sends all sales invoices simultaneously. It is, however, also possible to post an invoice for each individual order. Posting the invoice changes the status of the sales order ("invoiced"). Registration and processing the payment from the customer is handled by Alfred in the finance module.

5.5 Other Sales Module Functionalities

The sales module of an ERP system holds more functionalities than we have been exploring until now. This chapter will mention a few additional functions that one should find support for in an ERP system.

5.5.1 Sales Quotations

Most ERP systems support sales quotations. And sales quotation can be described as an order that is not yet been validated. A sales quotation allows a prospective buyer to review pricing and other delivery terms before he decides on a purchase. The way a sale quotation works in an ERP system has similarities to a sales order and can in some way be understand as a temporary sales order.

Maybe easiest way of solving sales quotation in an ERP system is in fact to use a temporary sales order that can be converted into an open sales order if the prospect is accepting the offer. However, most ERP systems have separate functions for dealing with sales quotations where both the prospects and the quotations lies in separate functions.

The sales order quotation process follows a similar structure in all ERP systems. First, a sales quotation is registered, and the sales terms are communicated to the prospect. Open quotations are monitored and updated regularly through the negotiations until the prospect either accepts or declines equations. Lost quotations are closed, and accepted offers are converted into open sales orders, and the prospect is transferred into a customer.

OPTISTREAM

Alfred uses the sales order quotation functionality when a potential customer asks for a price estimate to consider a potential buy. The first step for Alfred is to enter the new prospect and a sales quotation in Microsoft Dynamics 365 Supply Chain Management. This is done in a similar manner than for new customer and sales order.

After a new sales quotation has been created, and the desired item(s) with accompanying information is entered in the sales quotation's lines, Alfred sends the quotation to the prospect and awaits their reply. The sales department has its own screen in Microsoft Dynamics 365 Supply Chain Management to follow up on all expiring quotations and ensure that potential customers respond in time. If the quotation is accepted, Alfred converts the prospect into an actual customer and confirms the sales quotation. The sales quotation is then transformed into a sales order that can be processed with the other sales order at OptiStream.

5.5.2 Return Management

ERP systems for manufacturing supply chains provide support for managing the return of items from customers. All ERP packages have at least some basic support for this. For the simplest ERP systems these functions may be as basic as generating a "reversed sales order" for adjusting the inventories and financial accounts with the returned products, as well as generating a credit note to the customer.

Larger ERP packages have separate functionality for managing return orders. These return orders are integrated with the inventory and warehouse functions of the ERP system to manage the receipt of the returned items at the warehouses. The receipts process of the returned goods may involve doing an inspection of the items to see if they can return to the inventory for resale. Alternatively, if the items should be scrapped, or managed otherwise before inventory is adjusted and the customer credited.

As more and more of the trade is channelized toward internet, the need for structured return management has increased likewise. So, this is increasingly used and sought after functions by the users of ERP applications of manufacturing supply chains.

5.5.3 Direct Delivery

Direct delivery in an ERP system means that delivery skips parts of the manufacturing supply chain defined in the ERP system and rather go directly to the customer. The typical example supported by most ERP system is that a customer order can trigger a purchase order whereas the purchased items are directly delivered to the customer, instead of first arriving at the enterprises warehouse for then to be shipped to the customer at a later stage. Direct deliveries may help a manufacturing supply chains streamline their manufacturing supply chains by shortening these in a significant manner.

OPTISTREAM

OptiStream uses the direct delivery functions in Microsoft Dynamics 365 Supply Chain Management on spare parts that they have chosen to not have in stock. When an order on such a product comes in, Alfred or someone else in the sales team creates a sales order and triggers the direct delivery function. This function creates a purchase order in Microsoft Dynamics 365 Supply Chain Management toward the vender with delivery directly toward the customer on the sales order. When the OptiStream notices that the customer has received the items, they update the ERP system and the purchase order gets the status "received" simultaneously as the sales order gets status "delivered".

5.6 Key Terms

- Customer
- Sales order
- Sales order process
- Sales order type
- Sales order statuses
- Sales quotation
- Returns
- Direct delivery

5.7 Chapter Summary

The key data in the sales module are the customer master and the sales orders, where the sales orders consist of an order header and order lines. Basic functionality one should at minimum find in a sales order module includes sales order types, sales order statuses, sales price calculations, and order promising.

The sales order process is used for sales of items toward a customer. The standard steps are sales order entry, order confirmation, picking, packing, and shipment of the goods, as well as issuing the invoice and payment management. Advanced ERP systems support more advanced sales functionalities, some of these are sales quotations, return management, and direct delivery.

Chapter 6

Production Module

Learning Objectives

After reading this chapter, you will be able to:

- Describe on the key data components of a production module
- Understand the key functionality of the production module
- Know the principles of a production order process in an ERP system
- Get an overview over other production functionalities that may be included in an ERP system for manufacturing supply chains

6.1 The Production Module

Not all ERP systems targeted for managing supply chains have a production module, or alternatively they may have very limited production functions in this area. This means that some ERP systems are better suited for trading companies or other businesses where manufacturing is not a part of the supply chain. Therefore, having a good production module may be the key in order to claim that an ERP system is well suited for supporting manufacturing supply chains.

6.2 Data in the Production Module

The key data elements in the production module can be summarized as:

1. Master data connected to the bill-of-material (BOM)
   - The BOM defines the components and raw materials that are needed to produce an item.

2. Master Data connected to the production routes
   - Production routes describe the production steps ("operations") that must be executed to produce an item.
3. Business record in form of production orders
   - Production orders are used to manage the production process. Each production order copies the information from the end item's BOM and production route, so the production order holds information on what items are needed and what operations should be performed to produce this finish product.

The BOM is a hierarchical model of the all the components, subassemblies, and raw materials a company need to produce an end product. In an ERP system all parts of the BOM are registered as an item in the item master in the inventory management module. This includes the end product, the components, the subassemblies, and the raw materials. When a user creates a BOM in the ERP system, he or she starts with the item that should be the end product and then builds the BOM structure by selecting the correct items from the item master, their quantity, and other information and parameters needed to create the product.

By using the same items that may be purchased and sold through the sales and purchase module, the BOM is the key that links the supply chain throughout the facility of a manufacturing company.

The route describes the production steps, or operations, needed to produce the product. Each operation requires resources. The machines and other manufacturing resources are registered in the work center master and are linked to the operations in routes. On each operation in the route the user can define a processing time so that EPR system can allocate time on the resources when the route is used in a production order. The routes are linked toward an end item in the same manner as the BOM. Most ERP systems have possibilities to connect the operations in the production route to specific items in the BOM, so that the correct items can be picked from stock and consumed in production when the production step is performed by a worker.

Production orders are used to control and manage the production in an ERP system. On the production order the user can find information of the ordered item, the start date and finish date of the production, and other general information about the produced items and production processes. When creating a new production order, the system copies a new version of the item's BOM on order that can be used to allocate components, materials, and production resources. If necessary the user can change the BOM and route on the production order, without changes in the BOM and route on the item.

An overview of the elements of a production module is shown in Figure 6.1.

The figure shows a simplified view of the most important data elements and their relations in a production order module. These basic components are the BOM, routes, and production orders.

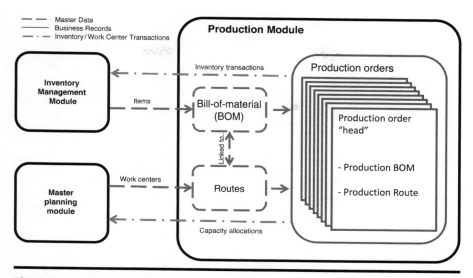

Figure 6.1 Key data elements in the production module.

The BOM uses items information from the inventory management module to connect the BOM to an end item and to define the items for the raw materials and components in the BOM lines. The routes are connected to the resources from the master planning module, where one operation in the route is connected to one or several resources. The BOM and route are interlinked since they are connected to the same end items, and sometimes the items in the BOM are connected to certain operations in route.

When creating a new production order, the ERP system copies the standard BOM and route from the end item to the production order. This BOM and route are unique for each production order, ensuring that user can change the BOM and route on one production order without altering the BOM and route in the master data or any other production order.

To clarify we will provide a basic example to illustrate how a production order can be constructed in an ERP system. Let's say that a manufacturing enterprise is producing stools. The BOM and route for a stool is shown in Figure 6.2.

The figure shows that the BOM of the stool consists of one seat and four legs. The route starts with a gluing operation and then a painting operation. Let's say that gluing takes 1 minute for each stool, and painting takes 1.5 minute/stool. When a new production order on, for example, 21 stools is made in the ERP system, the system knows that the requirement of seats is 21 (21 stools × 1 seat) and for legs it is 84 (21 stools × 4 legs) for this production order. Similarly, the processing time for the order (and capacity requirements toward the gluing and painting work centers) is 21 minutes for the gluing operation (21 stools × 1 minute/stool) and 29.4 minutes for the painting operation (21 stools × 1.5 minute/stool).

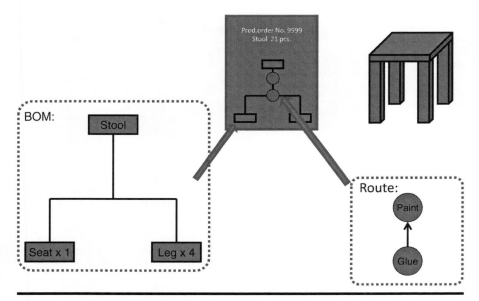

Figure 6.2   Example for use of BOM and route.

This means that the production order for these 21 stools will require 21 seats and 84 legs from the warehouse, as well as 21 minutes from the gluing work center and 29.4 minutes from the capacity of the work center for the painting.

OPTISTREAM

Peter, the production manager, registers all BOMs in Microsoft Dynamics 365 Supply Chain Management. He uses the same items that Alfred's team in the sales department will be selling as the "end product" and registers the BOM on this.

First, he creates a new BOM head before he enters the BOM lines where he adds information like the item, the quantity, and warehouse it should be picked from for each line. This provides input on quantity, cost, and resources consumption that are required to produce the end product. When he has completed a BOM, he approves and activates this according to the functionality of Microsoft Dynamics 365 Supply Chain Management. Microsoft Dynamics 365 Supply Chain Management will then use this BOM the next time he creates a new production order on the product. An example on a BOM in Microsoft Dynamics 365 Supply Chain Management is shown in Figure 6.3.

The routes are created in the same fashion. First, Peter creates a route head and then he registers each line in the route, where he adds information like the sequence number of the operation, the operation name, the

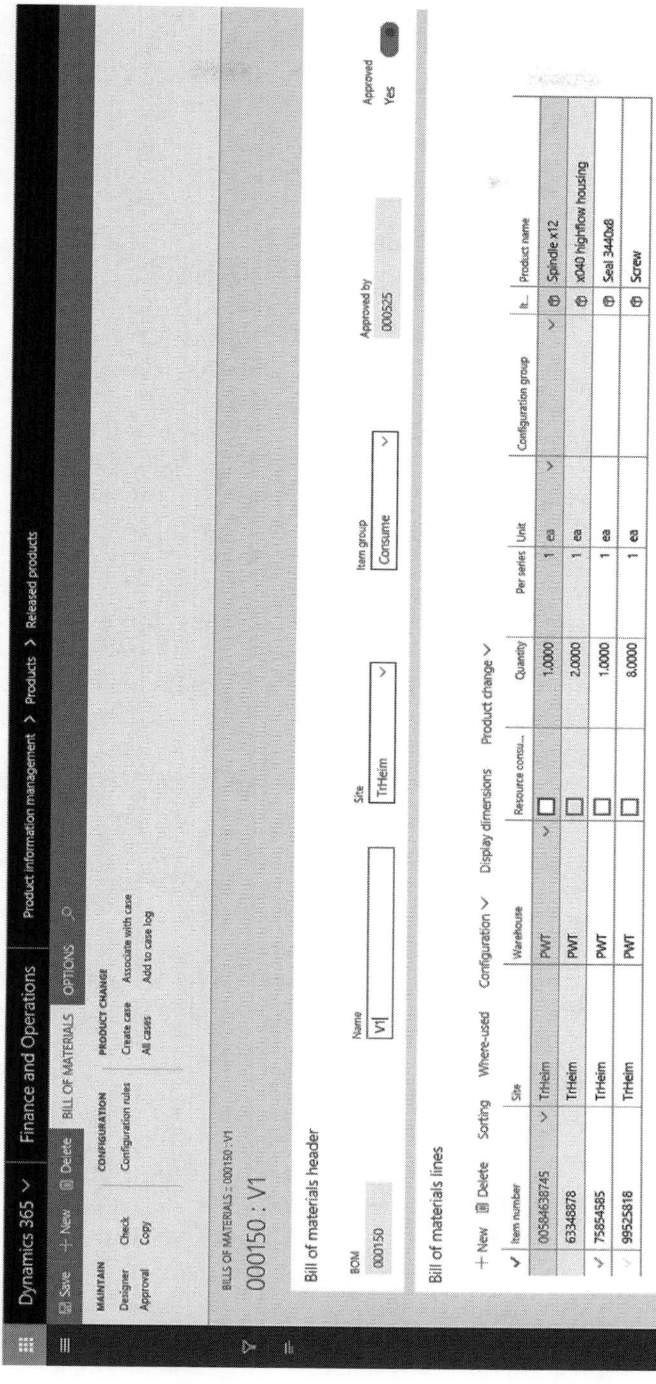

Figure 6.3   BOM in Microsoft Dynamics 365 Supply Chain Management.

items run-time in the operation, cost categories to manage the costing, and so on, until he gets a complete route for the product.

Then he adds the work centers to each line/operation in the route. They have organized the work centers as resource groups in Microsoft Dynamics 365 Supply Chain Management where, for example, all milling machines are defined as resources in the system and then grouped in a milling work center as a resources group. All resources and resource groups have capacity calendars in Microsoft Dynamics 365 Supply Chain Management that tracks the capacity load and availability on both the resources/resource groups.

This route (Figure 6.4) can then be used on production orders in Microsoft Dynamics 365 Supply Chain Management as soon as Peter approves and activates it in the system.

It is possible to store several BOMs and routes for a product, but Microsoft Dynamics 365 Supply Chain Management will always suggest the active BOM/route first when Peter makes a new production order. When he creates a new production order in Microsoft Dynamics 365 Supply Chain Management, the application copies the BOM and route from the item to production order. If Peter does any adjustments on the BOM and route in the production order, the changes will only be valid for this particular order. If he needs to do any adjustment that should be valid for all future production order, he needs to change or create new versions of the BOM and route that are registered toward the end item in Microsoft Dynamics 365 Supply Chain Management.

6.3 Basic Functionality

In the following section we will summarize the most common functions that a user should expect to find in production module. The amount of system support in a production module can vary in great degree between different software packages, and this section do only represent the basic production functions that are commonly found in most ERP systems.

6.3.1 Single-level versus Multilevel BOM

An item's BOM can be single or multilevel. This means that the BOM can include items that have their own BOMs as well. In an ERP system, the choice of using a single BOM in whole production or splitting into several multilevel BOMs, depends often on the amount of production orders the ERP system should generate and the level of work-in-progress storage in the production. The ERP system usually creates one production order per BOM and route. So, putting a complete production process in a single BOM will create a single production order for the

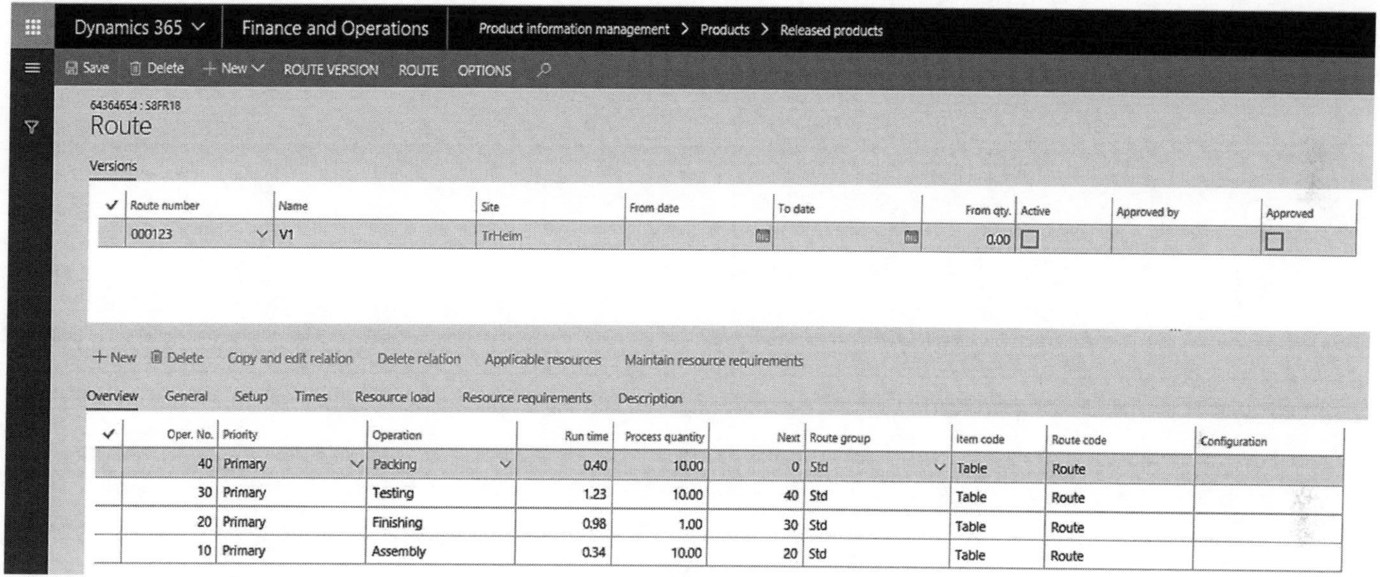

Figure 6.4 Route in Microsoft Dynamics 365 Supply Chain Management.

complete production process. Using BOM item in another BOM splits the production routing in several steps and thereby the production process into several production orders. When using multilevel BOM the ERP system requires the users to put the end item from each production order in a warehouse. This can allow the enterprise to design how the items flow through the factory floor and create more flexibility by placing buffers throughout the production process.

OPTISTREAM

Some parts of the pumps, like the pump housing, are included in many different variant of the pumps. Therefore, Peter has chosen to make separate production orders where he produces all the housings he need for a given time period and put these in a semi-finish production warehouse where they can be picked when needed. In order to do this, he has created separate items in Microsoft Dynamics 365 Supply Chain Management for each component we want to have in the semi-finish storage and has added a BOM and routes on these. He can then issue separate production orders on these components. The BOM and routes of the sales items are changed as well so that the components in the work-in-progress storage are picked when starting a new production order.

6.3.2 Phantom Items

Using phantom items in a BOM is like using another BOM item in a multilevel BOM, but for phantom item the ERP system will not create a separate production order. The items in the underlying BOM of the phantom item will be copied into the BOM of the end item every time a new production order is made on this product. Phantom items are normally used for easing the maintenance of large BOMs, by collecting similar items into their own sum-BOMs.

6.3.3 Routing Options

The operation in routing in an ERP system is normally structured in a sequential manner. Typically, the operation gets a sequence number that indicates the sequence that they are to be processed in on the shop floor, for example, the first operation gets number "10", the next operation gets sequence number "20", then next "30", and so on.

Not all production processes are sequential; some operations can go in parallel or overlap each other to get most of the production capacity. A company may also choose to use alternative routing toward the same item, for instance to select different work centers for different production order sizes. This means that some ERP systems have various functionalities for making more advanced routings. These options possibly can define parallel operations, possibilities for selecting alternative operations for parts of the routing, setup of overlapping operations, and so on.

As for most things with ERP system, the possibilities for making the routing may vary a lot from system to system. Smaller ERP packages may only hold basic functions for defining sequential routings, while more advanced ERP system may hold a near endless of possibilities in defining how the production process should be performed. Therefore, it is important that these possibilities are addressed before a company chooses an ERP system, to avoid costly modifications after an ERP software is purchased and the implementation project has started.

6.3.4 Production Planning

Production planning in an ERP system for manufacturing management is strongly connected to the master planning we will discuss in the next chapter, and in many ways use the same mechanism.

The production module in most ERP systems has production planning features. This functionality is based on analyzing the capacity situation on the work centers as well as material availability to find when a production order can be executed. ERP systems have visualization functions like Gantt and bar charts to help the planner to get an overview of the capacity shortages so he or she can plan the production manually to meet the time schedule.

Most ERP systems have automatic functions to help the users to schedule the orders; in such cases one or several of the work centers should be set to finite capacity. This means that the ERP system will distribute the production orders in time so that the preset capacity limits on these work center or work centers are not exceeded. There are several ways for doing this. Scheduling of the most common is backward planning, where the finish time of the production order is set as fixed and the operations are scheduled backwards in time to find a start time for the order. The opposite way is forward planning, where the production order start time is set, and the operations are planned forward in time until a finish time is found.

The production planning functions correspond with the planning that happens in master planning module. The master planning looks toward all orders within a company to create planned orders, while the production planning focuses only toward scheduling the production orders.

This is also one of the limitations of the production planning in ERP system. Since the production planning only considers production orders, a small change done in the production planning may have large consequences for the overall master plan in the manufacturing supply chain. For example, moving the start time of a production order earlier in time may have consequence on the purchasing side since the material for the production is needed earlier, while moving the finish date later may lead to delayed customer deliveries. A company must, therefore, be aware in how they are using the production planning features within an ERP-enabled manufacturing supply chain.

OPTISTREAM

Peter uses the "backward from required date" in Microsoft Dynamics 365 Supply Chain Management, to automatically plan all production orders so they are completed in time. He performs the production planning once a week, where he selects the order for the coming week and plans the productions for this time period.

He has set the milling work center group as a group with finite capacity since this is known to be the bottleneck in the production plan. The rest of the resource group is set with infinite resources since he can adjust the capacity on these according to the requirements of the milling machines.

However, he tries few possible changes to the start and stop times of the production orders while doing this planning. He rather uses the information provided by Microsoft Dynamics 365 Supply Chain Management such as resource Gantt charts as shown in Figure 6.5 to adjust the capacity by rearranging the personnel and other resources on different work centers.

The main reason for this is that he knows the production orders come as planned from the master planning as well, and a major change to the production orders in the production module will result in changes in other parts of the manufacturing supply chain. This is because the parts and material may already have been ordered by purchase department. Therefore, he is working to enable a flexible workforce and other activities on the shop floor to meet the overall plan set by the master planning, without doing any separate production planning in the ERP system. These activities will probably reduce the costs and extra work the disturbance extensive changes of the production orders may have on the overall manufacturing supply chain.

6.3.5 Shop Floor Activities

The production module of an ERP has at least some minimum functions to support the activities on the shop floor. Some of these include:

- Printouts of production documents
  - Most ERP systems provide document that describes the work at each operation/work station and card that describes production route that can attract the work piece as it flows through production.
- A printout of a picking list for picking needed material and components for production
  - These functions are related to the warehouse management functions, and the picking for production is often done by warehouse personnel.

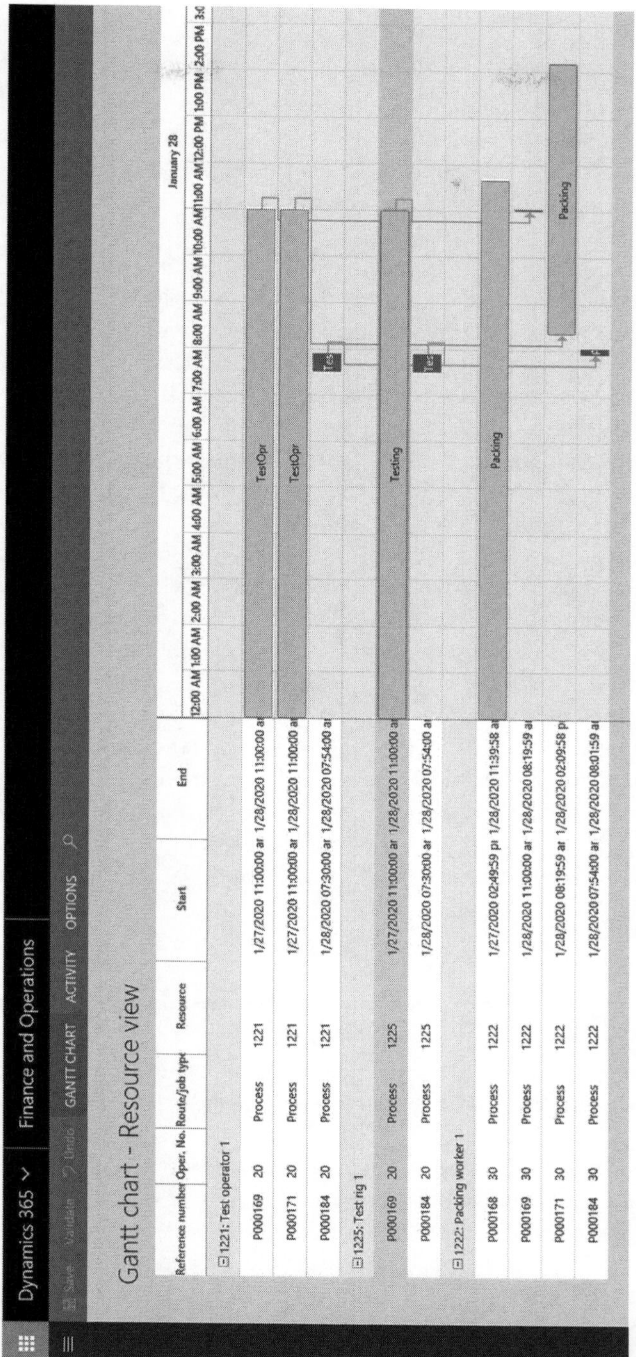

Figure 6.5 Resource view in Microsoft Dynamics 365 Supply Chain Management.

■ Possibility to report the progress on each operation, the amount produced, and the time consumed
  − In its simplest from this involves that the production workers write the progress on the production document and a foreman keys the progress back into the system.
■ Function for putting the finish products on stock and closing the order
  − The put away may be reported by the warehouse as a part of the function in warehouse functions.

As indicated in the following discussion, the basic shop floor support of an ERP system is based on physical paper documents that are printed and used as information carriers around the production floor. But most modern ERP applications have built-in functionalities for a more electronic approach. This can include automation of the picking and put away processes through handheld devices, proving screens on the work center where the worker can see the work orders, and reporting the progress on the operations directly on the workorders, either through a bar code scanner or other means of data acquisition.

Some ERP systems may provide functions like detailed planning of shop floor personnel, sequencing orders on work centers, providing work descriptions/ production drawings of the work to be performed. However, these functions vary a lot from ERP system to ERP system; so, the individual application must be studied toward the requirements of the company. However, these shop-floor capabilities of the ERP systems are limited in the respect that they are always directly connected to the production order. So any change in the shop floor will affect the production order and thereby have the potential to alter the overall master plan. Some firms therefore make use of an external manufacturing execution system (MES) in addition to their ERP systems among other things that provide flexibility between the manufacturing supply chain and the events on the shop floor.

OPTISTREAM

Nowadays the activities at the shop floor at OptiStream are handled mostly by using paper printouts and manual keying in Microsoft Dynamics 365 Supply Chain Management.

Microsoft Dynamics 365 Supply Chain Management hold advanced manufacturing execution functions in the "shop floor module". This module opens for automated data management on the shop floor and will cover most of the functions that Optistream needs in this area.

One of the main advantage of using Microsoft Dynamics 365 Supply Chain Management instead of an external MES is that shop floor control is seamlessly connected to other modules of the ERP system like the inventory management module and the human resources module (HR module). For instance, the HR module allows using a single employee master for both the data acquisition on the shop floor and the HR functions. Therefore, there is no need to register the worker two times, one for the user database in the MES system and other for the HR functions in the ERP system. The shop floor functions of Microsoft Dynamics 365 Supply Chain Management can also be integrated toward time and attendance (with clock-in/clock-out) in the HR module. This may have several advantages such as using same data capture equipment (like scanners, tags, etc.) for both purposes. Also, if a worker clocks out after shift, he will be automatically logged out of all production orders if he has forgot to do so before he left.

However, Peter has decided not to implement these possibilities in Microsoft Dynamics 365 Supply Chain Management for now and rather wait until they can invest in a MES system and integrate this toward the ERP system. This integration will probably be designed so that all information for the production order will be transferred to the MES that takes care of all production planning and shop-floor activities, and data capture. Production data will be transferred back to the ERP system so that the production orders can be updated.

An external MES will probably be more tailored and user-friendly for the production workers daily work. An external MES will also allow OptiStream to continue production even if Microsoft Dynamics 365 Supply Chain Management goes down, for example, maintenance or unplanned events. But most importantly, the detailed production planning and other changes they are doing on shop floor (like sequencing the operations on each machine), will affect the production order in the ERP application, and thereby, the overall master plan in Microsoft Dynamics 365 Supply Chain Management will be affected.

6.3.6 Production Cost Calculation

Providing insight in the costs of production is one of the most important tasks of an ERP system. An ERP system calculates the cost of each production order according to the consumption of materials, components, and resources for completing a production order. The ERP system adds up the costs for all items on the BOM, cost of the work center use, and other indirect cost elements defined in the pricing parts of the ERP system to find the cost of the manufactured product.

The price calculation consists of two parts. Before the production starts, the system calculates the planned production cost according to the planned data. After the production is finished, it calculates the cost of the same but with the actual data reported from the shop floor. A production manager can then compare the planned and the actual production cost calculations and get a picture of the economic contribution of each order and the quality of the production processes.

OPTISTREAM

Peter checks the cost in Microsoft Dynamics 365 Supply Chain Management on all products before he starts to produce the product. He uses the cost sheets in Microsoft Dynamics 365 Supply Chain Management to check the precalculated cost of production orders, to find if he should avoid any actions to keep the cost down, or if there are some errors in the costing data that he needs to correct before the production starts.

When an order is finished in production, he uses the costing sheet to check the real costs before he finish marks the order. If there are some large deviations between the precalculated cost and the real costing, for instance deviations caused by more material consumption or more than expected production time in one of the work centers, he investigates what must have happened to find the root cause of the issue. Depending on his findings he will take actions to correct the issue on the shop floor, or correct the data in the ERP system so this bias between the precalculated cost and real production cost do not happen again. Figure 6.6 shows an example of a costing overview of production order in Microsoft Dynamics 365 Supply Chain Management.

Todd in finance acts like a production controller and checks the real costing in the costing sheets on all production orders. He uses this data to see what products are most profitable to set the product strategy of OpitStream and potentially correct the sales prices if the profitability is low on some products. He also checks if all input from the production is correct before production order updates the general ledger.

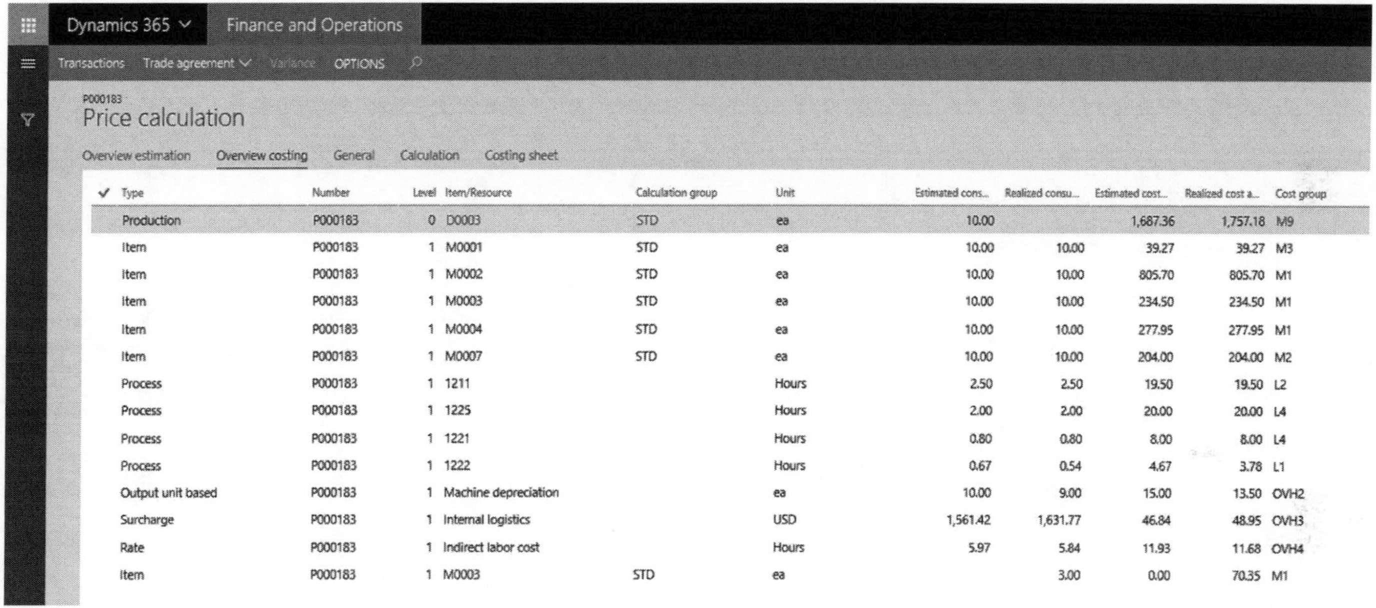

Type	Number	Level	Item/Resource	Calculation group	Unit	Estimated consu...	Realized consu...	Estimated cost...	Realized cost a...	Cost group
Production	P000183	0	D0003	STD	ea	10.00		1,687.36	1,757.18	M9
Item	P000183	1	M0001	STD	ea	10.00	10.00	39.27	39.27	M3
Item	P000183	1	M0002	STD	ea	10.00	10.00	805.70	805.70	M1
Item	P000183	1	M0003	STD	ea	10.00	10.00	234.50	234.50	M1
Item	P000183	1	M0004	STD	ea	10.00	10.00	277.95	277.95	M1
Item	P000183	1	M0007	STD	ea	10.00	10.00	204.00	204.00	M2
Process	P000183	1	1211		Hours	2.50	2.50	19.50	19.50	L2
Process	P000183	1	1225		Hours	2.00	2.00	20.00	20.00	L4
Process	P000183	1	1221		Hours	0.80	0.80	8.00	8.00	L4
Process	P000183	1	1222		Hours	0.67	0.54	4.67	3.78	L1
Output unit based	P000183	1	Machine depreciation		ea	10.00	9.00	15.00	13.50	OVH2
Surcharge	P000183	1	Internal logistics		USD	1,561.42	1,631.77	46.84	48.95	OVH3
Rate	P000183	1	Indirect labor cost		Hours	5.97	5.84	11.93	11.68	OVH4
Item	P000183	1	M0003	STD	ea	3.00	3.00	0.00	70.35	M1

Figure 6.6   Production cost calculation.

6.4 The Production Order Process

The sequence and details of the activities within the production order process can vary to a larger degree between the different software packages than for the previous discussed processes. However, the way most ERP systems supports the production order processes follows a pattern, with some variation. For instance, some ERP systems can perform automatic material check when creating a production order, while other software packages sees this as a part of a planning process that are done after the production order is created, and so on. In Figure 6.7 we suggest a simple process that will fit the basic production order processes in most ERP systems.

As the figure indicates, the production order process starts by making the production order in the ERP application. A user can create the production order manually or the system can automatically create the production order from a sales order. A transfer order releases this from a planned production order in the master planning module (see more on master planning in Chapter 7).

The next step is usually to plan the production order. The production scheduling involves material check and controlling the orders toward the work center capacity. The production planning is often performed in batches of orders in a timely fashion. How often the production planning is run rely on type of production. For instance, a bakery must set a detailed production schedule each day, while a producer of mechanical equipment may need to set their production plan each 14 days or even for a longer time interval.

Sometimes the production planner does major adjustment that requires replanning of the order or the whole plan by the ERP system, like changing the finish date of one or several production orders to meet customer commitments. Sometimes, the planner may do a manual adjustment that does not require a replanning like changing the work center on the route of the production order to level the load on work centers, or he/she must perform something outside the system, for instance rearranging the personnel or using overtime work to meet capacity restrains.

As previously mentioned, some production orders may already be planned through the master planning functions. The degree of production planning relies

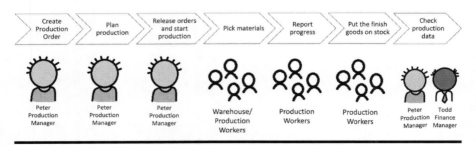

Figure 6.7 Production order process.

on many factors, and some of these, like time fencing, will be discussed in later chapters.

Releasing and starting the production orders is the next step in the production process. This involves handing over of the orders to the production floor and printing the picking lists for the materials as well as the production papers. The information from the production orders can be communicated electronically to the shop floor as well, either through built-in data acquisition functionalities in the ERP system or through an integrated shop-floor data collection solution.

Further, the production workers pick the needed materials before they can start the work and report the progress in each operation on the production order. The production order is then monitored through the production as the workpiece flows throughout the production floor, depending on how often the ERP system is updated from the input from the production workers.

When the production is completed, the production workers put the finished goods on stock and reports the production orders as complete in the ERP system. The produced goods are then available in the warehouse of the ERP system.

The final step is to check the reported production data and resolve any mistyping and other errors in the data collected on the shop floor. When the data is OK, the ERP system can then calculate the real costing of the production order. The management can then use this information to analyze how the orders were executed and potentially correct issues on how future orders are being managed. This last step includes closing the production order as well. By closing the production order, the financial ledgers in the ERP system are updated with the cost information from the production order.

OPTISTREAM

OptiStream uses a straightforward production process in Microsoft Dynamics 365 Supply Chain Management. Their production orders on pumps come from two sources:

- Alfred from the sales department releases the production orders from sales orders on pumps that are made or engineer-to-order.
- Peter releases planned production orders in the master plan on pump that are sold from stock.

Peter has the option to manually create production orders as well, but this is mostly done in special cases, like when creating prototypes or for pumps used for sales exhibition and similar.

Peter performs most of the updating and works on the production orders in "all production orders" application in Microsoft Dynamics 365 Supply Chain Management where all the production orders are listed (Figure 6.8).

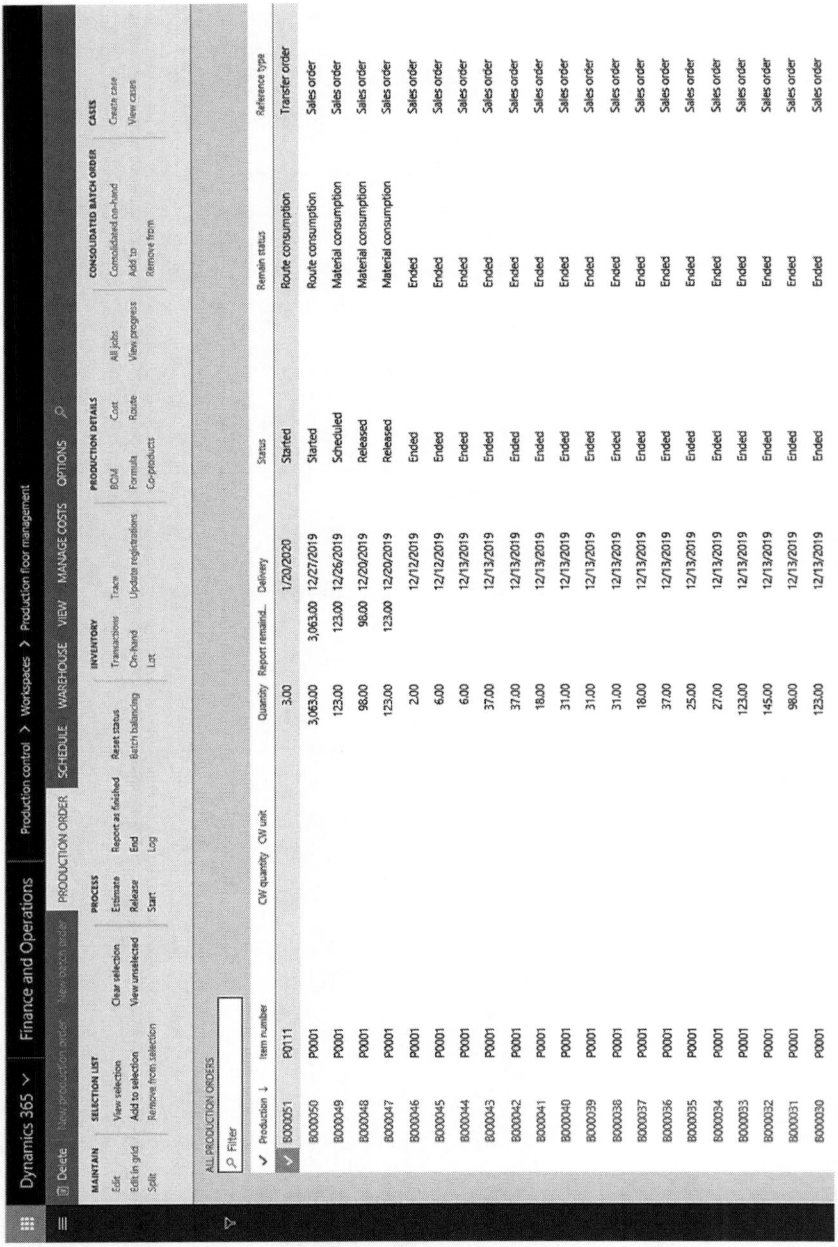

Figure 6.8 "All production orders" in Microsoft Dynamics 365 Supply Chain Management.

All new production orders get the status "created". On engineered pumps, Peter uses "estimate" function in Microsoft Dynamics 365 Supply Chain Management so he can calculate the expected production costs. He then checks the pre-calculation production cost to see if these seems OK, or if he needs to discuss something with the engineering department before he goes further with the order.

Every Thursday Peter runs a production planning process to plan the production orders for the next week toward the available capacity and material availabilities. This process was explained earlier in this chapter.

The planned production order must then be released. When Peter releases the production order, he simultaneously prints a job card for each job on the production order and a route card. The job card describes the job that should be performed at each workstation while the route card describes the production route of where the workpiece should go through the production floor. He hands the job card to the workers at work stations and the route card to workers at the first work station of the production process. The workers at the work station use the job card to plan and report the work at each workstation, and the route card is attached to the workpiece at the first workstation to identify this item to the following workstations.

Every morning, Peter starts the production orders in Microsoft Dynamics 365 Supply Chain Management that have the start date equal to the current date. He does this by selecting all relevant production orders and pressing "start" in the "all production orders" application. When pressing OK on the "start" screen, Microsoft Dynamics 365 Supply Chain Management prints picking lists on a printer in the workshop. Now, the production order has the status "started".

The production workers go to the warehouse with the print of the picking list to get the required materials for this order. The warehouse personnel picks the items and register the issued goods on the production order's picking list in Microsoft Dynamics 365 Supply Chain Management.

The production can now start. As the orders process the workers write down the progress and time consumed on the job cards and hand these over to Peter every evening. Peter then updates the order in Microsoft Dynamics 365 Supply Chain Management with the information on the cards.

When the order is finished, the production workers take the finished product over to the warehouse and put these in an area for finish products. The worker takes the route card from the item and notes the final produced quantity and error quantities (if any) and sends it to Peter together with the last job cards. Peter reports the produced goods along with the error quantity and checks the production input and the final cost of the order and corrects any potential errors. With this action, the produced items are put on stock in Microsoft Dynamics 365 Supply Chain Management.

Erica and the warehouse workers can then see in Microsoft Dynamics 365 Supply Chain Management that there are goods in the finished products areas and put these into the correct place in the warehouse.

The product orders now have status "completed". Every Friday, Todd in finance goes through all production orders with status "completed", checks the production costs, and talks with Peter if he finds some larger deviations on the orders. Then he sets the production orders status to "end" which updates the financial ledgers in Microsoft Dynamics 365 Supply Chain Management.

Now the overview of the estimated versus the real cost on the production order can be retrieved. OptiStream's management uses this production calculation data for reviewing the product portfolio and product pricing, as well as reviewing their internal production processes.

6.5 Other Production Module Functionality

This book covers the fundamental support of each module in an ERP system for manufacturing supply chains. It will be a near endless task to cover all production functionality found in all ERP systems; therefore, we have only mentioned a few of the most common extra features and functions one should expect to find in the production parts of an ERP system.

6.5.1 Subcontracting

Some manufacturing enterprises do not execute all the steps of the production process themselves but makes use of an external partner for parts of the production process. Subcontracting involves the process when a part of the production order is done by an external producer.

Subcontracting can be solved through standard ERP functionality by issuing purchase orders for the external production and then handling the integration with the production orders manually. However, this can require a lot of manual work in order to get the costing and other information correct in the system.

The built-in functions for subcontracting in ERP systems use purchase orders as well, but these purchase orders may be generated from master planning and integrated with a subcontracting operation on the route of the production orders. This enables the ERP system to manage the planning and cost allocation of the subcontract within the production process.

OPTISTREAM

OptiStream performs most of their production in-house, but at the time of peak in demand they may temporarily use a local workshop sited on the other side of the town as a subcontractor for some of the machining. In such cases, Peter adds an outsourcing operation in affected items production route. When he creates the production order on these items, Microsoft Dynamics 365 Supply Chain Management generates purchase orders for the machining that are to be done at the other workshop. He coordinates with Erica in the warehouse and Rita in purchasing to process the outsourcing purchase order and connected material flow from and to the outside workshop.

6.5.2 Back Flushing and Order-less Production

A company may, for various reasons, not want to report the actual time and material on each operation on a production order. In such cases, they may use back-flushing on their production orders. This means that one or several operations in the production route may be automatically reported when a later operation is reported, or alternatively, all operations and material consumption are being automatically reported when the finished items on the production order are put into stock.

Order-less production is even simpler than using back-flushing. The ERP may not produce orders at all, but the items (components, semi-finish components, etc.) are automatically drawn from stock according to the BOM when an item is put into the stock. In this way the ERP maintains the correct stock levels in stock without using production orders.

The advantage of using back-flushing and order-less production is less administration and works with production orders. The main downside with these methods is there are less, or no production data reported into the ERP system. As a result, all reporting on other data for analyzing cost, time consumption, errors in production etc. are not found in the ERP application. Therefore, back-flushing and order-less production are often applied in stable, repetitive production environments.

OPTISTREAM

OptiStream do not use back-flushing, and the workers report the exact material and time they consume toward each operation in the ERP system. Peter seeks to minimize the work of entering data in the ERP system by simplifying the routes and BOM on the items so it will be as few elements to handle as possible. If he finds an operation that could be back-flushed, he rather seeks to integrate this with another operation in the system to keep the system as simple and maintainable as possible.

OptiStream uses order-less production in a part of production where they produce in high volumes the fixtures used in all pumps. The actual production is managed by physical Kanban card outside the ERP system (Kanban uses physical cards to control the production instead for production orders). The production workers report everyday how much of each product they have produced, whereas Peter uses a function in Microsoft Dynamics 365 Supply Chain Management named "BOM-calculation" that subtracts the item on the BOM from stock and adds the finished products or the end item on stock.

6.5.3 Defective Quantities, Scrap, and BI-products

Almost all production processes generate some scrap and defects in production. The ERP systems reflect this, and most of them have functions for reporting erroneous products in production, as well as defining the scrap percentage for each operation on the production route as well as the BOM.

By-products are better than scarp and defectives, because these items can be put in stock and either be sold or processed further. By-product functions in an ERP system as a negative BOM line, where items are put into stock instead of consumed as the production order is processed. Some ERP systems have function for co-products as well, where producing one item automatically creates another sales item. Co-products are most commonly used in process industries but can be found in other industries as well.

OPTISTREAM

The production workers report the defective quantity on the job cards if something has gone wrong in the operation. The job cards are handed to Peter who updates the production orders in Microsoft Dynamics 365 Supply Chain Management so the expected quantity from the production order is reduced.

Peter has defined the metal spoon from the machining operations as a by-product in Microsoft Dynamics 365 Supply Chain Management. OptiStream sells this metal spoon to a local forgery to make some additional revenue for the company.

6.5.4 Tooling

Some ERP applications with more advance functionality have possibility to control the tooling of machines as well. If a special tool is needed for production the ERP system can reserve this from the tooling master to make sure that this will be available when the production order starts. A tooling module may include functions such as tool sequencing and services schedules, to ensure an optimal use of tools throughout the production facility.

6.5.5 Engineering Change

Engineering change describes the process of handling design changes of a manufactured product. The engineering change functions of an ERP system are often supplemented by a product lifecycle management (PLM) system. In such cases the PLM software manages the engineering changes on the product side, while the ERP system handles the impact these changes have on the production orders and manufacturing supply chain.

A company must track and follow up all changes made to a product and sometimes stop ongoing production and/or withdraw a product from the market with critical design flaws. Larger ERP systems support engineering change. This is typically done through engineering change orders that may be issued for any production changes, like alterations in the BOM, route, drawings/documents, etc. The engineering change orders can stop and withdraw all ongoing production orders on product, and issue new production orders if the engineering change is of severe character. Alternatively, the engineering change can be applied to the BOM/route for all new production orders after the ongoing orders are completed.

Not all ERP systems have functionality for engineering change. In such cases, the engineering change process is usually supported through a manual routine or by an external software application.

6.5.6 Other Production Modes and Industry Specific Functionalities

The specifics of each industry are not a topic of the book, but the reader should be aware that some ERP systems have enhanced the basic functionality described in this book to meet the production requirements for specific industries. This industry functionality can also be connected to specific production modes like the project, process industries, and lean functionality. Alternatively, the ERP system may be tailored toward a specific industry.

For instance, poultry production, where there are ERP solutions that have ready functionality for things like breeding and slaughterhouse management, reversed BOMs (one chicken may end up in many products, that is reversed than in a normal BOM where many items will end up in a few), and forecasting with anatomic balancing, ingredient management for processed products, and so on.

Typically, the larger ERP systems have some industry-specific functions built-in the standard application (that will be discussed later in this book), but to get an application that are specified toward a specific industry, one probably needs smaller

ERP vendors, or software providers that are building partner solutions "on top" of standard ERP solutions. For instance, Microsoft Dynamics 365 Supply Chain Management has some functionality to cover process industries, but to get a complete solution for food industry, or for example, a tailored ERP-solution chicken production, you need to go to one of Microsoft's partners that makes the solutions which enhances Microsoft Dynamics 365 Supply Chain Management' functionality.

The more specialized the industry focus of an ERP system is, the smaller the user base and the support team is. This, and that these enterprises are 100% focused on one industry only, may be the reason that larger enterprises often end up with an ERP system from a larger software house, and then solve any potential industry requirements outside the standard application.

6.6 Key Terms

- Production
- Bill-of-material (BOM)
- Production route
- Production order process
- Phantom items
- Production planning
- Shop floor
- Subcontracting
- Back-flushing
- Tooling
- Engineering change

6.7 Chapter Summary

This chapter has shown that the production module of an ERP system holds information about BOM, routes and production orders. Basic functionality of the production module includes production BOM, production routes, and production cost accounting.

The production process starts when the production order is initiated. Then, a production planner schedules and plans the orders. The shop floor personnel start the order and report the consumed material. The workers do also report the progress of the production order throughout the production order process until they put the finished goods on to the stock. The last step is to report and follow up the reported numbers and end the production order so that the financial ledgers are updated.

Chapter 7

Master Planning Module

Learning Objectives

After reading this chapter, you will be able to:

- Understand the basic data structure of a master planning module
- Describe basic functions found in the master planning module
- Describe a normal master planning process supported by an ERP system for manufacturing supply chains

7.1 The Master Planning Module

The master planning module is the key factor when it comes to driving the flow of items throughout the manufacturing supply chain. Master planning triggers replenishment for items in the warehouses to account for sales orders, issues to production, items in transfer between warehouses, and other events in the manufacturing supply chain. The master planning module can be understood as the part of the ERP system that connects and coordinates the other modules for manufacturing supply chains together, and thereby, manages the flow of items through the manufacturing supply chain.

7.2 Data in the Master Planning Module

The master planning module is closely connected to the other modules of an ERP system for manufacturing supply chains. The master planning module can of course be designed differently in different ERP-software packages. However, there are four kinds of basic data components that we will pinpoint as a part of the master planning module in most ERP packages:

- Master data in the form of planning parameters
  - Various parameters and data dictating how the master plan should be formed. These settings are mainly done for each item at each warehouse, and include things like planning methods, lead times, safety stock levels, planning time fences, optimal order sizes, and so on.
- Business records in from of forecasts
  - A forecast in the ERP system predicts the consumption of an item in a specific warehouse. The forecasts can either be created through a qualitative process that includes human interactivity, or through quantitative methods, for example, by using forecasting functionality in the ERP application.
- Master data on work centers
  - Work centers consist of production resources like machines and/or workers and some ERP applications named "resource groups". The capacity of each resource is summarized in the work center's total capacity calendar that provides an overview of its future load and availability. The work center's capacity calendars define capacity restrains in production and can therefore influence the production time of each production order.
- Master plans
  - A master plan in an ERP system in its raw form is a set of planned orders generated from a master-planning run. The planned orders in the master plan can then be released to "real" purchase, production, transfers, and sales orders.

The key input used by the master planning module is the inventory transactions that are stored in the inventory management module. The inventory transactions hold information on all current and historical events in the warehouses created by purchase, production, transfers, and sales orders, and other sources. The master planning can use the inventory transactions to find future requirements through analyzing the receipts and issues from open orders registered in the system.

The information on future requirements calculated from the inventory transactions can be combined with forecasts to extend the reach of the predictions further into the future. This information from inventory transactions and/or forecasts are used by the master-planning run in a gross/net requirement calculation that are combined with BOM/routes, and planning rules to generate planned orders that make up a master plan.

The master planning uses the BOMs (bill-of-materials) from production module to perform "BOM-explosions" for calculating the requirements for subcomponents, so that item in all levels of the production is accounted for in the plan.

The production routes are used to estimate the capacity requirements of the planned orders in the master plan, that again are balanced with the available capacity in the works centers. One or several of the work centers can be set up with restricted capacity. In such cases, the ERP system will create master plan where the planned order is organized in such way that the restricted work center's capacity is not extended. Alternatively, a planner can change the planned orders manually to meet capacity restrains for one or several work centers and do replanning. When the planner is satisfied with the plan, he or she can release the planned orders in the master plan into "real" production, purchase, or transfer orders.

Figure 7.1 shows the key components of a master planning module.

The figure indicates that the main component of a master planning module is the master-planning run that generates a master plan consisting of planned orders. The master-planning run uses the inventory transactions that sometimes are combined with forecast, to find the items that are on hand currently, and future requirement in the warehouses.

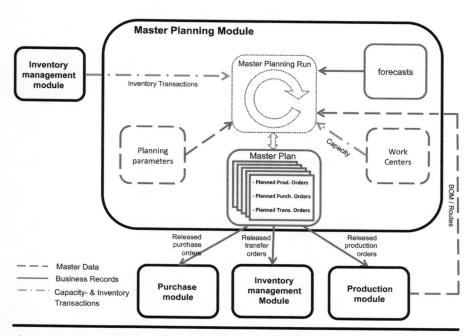

Figure 7.1   Key data components of a master planning module.

The BOM from the production module is used in a BOM explosion to break down the requirements to each subcomponents and materials, while the production route is used to estimate the resources requirements that is balanced toward the available capacity in the work centers. The master plan run uses a set of master data and parameters that dictates how the planned orders in the master plan should be formed. The planned orders in the master plan can then be released into "real" purchase, production, transfer, and/or sales orders.

OPTISTREAM

Greta, the supply chain planner, has the responsibility for master planning at OptiStream. She has the responsibility of maintaining master data for the planning, as well as running the master plan and executing the plan in cooperation with the other departments.

Greta can access the demand forecasts through the "released products" application in Microsoft Dynamics 365 Supply Chain Management (item master). On the released products she can also reach and set most of the item's planning parameters through an application named "item coverage".

The master data on resources was registered back when OptiStream was implementing the system. The types of resources that can be defined in Microsoft Dynamics 365 Supply Chain Management are machine, vendor, tool, location, and personnel. To simplify the setup Greta only uses resources with the type "machines". She grouped the resources into resource groups in Microsoft Dynamics 365 Supply Chain Management, defined their work centers, and cooperated with Peter in production in defining the capacity calendars.

The master-planning run is accessed through the master planning module in Microsoft Dynamics 365 Supply Chain Management. She has set some of the master plans to run automatically at nighttime so that these are updated when they need them in their internal planning routines. She accesses the master plan through the "planned orders" application, where she performs most of the planning as well. An example of the "planned orders" application (master plan) in Microsoft Dynamics 365 Supply Chain Management is shown in Figure 7.2.

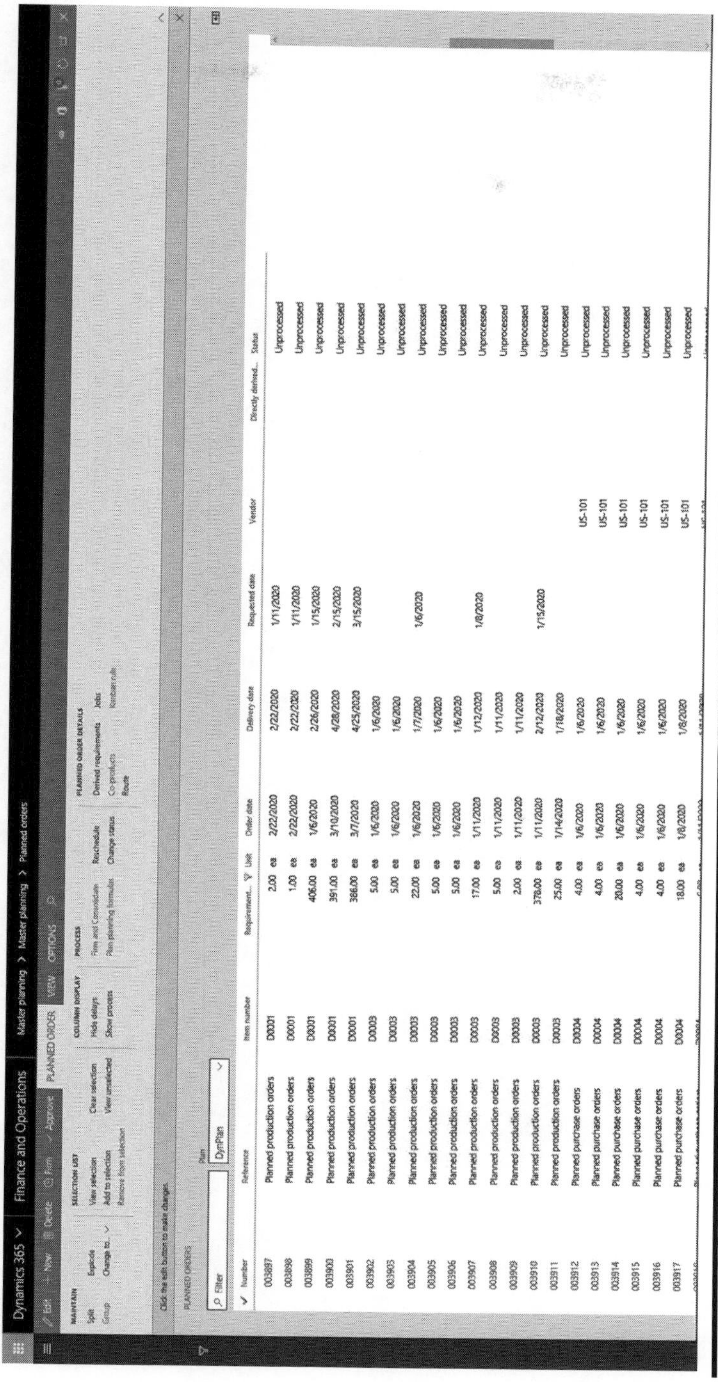

Figure 7.2 Planned orders application in Microsoft Dynamics 365 Supply Chain Management.

7.3 Basic Functionality

In the following sections we have listed some functions that are commonly found in an ERP system's master planning module.

7.3.1 Master-Planning Run

The master-planning run is a key function in a master planning module, and this application is used as an engine to create all material plans in an ERP system for manufacturing supply chains. A master-planning run in an ERP system first calculates the gross and then the net requirement for the different items in each warehouse, before finally generating the planned orders in the master plan using the planning methods and other parameters. One important system-generated parameter used by the master-planning run is using the low-level code. The low-level code dictates the lowest level an item is using in BOM, as indicated in Figure 7.3.

The figure shows a bill-of-material (BOM) with the respective low-level codes of four items: "A", "B", "C", and "D" (for illustration sake, let's say that these items are only used in the BOM in the figure). Item "A" is only used as an end product and gets low-level code of "0". Item "B" is both used in level 1 and 2 in the BOM, and therefore gets highest low-level code of these two (low-level code "2").

Item "C" and "D" is only used in level 1 and level 2 in the BOM respectively, which means item "C" gets low-level code "1" and item "D" gets low-level code "2".

The low-level code is used to organize the sequence of the items that is calculated by the master-planning run and ensures the "BOM explosion", so that the demand from the planned orders on items that are at the top of the BOM (with a

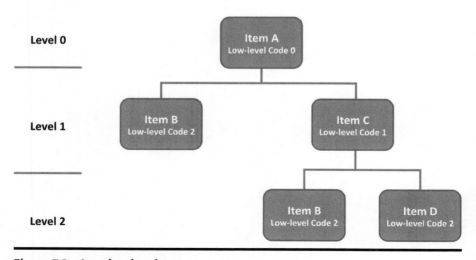

Figure 7.3   Low-level code.

lower low-level code) will be considered when calculating items with a higher low-level code further down in the hierarchy.

We will not go into the details of the master planning algorithms, but only outline some steps to illustrate the principles a master-planning run can use to calculate the planned orders in the master plan.

1. First, the master planning calculation starts with all the items with the lowest low-level code (end products with low-level code "0") and finds the gross requirement from future outbound inventory transactions (like future sales orders, requirement from production orders, etc.), and/or forecast if the item is forecast planned.
2. Then, it calculates the net requirement for these items by considering the current and projected future on-hand levels, as well as the inbound inventory transactions (e.g., from future inbound inventory transactions from purchase orders or inbound production orders).
3. Finally, the net requirement is reviewed toward planning data and parameter, and the master planning application creates the planned production, purchase, and transfer orders in the master plan, and if applicable, balances the capacity consumption of the planned production orders toward the available capacity of the work centers.

When the master planning is finished with making planned order in the master plan for items with the lowest low-level code (like "0"), it repeats steps 1 to 3 for items with the next low-level code (like "1"), but here it also takes the planned inventory transactions made from planned orders that just have been made on the items with a lower low-level code into account. Then it repeats the process for the items with the third low-level code (like "2"), and so on until there are no items with a higher low-level code.

When creating the planned order, the master planning calculation uses planning parameters such as planning methods, lead times, safety stock, etc. to suggest delivery dates on the planned orders. The start and stop time of the planned production orders can be adjusted according to the calculated capacity requirements on their production route that are balanced toward the available capacity of the work centers. The work center can be set with finite or infinite capacity. The master-planning run will automatically adjust the start/stop time of the planned production orders to meet the available capacity on the work centers with finite capacity. On work centers with infinite capacity the planner can choose to manually adjust the planned production orders to meet capacity restrains and potentially do a new master-planning run. These considerations can form a "closed loop" planning circle to meet capacity shortages and other capacity issues in the plan.

In this way the master planning application of an ERP system has in extremity the potential to create a complete master plan where all BOMs are exploded and the real orders, current on-hand, forecast, work center capacity, as well as planned orders are organized in a consistent manner.

OPTISTREAM

Greta use up several plans for different purposes within OptiStream's planning processes. These plans use the same master planning application in Microsoft Dynamics 365 Supply Chain Management but are set up to run toward different items using different parameter settings. Some of these plans are set up to run automatically, while other plans she chooses to start the master-planning run manually, as shown in Figure 7.4.

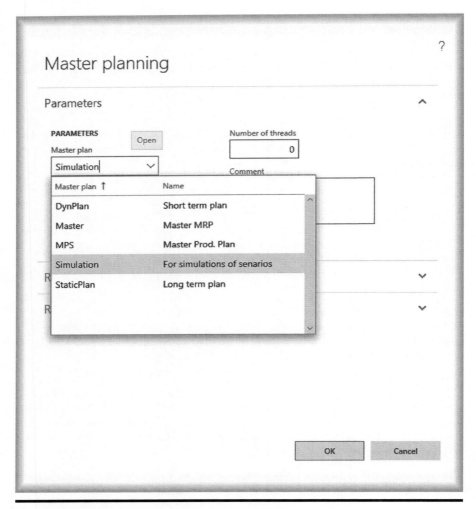

Figure 7.4 Staring a master plan run manually.

7.3.2 Planning Methods

The planning method maybe the most important master planning parameter when setting up an ERP system to support manufacturing supply chains. The planning method controls how an item shall be replenished in a warehouse and is used by the master-planning run to generate planned orders in the ERP system's master plan.

There is almost an endless variation of different planning methods that can be configured in the different ERP packages. Most of them can be organized under one of these three categories.

- Order-driven planning methods
- Requirement-based planning methods
- Reorder point-based planning methods

With an order-driven planning method we mean that a replenishment production, purchase, or transfer orders are directly triggered from a downstream requiring order. Table 7.1 shows an example of how an order-driven planning method can function between sales and production orders of a make-to-order item.

The columns in the table show future days ahead. The first four rows in the table illustrate the quantity on incoming sales orders and the last four rows show the corresponding replenishment production orders. The markings show that under an order-driven planning method, the ERP system will create a single replenishment order for each downstream order.

In most systems the order-driven approach can be configured so that the replenishment order is triggered automatically without using a master-planning run, while other ERP systems require running the master plan to create and release the

Table 7.1   Example of Order-Driven Planning Methods

Order-driven Planning Method

Day	0	1	2	3	4	6	7	8	9	10
Sales order 1			23							
Sales order 2					45					
Sales order 3					56					
Sales order 4								40		
On-hand	0	0	0	0	0	0	0	0	0	0
Production order 1			23							
Production order 2					45					
Production order 3					56					
Production order 4								40		

planned replenishment order/orders. This means that two variants of the order-driven planning methods are commonly found in ERP systems.

■ The replenishment order is directly generated from orders downstream the manufacturing supply chain – no release of a planned order in master plan is required.
■ "Order-for-order" master planning – The master plan is set to create a single planned order for the replenishment made for each downstream order. For example, a single planned production order is created in the master plan to fulfill a single sales order line.

Our impression is that making replenishment orders directly from the downstream orders is the most effective. The master plan for achieving an order-driven approach should only be used if the ERP system doesn't have possibilities to create a replenishment order directly.

The second group of planning methods is the requirement-based planning methodologies. This means that the collective demand from downstream orders and/or forecast should create the planned production, purchase, or transfer orders in the master plan to replenish the warehouse with the needed items.

There are a lot of different variants on how requirement planning methods can be executed in an ERP system. We want to highlight the two simplest and most commonly used variants.

■ Requirement – Requirement from forecast and/or downstream orders are generating a net requirement that triggers a planned order in the master plan.
■ Time-phased requirement (TPP) – Similar as requirement-based planning, but the gross requirements from a fixed time period is used to create the planned order ("requirement" usually only consider 1 day at a time).

To illustrate this, we have made some simplified calculations showing how these two requirement-based planning methods work.

Tables 7.2 illustrates simplified calculations for two requirement-based planning methods that are commonly used in ERP systems. The first row in the table indicates the gross requirements for the item. This gross requirement can come from downstream orders and/or forecasts. The second row illustrates the projected on-hand. The last row illustrates the quantity on the planned order suggested by the master plan.

To simplify we have chosen not to take the replenishment lead time into account. The safety stock is set to 20 and initially it was 150 items on-hand.

The first table shows a "traditional lot-for-lot" requirement planning. Here we see that the calculation seeks to generate order proposals that reflect the gross requirement for each day holding the on-hand is constant at the safety stock.

Table 7.2 Examples on Two Variants of Requirement-Based Planning Methods

Requirement-based planning method – "Requirement" (lot-for-lot)
Safety stock = 20

Day	0	1	2	3	4	6	7	8	9	10
Gross requirement		100	150	120	160	110	120	230	90	120
On-hand	150	50	20	20	20	20	20	20	20	20
Order proposal		0	120	120	160	110	120	230	90	120

Requirement-based planning method – "Time-phased requirement "
Coverage time 3 days, Safety stock = 20

Day	0	1	2	3	4	6	7	8	9	10
Gross requirement		100	150	120	160	110	120	230	90	120
On-hand	150	290	140	20	250	140	20	230	140	20
Order proposal		240	0	0	390	0	0	440	0	0

The lower part of the table shows a "time-phased requirement" planning that is similar to the requirement, but here the requirements for several days are collected together for a defined period.

We see that the inventory is held at a lower level when using "requirement", but it creates more frequent replenishment orders. "Time-phased requirement" may result in more variable on-hand levels but less frequent replenishment orders. Therefore, "time-phased requirement" is typically chosen if the company wants to reduce the number of planned orders in the master plan to a minimum, for example, reducing the total ordering costs.

As the table indicates, a safety stock is commonly used in connection to a requirement planning method to hedge for uncertainty in forecast and unforeseen events in the supply chain.

The third group of planning methods found in ERP system are planning methods based around the "reorder point" principle. This principle uses on-hand to create the planned order. Two variants are commonly used in ERP systems:

■ Reorder point – A fixed-order quantity is reordered when the on-hand stock reach a certain level.
■ Min/Max – An order is issued to reach the max quantity when the on-hand stock reaches a minimum level.

A simple illustration of these variants is shown in Table 7.3.

We have left the replenishment lead time out here as well to simplify the table. The upper part of table shows a "traditional" reorder point, where the reorder point

Table 7.3   Examples on Two Variants of Reorder Point-Based Planning Methods

Reorder point-based planning method – "reorder point"
Reorder point 50, order quantity 300

Day	0	1	2	3	4	6	7	8	9	10
Gross requirement		100	150	120	160	110	120	230	90	120
On-hand	150	350	200	80	220	110	290	60	270	150
Order proposal		300	0	0	300	0	300	0	300	0

Reorder point-based planning method – "min/max"
Min = 50, Max = 300

Day	0	1	2	3	4	6	7	8	9	10
Gross requirement		100	150	120	160	110	120	230	90	120
On-hand	150	300	150	300	140	300	180	300	210	90
Order proposal		250	0	270	0	270	0	350	0	0

is set to 50 and order quantity is 300. Initially there are 150 items on-hand. Here we can see that the system will propose a planned order with a fixed-order quantity when the on-hand will fall below 50.

The lower table shows a min/max planning method where the minimum is set to 30 and the maximum is set to 300. The min/max function is similar to the reorder point but here the order quantity is adjusted to match the max level.

To summarize, these two reorder approaches are quite similar, but with min/max can achieve a steadier inventory level of the expense on a varying replenishment order size. Therefore, a reorder point may be chosen in favor of the min/max if a fixed-order size is important in the replenishment.

Another reorder point-based planning method that is well-known in the literature and in the industry is "periodic review". "Periodic review" means that the replenishment is done by reviewing the inventory in a periodic fashion and ordering fixed-order quantity or an order quantity to achieve a max level. However, in an ERP system, this approach is usually achieved through using min/max or a reorder point and then running the master plan in timely intervals. Therefore, we will not discuss this variant further in this book.

Some items in an ERP should not be part of the master plan and not generate planned orders. These items are usually set as a "not-planned" or "manual planned" planning method in the ERP system.

The planning methods and calculations shown in this section are only examples to illustrate the three principles for planning methods that an ERP system operates with. In real-life ERP applications these planning methods can be tweaked in various ways to achieve the desired result, for example, by combining the requirement or min/max method with a fixed reorder quantity. This means that the possibilities of each ERP package must be explored to be able to set the optimum planning method for each situation.

OPTISTREAM

Greta uses the parameter "coverage code" that configures the planning methods in Microsoft Dynamics 365 Supply Chain Management. This parameter has the following settings.

- Period
- Requirement
- Min/Max
- Manual

Greta sets the "coverage code" settings and other replenishment parameters for each item at each warehouse where they should be managed in Microsoft Dynamics 365 Supply Chain Management. In this way she makes sure that the replenishment is triggered in a correct manner throughout the facility.

7.3.3 Time Fencing

An ERP system should have time-fence control mechanisms to make a sound, stable, and well-functioning master schedule. Time fences are boundaries between different zones in the planning horizon. There are time limits related to due dates that sets restrictions to changes in the master plan.

Changes to the master plan will happen. For example, customer orders will be canceled, machines will break down, components will be defected, or supplies will not be delivered as promised. A fixed plan will reduce production costs due to rerouting, extra set-ups, expediting, and extra work-in-process inventory. However, a manufacturing enterprise wants to be flexible and adapts to changing needs. The flexibility to changes is larger further off the planning horizon. The master plan can be altered for an item beyond its cumulative lead time, with little effect on related material and capacity plans. Closer to due date however, changes can cause major interruptions and costs in the manufacturing supply chain.

The enterprise should define the planning time fence and the demand time fence for each item. They define zones in the planning horizon with different levels of commitment to the plan.

Time fencing in an ERP system should at least include:

- A planning horizon – This is how long in the future the plan should be set. This horizon is mostly used to limit the master planning calculations to optimize performance of the software and reduce the time consumption of the master-planning run.
- A planning time fence – This time fence is the time within the planning horizon where the planned orders are starting to affect confirmed delivery of components, scheduled capacity, and other physical events in the supply chain. The planned orders inside the planning time fence should not be planned by the ERP system but should only be rescheduled under the supervision of a human planner/scheduler.
- A demand time fence – The demand time fence is set within the planning time fence. Inside this time fence only real orders (no forecasts) are included in the total demand. The plan should not be replanned at all within the demand time fence since this will affect confirmed sales to customers.

The planning horizon is the period of time that plans are made for. The planning horizon for master planning should be long enough to include the longest cumulative lead time among the products to be produced. Most companies use longer planning horizons to form effective plans.

The demand time fence is the point in time when unrealized forecast is dropped from demand. Typical manufacturers set the demand time fence as the cumulative lead time for an item. Inside the demand time fence, the plan is frozen and driven purely by customer demands because the lead time is very short. The planning time fence is set between the demand time fence and the end of planning horizon.

The zone beyond planning time fence contains only forecasted customer orders, and any changes can be done automatically by the ERP system. In the zone between demand time fence and planning time fence, actual customer orders gradually replace the forecast quantities, and changes can be made manually by the planner. Inside the demand time fence orders are confirmed toward customers and no alterations to the plan should happen beyond this point in time.

OPTISTREAM

Greta has defined time fence on the coverage group in Microsoft Dynamics 365 Supply Chain Management. The time fences in this ERP system are a bit different than time fences Greta have worked with previously, but she uses the following settings to meet her requirements.

- Planning horizon – Greta sets "coverage time fence", "forecast plan time fence", "BOM explosion time fence (days)" and "capacity scheduling time fence (days)" to limit the extent of the master planning calculations.

- Planning time fence – Greta uses the "freeze time fence" to lock the plan for automatically replanning of new orders, as well as "reduction key" setting for managing the reduction of forecast in favor of customer orders.
- Demand time fence – Greta has not found a setting to define the demand time fence in Microsoft Dynamics 365 Supply Chain Management. There is a "firming time fence" for specifying when Microsoft Dynamics 365 Supply Chain Management should automatically make "real orders" from the planned orders in the master plan. Greta has chosen not to use this, and all planned orders should rather be released manually.

Greta finds these time-fencing fields on the "coverage groups" in Microsoft Dynamics 365 Supply Chain Management as shown in Figure 7.5.

In this way Greta tries to manage setting up the system in correspondence to the planning theory she learned at school, but the interconnected logic of the ERP system makes it difficult to implement these time fences.

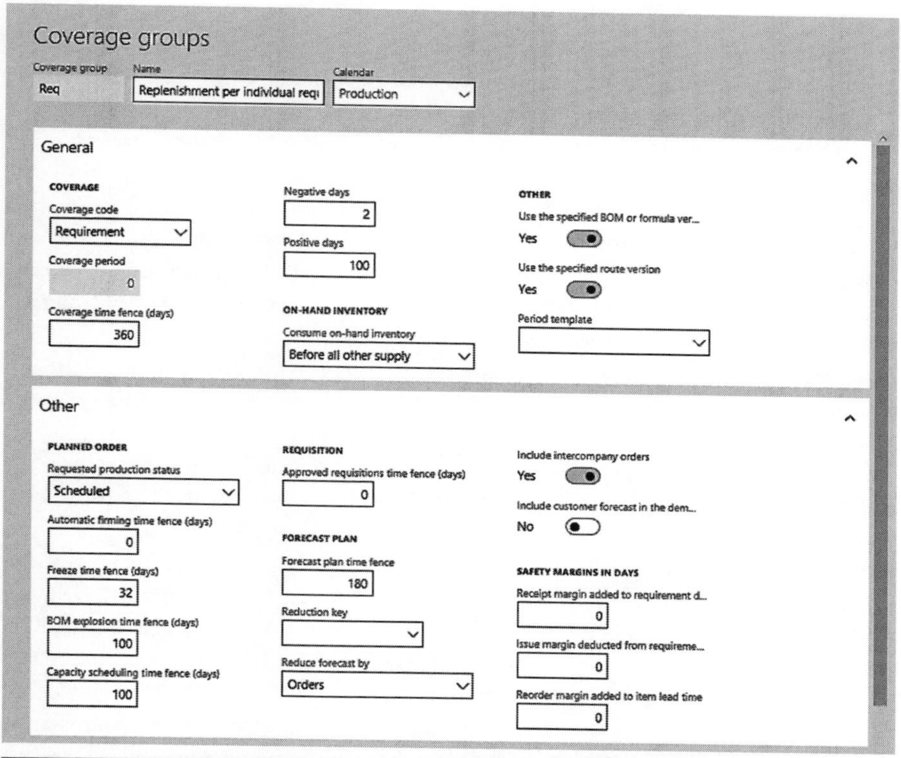

Figure 7.5   Coverage group settings.

For instance, other updates that Peter does to the production orders in production planning make it difficult to freeze the plan within the demand time fence. If Peter is moving a single ongoing order on the production floor, it will trigger changes in the whole master plan. Therefore, Greta and Peter have agreed on investing in an MES system, so that the detailed planning of the production and other events on the shop floor can happen in this application without affecting the master plan in the ERP system.

7.3.4 Other Planning Rules and Parameter

A master-planning run is using a lot of other planning rules, settings, and parameters when generating planned orders in the master plan. We have summarized the most important of these in this section.

The type of replenishment – In ERP systems there is a setting for what kind of planned order the master planning should create for the replenishment. These options are planned purchase order, planned transfer order, or planned production order. The users can change the planned order types in the master plan. For example, if the master planning suggests using a planned purchase order for buying an item that are in stock in another facility at the company, the planner can change this planned purchase order to a planned transfer order so the warehouse will be replenished from a company internal transfer instead.

Lead times – Lead times is used to set delivery dates in the system, both at order entry and within the master planning functions. Normally, there are lead time settings on each item for purchasing, transfers, and production. The production lead time depends on the quantity of each order and the work center capacity. Therefore, any fixed production lead time set in the ERP system is only used for a first estimation and overruled with when start/stop times are calculated on the production order/planned production order.

Order quantities – Most ERP systems support setting fixed-order quantities on the items. These order quantities can overrule the calculated replenishment quantities on the planned orders in the master plan. The reason for using fixed-order quantity can be that these are required for the ordering, transportation, or storing of the item (like meeting the number of items that fit a specific box size). Alternatively, a specific order quantity can be more economically favorable than others. A formula named economic order quantity (EOQ) can be used to find the optimal ordering size. The EOQ formula can be defined as $EOQ = \sqrt{(2DS)/H}$, where "D" is the daily demand in units, "S" is the items ordering cost, and "H" is the item's holding cost per day in the inventory. The EOQ is often connected to the reorder point-based planning methods but can be used in connection with other planning methods in an ERP system as well. The fewest of the ERP systems have built-in functionality to perform EOQ calculations; so any ordering quantities are usually estimated and set manually in the application.

Safety stock – The safety stock setting in ERP systems is often used in combination with forecast and "requirement" planning types. In some ERP systems the safety stock must be set manually, while other ERP-software packages have possibilities for automatic calculation of these settings. There exist a lot of algorithms for setting safety stocks, and one of the easiest can be expressed in the following formula: SS = (Maximum D × Maximum LT) – (Average D × Average LT), where "D" is demand and "LT" is lead time. For example, for a specific pump the average production time is 7 days and average demand is 10 pieces per day. The demand can peak up to 15 pieces per day that is stretching the production time to 10 days. The safety stock can then be estimated to 80 pieces (15 pcs/day × 10 days) – (10 pcs/day × 7 days).

Reorder point levels – The reorder point levels must be set on all items that are using a reorder point-based planning method. In most systems the reorder point must be set manually, while other ERP packages have possibilities to calculate and set a correct reorder point levels automatically. The order point must allow enough inventories to satisfy demand during lead time, that is, the time from the order is placed until it is fulfilled. If it is necessary to protect against stockouts, safety stock can be added to the reorder point. For example, a distributor of maritime equipment needs to find when it should place orders for a specific item from its manufacturer. The average sales are 100 per week, the lead time is 2 weeks, the safety stock is 50 units, and the order quantity is set to 500 units. The reorder point should cover demand during lead time + safety stock = 100 × 2 + 50 = 250 items. The distributor should order 500 items from the manufacturer each time its inventory level falls to 250 pieces. Similar settings can be done if the item uses a min/max planning method. The difference between the "max" and the "min" is usually the EOQ that where described above. Min/max settings can also be dynamically adjusted to offer better inventory performance, but that is not covered here.

7.3.5 Forecasting

Manufacturers are using data and information from a range of sources to create sound predictions of demands and trends. Companies must cope with seasonality, sudden changes in demand level, price-cutting actions from competitors, and financial crisis. Forecasting can help them deal with these troubles. The entire supply chain would be more efficient if the different members could collaborate to create a common forecast and make all their plans based on a single forecast. This would take out a lot of the uncertainty from the planning. ERP systems can help ensure that sales, delivery, production, and purchasing in each company are using only one forecast, because it is the common database for the main processes. The next step is to agree on a shared forecast with customers and suppliers. Collaborative planning, forecasting, and replenishment is the most known initiative to provide integrative forecast and keep all the supply chain members in tune with the end customer. The initiative is not implemented in many supply chains, and there is still a lot to do before collaborative planning, forecasting, and replenishment is a common practice.

Forecasting is done by a mix of qualitative or quantitative methods. In situations where little demand data are available, or the data are no longer relevant for future sales, qualitative judgments are required from experts who can use their industrial insight to predict demand. These experts, however, will often use some historical demand data to support their judgment. When extensive historical data are available for a product, quantitative models can be used to project future demand, and there is little need for human judgements. However, some judgement is needed to adjust the models in cases where the demand no longer follows historical trends.

Qualitative methods are best guessed projections based on judgment, intuition, and informed options. The quickest and maybe least accurate qualitative method is that the planner makes projections based on his personal insight. More logical, unbiased, and systematic ways to bring together information and judgements is market research, for example, the sales force collaboratively estimate future demand. In situations where market acceptance and penetration rates are highly uncertain and long term, such as when developing new technology, it can be a good alternative to use more time-consuming approaches such as expert panels. For example, the Delphi method is a structured method where individual experts make a forecast, and then iteratively correct them until they have agreed on an aligned forecast.

Quantitative methods involve the estimation of values we don't know by using values that we know. Numerical facts and historical data are used for making projections about the future. There are two main types of quantitative methods, causal models, and time-series analysis. The goal of causal forecasting model is to develop the best statistical relationship between a dependent variable and one or more independent variables. The most common casual model used in practice is linear regression analysis. In this model, the dependent variable is a function of only one independent variable, for example, sales volume for the next year depends on marketing costs. A straight line of the form "$Y = a + bX$" is used to describe the relationship between the dependent variable "Y" and the independent variable "X". The line should be positioned in a set of data points so that the squared distance from the line is minimized (a least square fit).

Time series analysis produces forecasts based on historical values. They are widely used in situations where forecasts of the sales in the next year or less are required. They are especially relevant for items that are sold frequently because time-series methods can be computer-aided and to a large degree automated. They are best suited to relatively stable and reliable datasets. The easiest time series method simply projects future demand based on the last period's demand. However, historical data contains historical patterns such as seasonality, trends, and random noise. Time series forecasts based on such raw data may give relatively poor results. Time series analysis therefore has two goals, both to identify the nature of the historical demand and to forecast future demand. Both of these goals require that the pattern of observed time series data is identified and more or less formally described.

Historical patterns need to be separated or decomposed before the data can be used to create forecasts that are more accurate than a simple trend line. A well-performing time series model will provide indexes for seasonality, trends, and randomness. The model will usually not take event-based demand changes, such as price changes or new product introductions, formally into account. Forecasts are often run on time-series models and then adjusted based on events such as price discounts or campaigns.

The forecasting module of the ERP system can be used to run statistical forecasting on individual products, and construct aggregate-level forecasts by summing the low-level forecasts. The problem with such a "bottom-up" approach is that lower-level forecasts are likely to be less accurate for long-time horizons. They tend to miss trends that are obvious at the aggregated levels. Patterns that are easy to identify the aggregated level can be masked at the lower level by the stochastic behaviour of individual demand. High-level statistical forecasting will give better results, but usually require a separate demand planner tool that enables efficient aggregation and disaggregation of forecasts. This is not standard ERP functionality and is not explained in this book.

You can choose from several different forecasting methods. The two most frequently used methods are moving averages and exponential smoothing. The moving average method assumes an average is a good estimator of future behaviour. It consists of making the average of the last "n" observations to forecast the next observation. For example, if n = 4 weeks, the forecasted sales for week 12 is the average sales for week 8, 9, 10, and 11. Its advantage over the simple projection model is that by averaging, the forecast will not fluctuate as much. The level of fluctuation depends on the number of observations used. An average of a high number of observations will provide a very stable and insensitive forecast. A drawback with this method is the need to keep several periods of history for each forecasted product.

The exponential smoothing methods give similar results but without the need for so much data and with easier calculations. The previously calculated forecast includes the history of earlier observations. The basic idea is that exponential smoothing corrects your next forecast in a way that would have made your prior forecast a better one. That is a good idea, and it usually works well. The new forecast is based on the old-calculated forecast plus a percentage of the difference between that forecast and the actual value at that point. That is: New Forecast = Old Forecast + a (Actual − Old Forecast) where "a" is a percentage, known as a smoothing constant and Actual − Old Forecast represents the prediction error. Because exponential smoothing relies on only two pieces of data (the last period's actual value and the forecasted value for the same period), it minimizes the data storage requirements. The nice thing about exponential smoothing is that you can take the error in your last forecast and use that error, and hopefully improve the next forecast. However, this method is only accurate when a reasonable amount of continuity between the past and future can be assumed.

While this kind of assumption may sound reasonable in the short term, it creates problems the further the forecast goes. This method is most suitable for forecasts that are short term and in the absence of seasonal or cyclical trends. That said, there are more advanced variations of exponential smoothing that can handle trend patterns, but they are not handled in this book.

Some ERP systems have built-in functionality to support the creation of forecast through both qualitative and quantitative methods. However, the focus of forecasting in ERP system is often more toward using the demand from forecast in the master planning function. Therefore, enterprises do often use a "best of breed" forecasting software or other tools to create and maintain the forecasts, and then transfer this to the ERP system for further processing in the master planning functions.

There are two ways an item can be forecasted in an ERP system. The first is that forecasts are made directly toward the item. These forecasts are usually set toward end products and/or critical components within the production process. Alternatively, the forecast can be inherited through the master planning process from forecast on items downstream the manufacturing supply chain. The forecast is then a part of what is called "dependent demand", that describes the part of an item's demand are influenced by the demand of other products.

OPTISTREAM

Greta uses an external forecasting software tool in connection to OptiStream's sales and operations planning (S&OP) process where she creates forecast through a collaborative process. She transfers the finish forecast to the forecasting functions in Microsoft Dynamics 365 Supply Chain Management, where it is used in the master planning functions during the master production scheduling (MPS) process.

She makes separate forecasts on sales items that are produced to stock, as well as critical components in production, to ensure the replenishment of these. Some of the components use the dependent demand from forecast on the parent products to trigger their replenishment in the master plan.

It is possible to make forecast through machine learning from historical data in Microsoft Dynamics 365 Supply Chain Management. But Greta has not yet set these functions in use and still prefers to focus on the forecasts that are made from their future plans.

7.3.6 Capacity Planning

Capacity planning is the process of determining the capacity needed to execute manufacturing plans. ERP systems usually provide capacity planning support on two levels of aggregation. Rough-cut capacity planning (RCCP) is performed to validate initial MPS runs. Detailed capacity requirement planning (CRP) is performed to validate a fully exploded master plan. How much effort is to be put into ERP-based capacity planning depends on the overall capacity situation. A rough-cut capacity check on one or two critical resources is often sufficient for stable supply chains that operate with one or two shifts per day. A more detailed CRP might be beneficial to optimise the use of resources when demand for products is high.

RCCP – It is a process of validating if the supply chain has capacity to execute the MPS (the MPS process will be discussed later). RCCP attempts to do this by checking the capacity of key resources or resource groups/work centres. RCCP uses a "bill of resources" defined in the ERP system to check if the available resources have enough capacity to cover each time period in the plan. The bill of resources specifies the number of hours required at each resource group to make a particular end item and its components. The RCCP calculates the total number of hours required for each resource group to fulfil the MPS. Since the RCCP does not consider lead time offsets, the time periods must be large enough so that end items and all their components are completed within a single period. Such an aggregated calculation often makes RCCP too optimistic about what can be produced.

Bill of resources can be generated for resource groups such as a department or a production line. ERP systems allow defining resource groups and allocating critical resources to these groups. A bill of resources specifies the number of hours required at a resource group to make a particular end item and its components. Such bills can be generated automatically. A BOM explosion is performed for each item in the resource group. The ERP system determines the number of hours required for all components and subassemblies in the BOM, and calculates the cumulative resource requirements for the parent items.

CRP – It refers to the process of determining in detail the amount of capacity needed to accomplish the planned production requirement. CRP is performed after a multiple-level master planning runs with full explosion and offsetting is complete. CRP is usually restricted to key or critical work centers that are defined as finite capacity resources. CRP requires that routing, sequences, and operation times are specified for these resource groups. Released and planned orders from the master planning are the basis for creating load in the ERP system. The CRP results are presented as the total workload per calendar day or week for each work centre. CRP is a more detailed capacity planning tool than RCCP because it also considers scheduled receipts, on-hand inventory, and routings when calculating capacity requirements. Even though RCCP may indicate that sufficient capacity exists to execute the MPS, CRP may show that capacity is insufficient during specific time periods.

OPTISTREAM

It is currently not possible to register a "bill-of-resources" in OptiStream's version of Microsoft Dynamics 365 Supply Chain Management". Greta is, therefore, extracting information from the ERP system for doing a separate rough capacity estimate for her planning processes.

CRP is calculated in the system. They have set all the work centers with infinite capacity in Microsoft Dynamics 365 Supply Chain Management. Therefore, the CRP calculations are only used to monitor the capacity situation in order to replan and adjust master plan manually to meet any capacity restrains.

7.3.7 Planning Alerts

The master planning in ERP systems do often handle large number of items and planned orders. This means that it is near impossible for a human planner to have a complete overview over the whole plan. Therefore, he or she must concentrate on solving the exceptions and problems in the plan. Hence, most systems have an alert or warning system that notifies the planner and helps him/her to focus on the right things. Typically, when the quantities from a master plan are netted against each other, the ERP system provides action messages. Action messages might be suggestions to create a new order, change the quantity or date of an order, or cancel an order. The planner can then focus on solving these action messages rather than reviewing the whole plan for issues.

OPTISTREAM

Microsoft Dynamics 365 Supply Chain Management can generate both so-called "future messages" and "action messages" to help Greta with the planning process. Action messages can make suggestions for changing a planned order, while future messages are generated when an order does not reach its due date based on lead times estimations.

If the system is correctly configured, Greta should only have to review and confirm these exceptions of the plan. However, such an ideal way for working requires an extensive setup and maintenance of the master data in Microsoft Dynamics 365 Supply Chain Management. So, Greta has set up the system to only show the most important of the action message the ERP system can generate.

7.3.8 Planning Overview

Most ERP systems provide several ways to look at the master plan. The most common of these involves splitting the master plan in separate plans from production, purchases, and planned transfers. The production planning application is usually identical with the master plan application but only the planned production orders are listed, allowing a production planner to focus on the orders that are relevant for him or her. The same goes for the purchase and transfer planning screen. This is fundamentally the normal master plan application, but only with the planned purchase orders or planned transfer orders listed.

Normally, an ERP system provides an overview that shows all orders and other inventory activities of a single item. This is usually some of the most used tools of the master planning application that helps the planner to take decisions and solve issues on the setup of the item.

Most ERP systems have several other screens, views, and functions to help in the planning of the supply chain. But these functionalities may vary from software to system, and each software application must be explored to find their unique strengths and weaknesses.

OPTISTREAM

Greta and the others at OptiStream can view the master plan in several ways in Microsoft Dynamics 365 Supply Chain Management. Some of the most used applications are:

- "Planned orders" – Show the complete master plan with all planned orders
- "Planned purchase orders" – Identical with the "planned order" application but only show the planned purchase orders
- "Planned production orders" – Identical with the "planned order" application but only holds the planned production orders
- "Planned transfers" – Identical with the "planned order" application but this function only displays the planned transfer orders

Greta is mainly using the "planned orders" application when she is doing her planning activities across the departments. Rita, Peter, and Erica use the "planned purchase orders", the "planned production orders", or the "planned transfers" applications when they are reviewing the plan and releasing planned orders for their departments.

Another planning application in Microsoft Dynamics 365 Supply Chain Management that is commonly used at OptiStream is the "net requirement" screen. This function shows all inventory activities related to a specific item. Greta and the others at OptiStream use this function to see all inbound and outbound orders on an item, as well as the planned orders the master planning function is suggesting to fulfill the replenishment of this item. A screenshot of the "net requirement" application is shown in Figure 7.6.

By using these applications, Greta can solve most of the issues she has with the plans in Microsoft Dynamics 365 Supply Chain Management. The ERP systems have many other tools and applications that may help her in the planning processes, but Greta usually finds what she needs through the "planned orders" and "net requirements" applications.

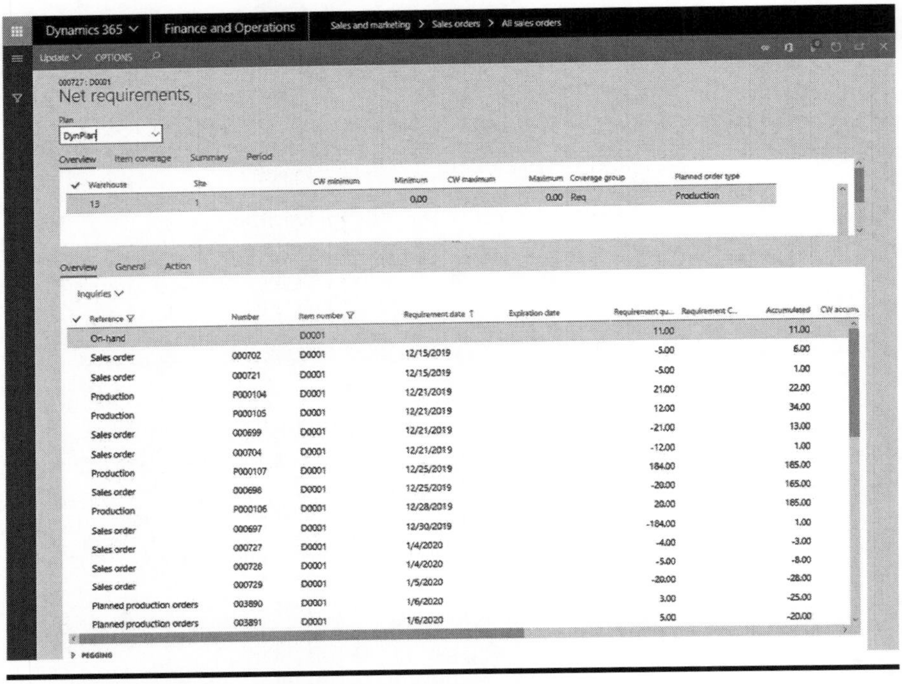

Figure 7.6   The net requirements application.

7.4 Planning Processes

As described, the master-planning run has the potential to calculate a single and large master plan including all requirements from all items in all warehouses. This affects how the master planning in an ERP system is performed in many enterprises: A single, complete master plan is calculated in a nightly run and is then used as the main source in the planning efforts within the company. But such "Big-Bang-plans" can be very confusing and comprehensive to manage, and therefore, this may not be the optimal way for performing the planning processes.

The master plan module can support a hierarchy of planning processes that are performed to cover a range of purposes. Plans are needed with different time horizons, level of detail, and updating frequencies. Planning attributes and parameters are set to meet the needs of items with different requirements, value, and production methods. Even if it is the same master plan, a company can set up separate planning "runs" for product families, end items, and components. The most common planning processes are S&OP for product families, MPS for end items and key components, and a detailed material requirement planning (MRP) for a full explosion of the plan. The master planning module of an ERP system can support the S&OP process with demand and supply data, but actual S&OP calculations are usually done in a separate tool or module. The master plan module is rather used to calculate the MPS or MRP on request.

S&OP is concerned with long-term, volume-level plans and aims to balance the sales/marketing plans with available production resources. Calculations of aggregated demand and supply are done several months ahead. This information is used for assessing production capacity and constraints and finds out if the proposed demand plan is doable.

MPS items are usually end items or products options that manufacturing will build in the near future, as well as critical semi-finished products and components for purchases. An MPS run can be conducted without a BOM explosion to ensure that critical items are correctly planned before the complete master-planning run takes place. MPS items are a subset of the overall product database. Such items have a demand from a forecast or a sales order line and can be allocated automatically before an MPS run. The MPS forms the basis for calculation of resources and capacity needed, and helps the enterprise to provide on-time delivery to their customers.

MRP is a detailed scheduling with a full explosion of the BOM, and replenishment calculation of all components. In a complete MRP run, the master plan determines the materials, parts, and subassemblies that are required to manufacture a planned quantity of end items on time. A complete MRP run includes work-in-process inventory, scheduled receipts, and planned orders. The calculation of material requirements is based on actual requirements for components and the demand forecast on the component level. The full MRP plan often calculates the replenishment of reorder point in planned items as well. The purpose of MRP is to provide time-phased plans, by item, so end items can be delivered on time.

The configuration of the master planning is therefore quite complex and includes a range of choices and parameter settings.

7.4.1 Sales and Operations Planning

Sales and operations planning (S&OP) is a process for better alignment of a manufacturer's supply with demand by having the sales department collaborate with operations to create an aggregated production plan. The aim is to establish proper production rates and capacities in a plan that considers inventory levels, customer backlog levels, and work force stability. The time period is usually a month and the time horizon are up to 12 to 18 months. S&OP is typically carried out once a month, and bring together sales, operations, and other departments that are closely involved in supply or demand, such as marketing, development, procurement, transportation, and finance. Plans from each department are aligned through a reconciliation process that takes decisions regarding production, inventory, and workforce. During this process, trade-offs between volume and product mix are made so that demand and supply are in balance. The main result is an aggregated sales and production plan for what to do in the next months.

Figure 7.7   The sales and operations planning (S&OP) process.

A schematic overview of the S&OP process is presented in Figure 7.7. S&OP is based on forecasts about aggregate demand, and the current status of inventory, production rate, and workforce levels. Such an overall planning is not the core functionality in ERP systems. Many companies therefore handle S&OP in spread sheets or specialised software. However, the outputs of ERP systems are utilised in the planning process. The first phase is to extract sales history from the ERP system. The sales history is utilised to generate aggregated forecasts for product groups. Collaboration with the sales team and customers should be established to verify that the forecast numbers are as realistic as possible. With a consensus demand plan generated, the second phase is to extract inventory levels, production history, and production plans from the ERP system, and provide a comparable view of supplies. This information is used for assessing production capacity and constraints and find out if the proposed demand plan is doable. The planner will run alternative what-if production plans to see the impact of changes such as shifts in demand, product introductions, or supplier problems, on capacity and delivery ability. The third phase brings all plans and data together in a unified way to be used in S&OP review meeting where managers from sales, production, and purchasing are present. During this review step, what-if plans are reviewed to find a doable plan, and any key decisions that have not been resolved in the earlier phases are addressed. If it is not doable, the sales plan or the production plan has to be adjusted. In the end, the goal of the S&OP process is to generate a final, aggregated plan that is sent to cross-functional owners and distributed downstream to all affected areas.

Since ERP is a transaction-based system, it seldom stores aggregate or family-level data that can be used directly to create a long-term operations plan. However, the master plan is a good starting point to create such aggregated data. Data regarding planned production orders, purchase orders, inventory, routings, and lead times are available at the SKU level. Ideally, the product families used for S&OP are similar to a grouping in the ERP master schedule, and the aggregated data can be easily extracted. If not, the aggregated supply data need to be constructed in a spread sheet or through an automated S&OP tool.

Some ERP vendors offer sales and operations tools for handling all steps in an integrated system. Such software is sold as optional modules of an ERP suite or as stand-alone products. Some advance planning and schedule (APS) softwares may also come with sales and operations functionality. Most ERP systems provide the possibility to integrate sales and operations tools sold by third-party vendors.

OPTISTREAM

Every month Greta prepares the S&OP meeting. She uses data from Microsoft Dynamics 365 Supply Chain Management to estimate things like current status of inventory, sales numbers, production rate, and work-force levels. However, she only extracts data from Microsoft Dynamics 365 Supply Chain Management and use a Microsoft Excel spread sheet to create the outputs, that includes an aggregated sales plan and high-level operations plan for the production. She then conducts the S&OP meeting with Rita, Peter, and Alfred, the mangers of the purchase, production, and sales department, to coordinate and decide on these overall plans.

7.4.2 *Master Production Scheduling*

The master production scheduling (MPS) process aims to establish a time-phased plan for when and how much to produce of critical end items. MPS is a form of MRP that limits planning to items that have a major influence on company profit, or which dominates the entire supply chain by using critical resources. These items are selected for an initial planning run that takes place before the full MRP/master-planning run and is normally performed without a BOM explosion. The aggregate MPS at item level should match with the S&OP defined at family level. The time period is usually a week and the time horizons are up to 3 to 6 months. A typical MPS process is shown in Figure 7.8.

The first phase is to prepare planning data. The main sources of information for MPS are demand data for individual end items, inventory transactions, and

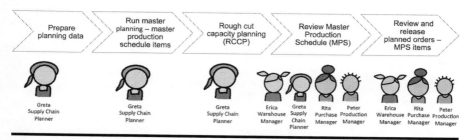

Figure 7.8   The master production scheduling (MPS) process.

capacity requirements. The MPS calculation is used for end items and key items that have a dedicated forecast. Forecasts and sales orders are structured in a time-phased demand plan. An initial check against the S&OP is needed. Planned MPS item's quantities must agree with the product family estimates of capacity requirements from the sales and operations plan.

The second phase is the master planning of MPS items. The definition of what is included as an MPS item will vary according to the manufacturing strategy. Typically, in make-to-stock manufacturing supply chain the end item will be defined as the MPS item. In engineer-to-order, make-to-order, or assemble-to-order environments raw-materials, components, or semi-finished products can be forecasted separately and included as an MPS item.

The MPS planning process uses the master planning capabilities of the ERP system. Demand data are transformed into net requirement signals based on inventory levels, order backlogs, lead time, and capacity. Safety stock policies and lot-sizing rules are also considered. The result is a time-phased supply plan proposal. The plan must meet the demand and be balanced against inventory costs and the capacity of important work centres in the manufacturing supply chain. After the master schedule is created, the next phase is to validate it to ensure that the production has sufficient capacity within the work centres. The methods for capacity planning are explained in the previous sections. Several master-planning runs might be necessary to find a doable plan. Finally, the MPSs are reviewed by managers from production, warehouse, and purchasing. The agreed upon MPS plan forms the basis for a full MRP run with complete BOM explosion and release of orders.

Finite material and capacity planning can be performed during the MPS run, and inventory levels and lead times are taken into consideration. This helps you plan purchase, production, and transfer orders more reliably, and optimize manufacturing flows in the supply chain.

Requirements can change a lot due to inventory adjustments, postponed or canceled sales orders, shorted or missed production quantities, and a variety of other reasons. The planner's job is to ensure that the correct requirement signals are used to update the plan, by monitoring and managing exception and action messages from the ERP system. The schedule provides useful support for the planner before actual release of orders. They serve as gatekeepers to ensure that execution activities in the manufacturing supply chains are not disrupted due to changes in demand or supply.

OPTISTREAM

Microsoft Dynamics 365 Supply Chain Management has no tailored functions for MPS planning, but Greta has managed to establish routines for this using the standard master planning in Microsoft Dynamics 365 Supply Chain Management and in combination with external tools (Microsoft Excel spread sheets).

The production at OptiStream combines different manufacturing strate-gies that affect items selected as MPS items. All their stocked pumps (MTS products) are MPS items. The stocked pumps are their high-volume products and accounts for approximately 70% of their production volume. To ensure the production of all pumps, both the stocked pumps and the MTO/ETO products, OptiStream has identified some key compo-nents and raw materials as MPS products as well. These purchased items are important because they either have long lead time items that are criti-cal to keep production going, or they simply are expensive products. So, they should keep a special focus on optimizing the inventory costs.

Each month Greta prepares a forecast on each of the MPS product. This forecast is made through a collaborative process that is managed outside Microsoft Dynamics 365 Supply Chain Management. This forecasting pro-cess involves incorporating the input from the aggregated sales plan made in the S&OP process into the forecasts of the MPS products. The forecasts are then transferred to the "demand forecast" of MPS items in Microsoft Dynamics 365 Supply Chain Management.

Greta then runs the MPS planning in Microsoft Dynamics 365 Supply Chain Management. This is done as "normal" master-planning run, but that are only executed toward the MPS items. Greta has configured a separate plan for this in Microsoft Dynamics 365 Supply Chain Management. Once a month she starts this plan manually when all forecasts are updated in the ERP application, as shown in Figure 7.9.

Greta has set up the plan that will only create planned orders on the MPS items. However, she has not managed to configure this ERP system to create an aggregated RCCP. Therefore, she extracts the capacity data from Microsoft Dynamics 365 Supply Chain Management and creates a RCCP in a Microsoft Excel spread sheet. This RCCP plan only accounts for the stocked pumps, so she ensures that 30% of the capacity ahead will be available for production of the standard and engineered pumps that they are making to order.

The MPS plan is then reviewed together with Erica, Rita, and Peter in the warehouse/purchase/production departments who later release the planned orders for the MPS items as early as possible. When a planned order from the MPS plan is released, OptiStream has set a rule that these should not be rescheduled without addressing this in the S&OP meeting. In this way they seek their plans as stable and predictable as possible.

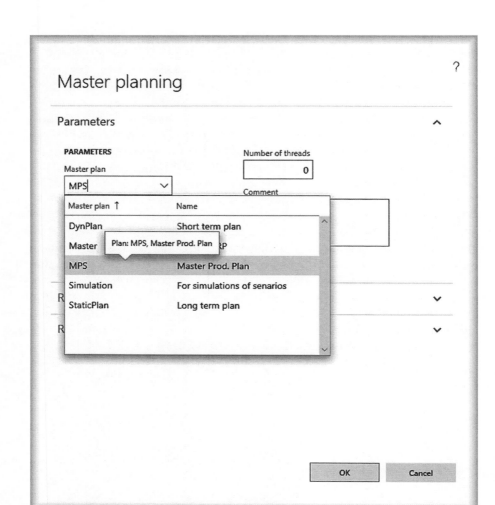

Figure 7.9 Starting MPS planning in Microsoft Dynamics 365 Supply Chain Management.

7.4.3 *Material Requirement Planning*

The master planning does also determine the replenishment of materials, parts, and subassemblies that are required to manufacture a planned quantity of end items on time. This is usually termed material requirement planning (MRP). The calculations of an MRP plan and the MPS scheduling are very similar, but there is one main difference. The demand from the MPS items is passed down in the MRP plan to get a complete plan overall needed replenishment for the items in the warehouses.

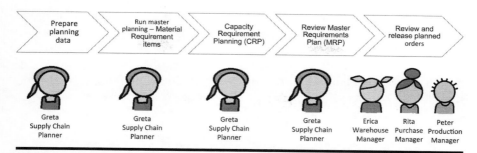

Figure 7.10   The material requirement planning (MRP) process.

The MPS plan provides the quantities and due dates for each end item. The bill-of-material lists all raw materials, assemblies, subassemblies, parts, and components, as well as the quantities of each, needed to manufacture a product. MRP planning uses the bill-of-material, routings, and inventory transactions, and other master planning functions to schedule the quantities and timing of supply. A simple MRP process is illustrated in Figure 7.10.

The MRP process starts with preparing the data and running the plan. The MRP plan must meet the required quantities for end times and be balanced against inventory costs and the capacity of important work centres. MRP planning is often capacity constrained. It is combined with capacity planning that computes the labour or machine capacity required to manufacture critical parts and components. The result of the MRP planning in an ERP system is a supply plan consisting of planned orders, where the users can release the plan into real orders in the other modules for manufacturing supply chains.

The planning algorithms used for both MPS and MRP are identical and are often calculated through the same master planning applications in the ERP system. But some ERP systems have functions helping the users to separate the plans to easily implement a hierarchical master planning process.

OPTISTREAM

OptiStream runs the master scheduling on their MRP plan two times a week. Greta checks the action message the morning after the MRP run to see if there are any new action messages that appeared during the night. If the action messages reveal any problems, for example, a purchase order is delayed and will affect the delivery of the end product to the customer, she will take this up with the appropriate department/departments in their daily morning meetings.

Every Thursday after the MRP run, she goes through all new planned production orders for the next week with Peter in production. Peter make any needed adjustments to the plan before he releases the planned production orders in the MRP plan into "real" production order. Thereafter, Greta does the same exercise with Rita in purchase and Erica in the warehouse, before they release the purchase orders and transfer orders for the coming week.

Ideally, if all production and purchase orders will be executed according to plan, it will create steady master plans and a hassle-free planning process at OptiStream. But in real life all productions, purchases, and transfers do not go according to plan. So, OptiStream starts each morning with an short planning meeting where Greta (planning), Rita (purchase), Peter (production), and Erica (warehouse), go through all changes, issues, and new action messages in the MRP plan in order to find a common ground on how these cases can be solved for the betterment of the total manufacturing supply chain.

Many manufacturing companies run a complete master plan for all items several times a week, and do not differentiate between different plans as well as MPS items and MRP items. However, there are four main reasons why Greta and OptiStream use hierarchical planning process starting with S&OP plans for running a separate MPS, before they do a complete MRP/master-planning run on all items.

- To focus on critical items – The planning runs that only include the MPS items enable Greta to test out different options without affecting the entire BOM. Greta can then conduct initial planning runs on critical items to ensure that the supply chain can meet due dates and capacity requirements.
- To increase planning speed – Plans that include all items in the product database might cause performance problems. Splitting the plans in smaller master-planning runs limits the strain of the Microsoft Dynamics 365 Supply Chain Management into smaller pieces.
- To avoid system nervousness – Frequent changes at the finished product level can make the complete MRP unstable. A complete planning process with S&OP, MPS, and finally a full MRP/master-planning run, will anchor key elements in the plan earlier, that again smoothens the plans and consequentially the material flows throughout the manufacturing supply chains.

7.5 Key Terms

- Master-planning run
- Master plan
- Time fence
- Forecasting
- Resources
- Planning policies
- Planning alerts

- Sales and operation planning (S&OP)
- Master production scheduling (MPS)
- Master requirement planning (MRP)

7.6 Chapter Summary

This chapter has shown that the master planning module consists of a master-planning run, a master plan, forecasts, work centers, and planning parameters. The master-planning run generates the planned orders in master plan by analyzing the inventory transactions, forecasts, bill-of-materials/routes, work-center capacity, and the items planning parameters. Important functionality of the master planning module is the planning parameters, planning methods, time fencing, forecasting, capacity planning, and planning alerts/overviews. The master planning process consists of S&OP, MPS, and MRP, but many manufacturing companies do choose to perform a single, large master-planning run to support their manufacturing supply chain.

Chapter 8

Using ERP Systems in a Manufacturing Facility

Learning Objectives

After reading this chapter, you will be able to:

- Describe how an ERP system can interact with the manufacturing supply chain within a single facility
- Know how the settings of the different planning methods in an ERP system can influence the manufacturing supply chain within a facility
- Provide guidelines for choosing the correct planning methods in the ERP system to meet different requirements and conditions in a facility's manufacturing supply chain
- Describe the relation between setting of the planning method of the ERP system and the chosen manufacturing strategy

8.1 How an ERP-System Affects the Manufacturing Supply Chain

In this chapter we will discuss how an ERP system supports the supply chain within a manufacturing facility. This describes the simplest installations of an ERP system for manufacturing supply chains. For example, implementation of an ERP system in a small manufacturing enterprise that consists of only one company holding a single physical facility, or an individual implementation in a small manufacturing company in a larger manufacturing group, as shown in Figure 8.1.

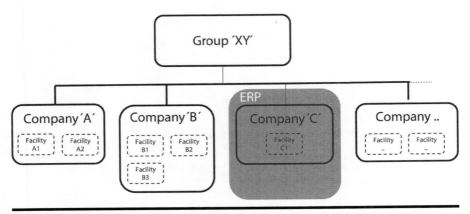

Figure 8.1   Example of using an ERP-system in a company with a single facility in a larger manufacturing group.

The figure shows a manufacturing enterprise ("Group XY") consisting of several manufacturing companies. In this chapter we will start by studying how an ERP system can be used in the simplest of the company of such a setup, namely a company consisting of a single facility (e.g., "Company C" in Figure 8.1).

The reason that we will first discuss the setup of a single facility, is that the use of an ERP system in a facility is the basic building block for establishing ERP support of an enterprise-wide manufacturing supply chain. Therefore, this should be explored before discussing the setup of ERP application to support a larger manufacturing supply chain that goes across facilities and/or companies.

8.1.1 The ERP-system's Role in a Facility's Manufacturing Supply Chain

As described in Chapter 1, a manufacturing supply chain can be understood as a network of facilities, each consisting of an inbound, production, and outbound part. By comparing these elements of a facility in a manufacturing supply chain with the core modules in an ERP system for supply chains, we can draw the following conclusions:

■ The purchase orders carry replenishment information that drives the inbound material flow of the facility, as the goods are ordered, delivered, and received from vendors.
■ The production orders are backbone information carrier for ensuring the material flow within the production process of the facility.

- The sales orders in the ERP system are used as an information carrier to register, confirm, and trigger outbound activities in order to deliver goods to the customers.
- The master planning in the ERP system uses inventory transactions, forecasts, and information from other sources to create the purchase and production orders that drive the replenishment of items throughout the facility. Therefore, we can say that this process controls and coordinates the replenishment of items, and thereby, the material flow within the facility's manufacturing supply chain.

This means that these orders that are managed by the ERP system are used as the main information source to drive the material flow within a facility in the manufacturing supply chain. The relation between the information flow of ERP system and the physical flow in a facility in a manufacturing supply chain is illustrated in Figure 8.2.

The figure shows the relation between the material flow within a facility and the different orders in an ERP system for manufacturing supply chains. This simple analogy indicates that the way the orders are triggering the replenishment in the ERP system may have large impact on how and how effectively the material flows through the facility.

The purchase and production orders are generated by the ERP system's master planning according to the setting of the "planning methods" that where discussed in chapter on Master Planning. This parameter or parameters dictate how the master planning creates the planned orders to replenish the items at each warehouse to

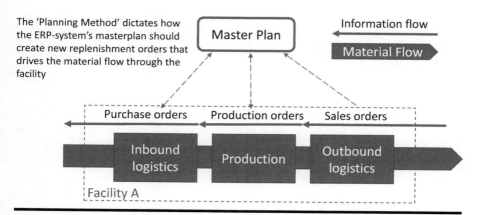

Figure 8.2 The information flow within the ERP system versus the material flow within a facility in the manufacturing supply chain.

fulfill actual orders and/or forecasted demand. The manufacturing supply chain performance is therefore affected on how the planning methodology is set in the ERP system.

As mentioned in the chapter on master planning, the planning methods used in ERP systems is often built upon three principles. These principles are visualized in Figure 8.3.

The figure shows three illustrations for the different principles used behind the planning methods in ERP systems. The illustration in the left of the figure shows an order-based planning method. If the item is set as order-based on the warehouse, a replenishment order will be triggered every time a requiring order is entered in the system. This means that there is no use for inventory or storage of items between the requiring order and replenishment orders, since the items that are replenished should immediately be delivered toward the requiring order. This method is often used between sales order lines and production orders in a make-to-order environment but can be used at other places in the manufacturing supply chain as well. For instance, order-based principle is used in cases where items are purchased for direct deliveries to an end customer. In most ERP systems the order-driven replenishment orders are created directly without using a master plan.

The illustration in the middle of the figure outlines the requirement-based principle. Items that are set as requirement-based are using future requirements from things like forecast, orders, and/or inventory levels to create replenishment orders. There are many subtypes of requirement-based planning methods; one of these is time-phased requirement that we did discuss in the master planning section. Typical examples of using a requirement-based planning method is make-to-stock items where sales order is selling items from stock and the production is mainly based on forecasts (what often is understood as the traditional "MRPII" approach, that was mentioned earlier in this book). A requirement-based planning method normally requires master planning, and that replenishment orders are released from planned orders in the master plan. A requirement-based planning method is usually combined with a safety stock level, to ensure a good service level and avoid stock outs.

The last principle in the right of the figure is the reorder-based planning methods. In this principle the system is only considering the items inventory level when doing replenishment. Traditionally, only the current on-hand are considered when doing replenishment, but in some reorder methods "min/max" can be combined with a forecast so that replenishment can happen toward future projected inventory levels as well (we are not considering this option, since such cases may also be solved by a requirement-based planning method). A typical example on items using a reorder planning method is spare parts where a replenishment purchase order is triggered every time the items inventory level comes down to a certain level. The reorder-based items are usually a part of the master plan, and replenishment production or purchase orders must be released from planned orders in the master plan.

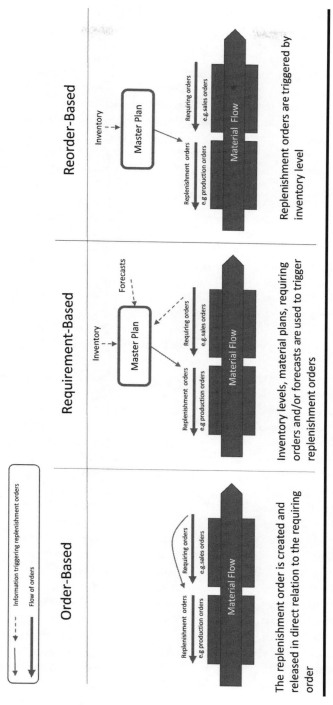

Figure 8.3   Three principles behind common planning methods in ERP systems.

8.1.2 The Setup of the Planning Method in Real-life ERP Systems

In real-life ERP packages the setup of the planning methods are not always straightforward. An ERP software may include lot of subtypes for the planning methods. The software package may use own terminologies, and there can be a lot of special parameters and configurations that must be taken into consideration when setting the planning methods. This means it is normal to consult with specialists on the specific ERP application to provide an overview on all the possibilities in the software and get the configuration correct according to how the manufacturing supply chain should behave.

However, there are usually one, or a few main parameters, that control planning method in the ERP system. The terminology used for describing the planning methods parameter may be different from package to package, and sometimes planning methods are achieved by setting several parameters and other configuration options in the application.

To illustrate the setup of the planning method in real-life ERP systems we have done a brief investigation of the main setting that affects the planning method in a selection of ERP applications. Table 8.1 gives an overview of the parameter or parameters that best corresponds with these configurations, and our suggestion of these parameters can be set to achieve the different planning method.

The table shows a rough overview over the terminology of the parameter for the planning method in selection of known ERP packages, as well as our suggestion for the setting of these to achieve some common planning methods.

The first column in the table describes the names of the parameter and the different planning methods used in this book. We have chosen to split the requirement-based planning method into "requirement" and "time-phased requirement" and the reorder point planning method into "reorder point" and "min/max" in order to separate the most commonly used options for these methods.

The second column shows the planning methods in Microsoft Dynamics 365 Supply Chain Management are mainly controlled by a parameter named "coverage code". The "coverage code" can be set on the items for each warehouse where these can be stored. The "coverage code" parameter does not control if the replenishment should be order driven, but here is a possibility to manually release production orders (and purchase orders) from the sales order line. The "coverage code" in Microsoft Dynamics 365 Supply Chain Management controls if the master plan creates planned orders following a requirement-based ("requirement") or a time-phased requirement ("period") planning method. There is no separate choice for reorder point, but this software package does rather use a "min/max" principle.

SAP S/4HANA separates the setting of the order-driven methods from the other planning methods as well. We found that the parameter named "strategy group" is controlling if the item is make-to-order product (if the item follows a "order driven" strategy or not), while the parameter "MRP type" dictates how the master planning should create planned orders. The MRP type includes a lot of variants of the

Table 8.1 Examples/Ideas to Key Parameters Settings in Different ERP Systems to Achieve the Planning Methods Discussed in this Book

Where	This Book	Microsoft Dynamics 365 Supply Chain Management	SAP S/4HANA	Infor M3	IFS Applications	Oracle E-Business Suite
Name of Main Parameter	Planning Methods	Coverage Code	MRP Type	Planning Method	Planning Methods	MRP Planning Methods / Inventory Planning Methods
Examples for parameter setting to achieve similar functionality between the inventory planning methods mentioned in this book and the functionality of the ERP applications	Order driven	(Manually released from sales orders)	("Strategy Group" is set to "20 – make-to-order production", etc.)	"3 = Order driven: acquisition orders are only triggered, created, and released by a requiring order"	(Handled through dynamic order processing [DOP])	(Through the "assemble-to-order" parameter on the item master)
	Requirement based — Requirement	"Requirement"	"PD – MRP"	"1 = Material requirement planned (MRP)"	"A – lot-for-lot"	MRP planning methods: "MRP planning" (with "lot-for-lot")
	Requirement based — Time-phased requirement	"Period"	"R1 – Time-phased planning"	"1 = Material requirement planned (MRP)" (with use of "order quantity days")	"G – Order cover time"	MRP planning methods: "MRP planning" (with "fixed days supply")
	Reorder based — Reorder point	N/A	"VM – Automatic reorder point planning"	"2 = Reorder point (ROP) planned per item/warehouse"	"B – Order point planning"	Inventory planning methods: "Reorder point planning"
	Reorder based — Min/Max	"Min/Max"	N/A	N/A	N/A	Inventory planning methods: "Min-Max planning"

- The notes in *(brackets)* are author's comments when the planning method can be archived outside the setting of the main parameter.
- The table represents the author's brief investigations of the software packages, so inaccuracies many accrue. The ERP system is a subject for change by the software vendors. Contact the software vendors for a full description of the ERP application's capabilities and how to configure the inventory planning methods in the specific software package.

"planning methods" that cover more principles mentioned in this book, but our brief investigation did not reveal a parameter choice for a "min/max" principle.

Infor M3 is the only ERP system in this selection where the order-driven principle as well as the other planning methods are controlled through a single parameter. Infor M3 has a planning method setting that covers all main planning principles, but as for SAP S/4HANA, Infor M3 does not have a parameter choice for the min/max principle.

IFS uses "dynamic order processing" (DOP) to control the order-driven approach. The DOP is a separate function in the ERP application that connects the sales order with connected productions. The planned orders in the master plan are dictated by the "planning method" parameter in IFS. IFS does not include a separate parameter setting for the "min/max" method, but this software included selections for the other planning methods in the table.

Oracle application uses two parameters to control the planning method: "MRP planning method" and "planning method". According to our understanding Oracle supports the principles mentioned in this book through these parameters, but the only parameter we could find for an order-driven approach was "assemble-to-order".

We must pinpoint that the information in Table 8.1 is only a rough illustration of the basic settings in the ERP applications. All these software packages have other settings and possibilities that may help an enterprise to achieve their required planning methods, and these software packages are constantly under development where new features and possibilities are being added. Therefore, even if a planning method is indicated as not applicable ("N/A") in the table, this does not necessarily mean that the system does not support this method. This may be achieved by other setup in the systems since we may have overseen several possibilities in our investigations.

We, therefore, recommend contacting the software vendors for a full and exact description over what planning methods are supported and how these can be configured in the application. However, the table indicates that real-life ERP applications for manufacturing supply chains do cover the three basic principles behind planning methods that are described in this book. The configuration, naming, and other details and how they are executed in the different software packages may differ.

8.2 Effect of ERP Systems Planning Methods on Flow of a Facility's Manufacturing Supply Chain

Normally the flow of information within a facility is not as simple as the previous analogy with the supply chain may lead to believe. An enterprise may need to control an item differently in each warehouse within the facility, and therefore, the planning method is usually set for each item and warehouse in an ERP system. This may be used for complex sub-manufacturing supply chains within the facility, as illustrated in Figure 8.4.

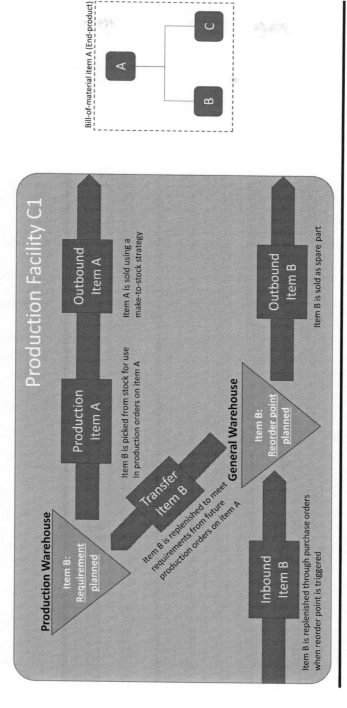

Figure 8.4 An illustration of why different planning methods are used on the same item in different warehouses.

The figure shows an example of the setup of the planning method of an "Item B" in a facility named "production facility C1". "Item B" is used as a component in the assembly of "Item A" and can be sold separately as a spare part as well. The bill-of-materials of the end product "Item A" is shown far right in the figure.

"Item B" is purchased and then stored at the general warehouse, where it either can be sold as a spare part or transferred to the production warehouse to be used as a component in the production.

The demand for "Item B" in the general warehouse is relatively steady for items that goes into production, but the sale of spare parts is lumpy and hard to predict, since there can be no demand for weeks before a larger order comes in.

In the general warehouse, the planning method of "Item B" is set as reorder point (with a defined safety-stock level, that are not indicated in the figure) in the ERP system, to ensure that items are always of a certain stock level to account for uncertain demand for both spare parts and components in production.

The enterprise is selling "Item A" according to a make-to-stock strategy. The production orders of "Item A" are made from forecast on future sales and the orders are triggered using a requirement planning method. The sales rate of these products is steady, and therefore, they have chosen to use a requirement planning methodology for "Item B" in the production warehouse as well to ensure that items will be transferred from the general warehouse according to forecasted consumption of "Item A".

This simple example with only one item shows that there can be a sub-supply chain within each facility where items flow between the different warehouses according to the setup of the planning method of the ERP system. In a real-life ERP installation there can be multiple items and warehouses, which will increase the complexity of the network of different sub-manufacturing supply chains and the setup of the planning methods accordingly.

Which planning method should be set for what item in which warehouse can be a complex and time-consuming job. This setting is often done on a basis of a lot of factors. We will explore three of the most important of these factors, namely:

- The decoupling point
- The relation between the requiring order/orders and the replenishment order/orders
- "Forecastability"

8.2.1 The (Customer Order) Decoupling Point

The decoupling point specifies the point in the manufacturing supply chain when the item no longer can be replenished toward a specific sales order. The decoupling point is related to the time it takes to produce and/or provide a product related to the delivery time promised to customers.

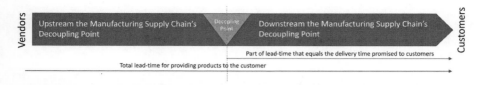

Figure 8.5   The decoupling point.

We can operate with the decoupling point (upstream and downstream) of the manufacturing supply chain. Decoupling point is illustrated in Figure 8.5.

The decoupling point can be set as the item's total lead time minus the time the customers will accept to wait for the delivery after ordering the goods.

The figure separates two parts in a manufacturing supply chain: upstream and downstream. Downstream the decoupling point the customer's exact demand can be known, and the sales order can be used to generate the production, purchase, and/or transfer orders that are needed to replenish the goods in time for the delivery. Upstream the decoupling point, the customer's exact demand is not known. Production, purchase, and transfer orders are therefore usually generated from forecasts and/or a reorder points that do not require a sales order to trigger the requirement.

The decoupling point is affected by the service level provided to the customers, as well as the item's throughput time in the supply chain. The longer a customer accepts to wait between he orders a product until it will be delivered, and the shorter the throughput time of item is, the further the decoupling point can be moved upstream the manufacturing supply chain.

Normally, there is an advantage to have the decoupling point far upstream the supply chain since this opens for less need for inventory buffers since a larger portion of the supply chain is driven by the exact customer demand. This can lead to improved service levels, cost reductions, less capital tied up in the supply chain, and less risk for ending up redundant stock levels of finish goods. However, this must anyway be weighted toward cost for managing customer orders individually, and the customer's willingness to wait for the product to be delivered.

8.2.2 The Relation Between the Replenishment Orders and the Requiring Orders

The second factor we want to highlight is the relationship between the replenishment orders and the requiring orders. This relationship is especially important when setting up the planning method downstream the decoupling point, and if there are a "one-to-one" or a "one-to-many" relation between the replenishment orders and the requiring orders. A different planning method is required if a single production order should be made for each requiring sales order than if one production order should fulfill several sales orders. Figure 8.6 illustrates an example of this relation.

This figure shows two examples on the relationship between the orders. Left side in the figure shows a "one-to-one" relation between the replenishment order and requiring order, where each sales order for a special designed pump is triggering a single production order. The example at the right shows a "one-to-many" relation where a single production order can fulfill the deliveries of many sales orders on standard pumps.

If the setup of the item in the warehouse follows a "one-to-one" or "one-to-many" relation between the requiring order(s) and the replenishment order is often dependent on if the product is unique for each order, or a standardized product to be delivered to lots of customers. For engineered products that are made exact to customers specifications, a single sales order should trigger a separate production order for each unique product and therefore follows a "one-to-one" logic. "One-to-many" is often used in standardized products where a lot for sales orders can trigger a single production order that runs the production.

The question of "one-to-one" versus "one-to-may" and other variants of relationship between requiring and replenishment orders is not only valid between the sales orders and production orders but may appear at other places in the manufacturing supply chain as well. But it is usually most critical when it comes to production of customer unique products versus standard products, and therefore we will focus our discussions on this around these parts of the manufacturing supply chain.

8.2.3 "Forecastability"

Last factor we want to highlight for setting up the planning method in an ERP application is "forecastability". "Forecastability" reveals if it is possible or feasible to provide a good forecast on the item. A forecast in an ERP system can either be set directly toward a specific item in a warehouse; alternatively the forecast is inherited or through dependent demand from forecast set on items downstream supply chain. For instance, a sales forecast set on an end item (like a finish pump), can also be used as a forecast through dependent demand on all components and materials (like pump housings, spindles, screws, and so on) provided that a requirement-based forecast is used in all parts of the chain.

With high "forecastability" we mean that it is feasible to predict future demand of the item in the warehouse with high certainty, either through dependent demand from downstream orders and/or forecasts set directly toward the

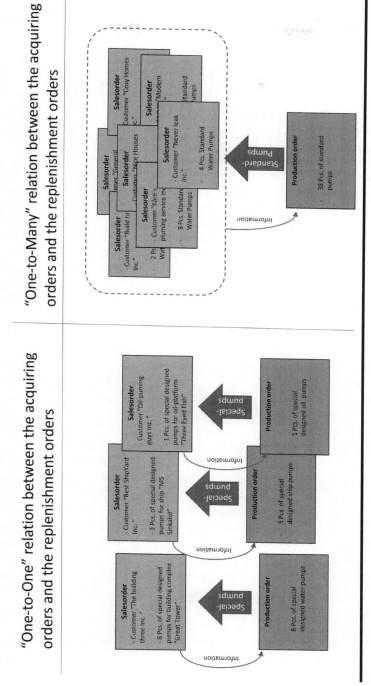

Figure 8.6   Example to illustrate "one-to-one" versus "one-to-many" relation between the requiring orders and replenishment orders.

item on the warehouse. With low "forecastability" we mean that it is not possible and/or feasible to predict future demand in a good manner from forecasts and/or downstream activates.

8.3 Setting the Correct Planning Method on Each Item/Warehouse Combination in the Manufacturing Supply Chain

Using the previous mentioned factors we can conclude that the planning method for a specific item in a warehouse should be set differently if the item is downstream or upstream the decoupling point. If the item is placed downstream the decoupling point, there is enough time to order and/or produce the item after a sales order is entered, and therefore a planning method that triggers orders from the exact customer order demand should be used either using a "one-to-one" or "one-to-many" relationship between the orders, depending if the items are order unique or not.

If the item is placed in a warehouse upstream the decoupling point, there is not enough time to replenish and/or produce the item after a sales order is entered, and therefore a forecast or a reorder point should be used as planning method in the ERP system to trigger the replenishment order. This is to ensure that there are items on stock when new customer order is entered.

Using this we suggest a decision tree shown in Figure 8.7 to provide some guidelines for what planning method can be set for each item in a warehouse in the ERP system.

The decision tree shows some questions that can be used as a guideline when setting the planning method for items in a warehouse in an ERP system. The first question that should be investigated is if it is possible to use sales orders to trigger replenishment orders (production/purchase order) for this item in this warehouse. Or said in another way, is the item will be located before or after the decoupling point in this warehouse?

If sales orders *cannot* be used to trigger the replenishment, the item in the warehouse is most likely upstream the decoupling point in the manufacturing supply chain. The selection between two choices in setting the planning method depends on forecasts. If it is not feasible or possible to use a forecast, the enterprise should probably choose a reorder point-based planning method. Alternatively, if they can and should use forecasts, they should probably use a requirement-based planning method on this item in the specific warehouse.

If sales orders *can* be used to drive the replenishment of the item in the warehouse, the item is most likely to be downstream the decoupling point. The enterprise should then investigate if this item is a standardized product where one production order can fulfill many sales order. If this is the case, the planning method should

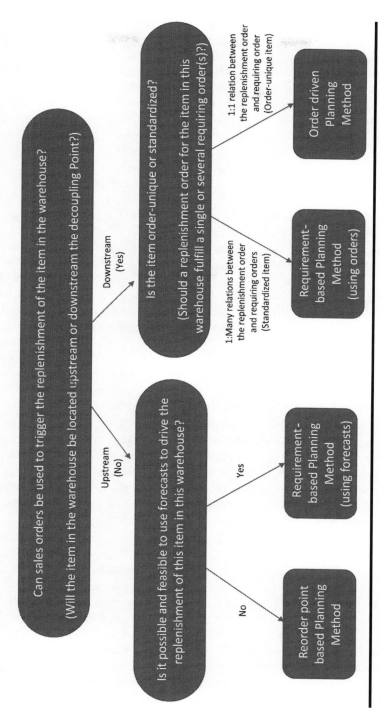

Figure 8.7 Decision tree providing guidelines for what planning method can be used for a certain item in a certain warehouse.

probably be set to a requirement principle so they can run the master plan to create a single planned production to fulfill the requirements from many sales orders. If the product is order-unique the enterprise should probably use an order-driven planning method on the item in the warehouse, to avoid going through a master plan run for each production orders that should be released.

The decision graph is also set up to first check if the replenishment orders can be done from sales orders. The reason for this is that setting the planning methods of the ERP system to as much as possible to fulfill the exact demand from customer orders is usually most favorable. By driving the facility's supply chain from the exact demand from sales orders as much as possible will reduce the need for excess on-hand safety stock or other buffers to meet uncertainties in forecasts or reorder point configurations.

This decision graph is only indicative and shows the most typical choices made by enterprises for setting the planning methods. It must only be seen as a starting point for further discussion for setting of these parameters. For example, a company may choose to combine the reorder-based method of "min/max" with forecasts if they think that this method will perform better than using a requirement-based principle at this specific item. Alternatively, an order-based planning principle can be chosen instead of a requirement-based principle on standard items if the production process requires that a single order should be triggered individually for each sale, etc.

OPTISTREAM

When configuring Microsoft Dynamics 365 Supply Chain Management in the Trondheim facility, OptiStream did set item's planning method and other configurations at the warehouses according to item's product group. The planning method is controlled by "coverage type" that is set in a "coverage group". This "coverage group" can be connected to each item and warehouse combination in Microsoft Dynamics 365 Supply Chain Management. The setting of "coverage type" in the "coverage group" parameter is shown in Figure 8.8.

Following is the discussion regarding setup of the planning method on four different groups of items.

Special pumps at the sales warehouse – The special pumps are engineered for each customer order. The customer does usually accept to wait up to 2 to 3 months for the delivery of these pumps after they enter the order, while the production time is around 1 to 2 months. This means production for special pumps can be triggered from a sales order, and OptiStream should use an order-driven planning method for these items in the sales warehouse.

Microsoft Dynamics 365 Supply Chain Management does not have a separate parameter setting for order-driven replenishment, but the user

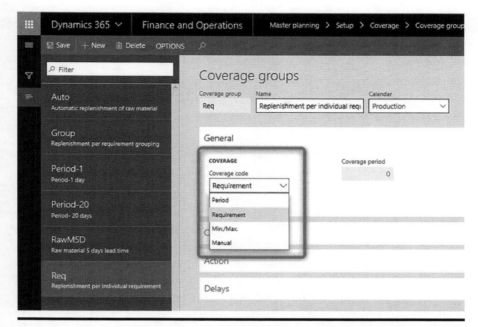

Figure 8.8 **"Coverage type" in the "coverage group" in Microsoft Dynamics 365 Supply Chain Management.**

must manually release a production order from the sales order line for each order-driven production. The items used for special pumps are configured with a "coverage type" set to "manual" at the sales warehouse, whereas as the user must perform release the production orders from the sales order lines manually, as shown in Figure 8.9.

Standard pumps at the sales warehouse – These are expensive pumps that are not stored in the sales warehouse but are made to order. OptiStream can get a few orders on these pumps each week and tries to collect the production of these in a single production run. The customers must usually wait approximately 1 to 2 weeks for a delivery, that are not far from approximately 5 days production time to manufacture most standard pumps.

The production of these pumps can be triggered by a sales order. However, a single production order should be issued for supplying all waiting sales order. Therefore, is it most sensible to use a requirement planning method for these items in the sales warehouse.

OptiStream has set the "coverage code" to "requirement" on these items. Every week when Greta runs a master plan, Microsoft Dynamics 365 Supply Chain Management uses the requirement from all open sales orders

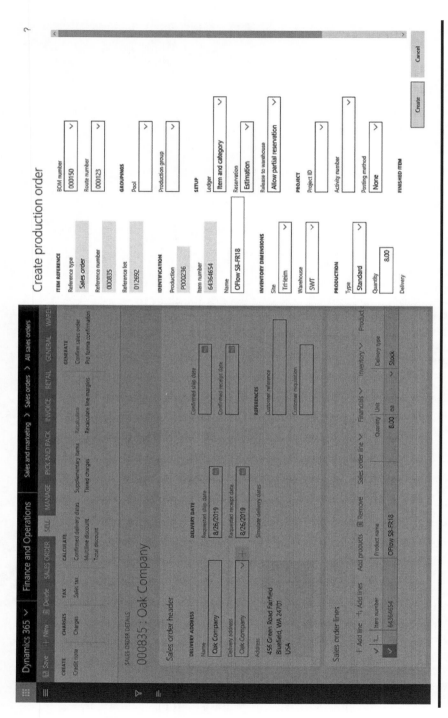

Figure 8.9 Releasing a production order from a sales order line in Microsoft Dynamics 365 Supply Chain Management.

on this item and creates a single planned production order for this item. This planned production order is then used in production to make the correct amount for the waiting deliveries.

Stocked pumps in the sales warehouse – These are standard pumps that are sold in high volume. OptiStream can ship these pumps 1 to 2 days after a sales order is received. It takes approximately 5 days to run an order of standard pumps through the production.

The orders from stocked pumps should not be triggered from sales order since the delivery time is shorter than the normal production time. OptiStream do invent time in making forecast on these items since they are of relatively high value and the demand is relatively steady.

As for the standard pumps, OptiStream uses the planning type "requirement" in Microsoft Dynamics 365 Supply Chain Management. In addition, they use a forecast on each item, and set a safety stock level in the ERP application to account for forecast inaccuracies fluctuations in sales. When Greta runs the master plan, Microsoft Dynamics 365 Supply Chain Management uses the current stock level, the safety stock settings, and a combination of both sales orders and forecast to create planned production order for these items.

Spare parts in the general warehouse – These items are usually with low value that are stored in the general warehouse for rapid delivery to both customers and the internal production. These items are usually shipped from the warehouse 1 to 2 days after a sales order entry.

Since most spare parts are purchased with lead time longer than the promised lead time of 1 to 2 days, their replenishment cannot be triggered from sales order. With a few exceptions, OptiStream has chosen not to use resources to make forecast on these items. This is because they are of relatively low cost and hard to make good forecasts since the demand for spare parts is uncertain and most of them may be used in production as well from time to time. Therefore, OptiStream has chosen to use a reorder-based planning method for the spare parts.

In Microsoft Dynamics 365 Supply Chain Management, OptiStream has set the parameter "coverage type" to "min/max" on most spare parts (Microsoft Dynamics 365 Supply Chain Management do only support "min/max" as reorder-based planning method). They have also set a safety stock level on all spare parts to be sure that there are always some spare parts on stock if there is an unexpected demand for some of the items. The master plan in Microsoft Dynamics 365 Supply Chain Management uses the current stock level, the min/max settings, and the configured safety stock level, to create planned purchase orders for spare parts.

8.4 Configuring an ERP System for Different Manufacturing Strategies

The ERP system can be set up to follow different manufacturing strategies, such as MTO (make-to-order), ATP (assemble-to-order), or ETO (engineer-to-order).

By defining the decoupling point and adjusting the planning methods, the ERP system can be configured to fit most manufacturing environments. And since the setup of the planning method is connected to each item and how they should be replenished in each warehouse, the ERP system allows different configurations of manufacturing strategies within a single facility as well.

This means that a single manufacturing facility may have several interconnected manufacturing supply chains following different manufacturing strategies. Figure 8.10 shows the relation between the manufacturing strategies and the setting of the planning method of the ERP systems.

The figure shows typical settings of the planning method to support different manufacturing strategies within a manufacturing facility. As the figure indicates the settings of the planning method of the ERP system should be different according to the placement of the item in the specific warehouse upstream or downstream the decoupling point.

Upstream the decoupling point, the setting of planning method is independent of the manufacturing strategy the item is following. A requirement planning method should be used if the demand of the item in the warehouse can, and should, be forecasted. This forecast can either be made and set to estimate the demand of the item on each warehouse, or the forecast can be

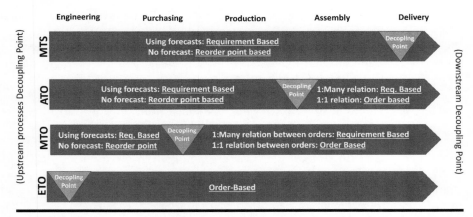

Figure 8.10 Connection between the planning method and different manufacturing strategies within a single manufacturing facility.

inherited through dependent demand from forecast on items further downstream the supply chain. If the item of the warehouse upstream decoupling point it cannot or should not be forecasted, and a reorder planning method must be considered for controlling the replenishment of the item in the specific warehouse.

Downstream the decoupling point, the settings of the planning methods should reflect the manufacturing strategy of the item and/or item group.

As the figure implies, to achieve an MTS strategy the decoupling point must set at the finish good stock at the facility, and therefore the sales orders cannot be used as an input to drive the replenishment upstream the manufacturing supply chain. This means that a requirement-based planning method in combination with forecast is often preferred in these environments. A reorder point-based planning method should be set in the ERP system if the enterprise cannot or will not use forecasts to drive the replenishment on certain items.

In an ATO and MTO environment parts of production, or the whole production process, is often driven by the demand from sales orders. The decoupling point is therefore set upstream the assembly and/or the production. The ATO/MTO products are often standardized, and a single assembly order and/or production order can be used to fulfill several sales orders. In such cases requirement planning method may be used in the ERP system to trigger the replenishment. This planning method enables the master planning to create a single planned assembly or production order that collects the demand from all sales orders that are waiting on the same product. In this way the facility can fulfill multiple sales orders through issuing and managing a single production order.

If the products are complex and not produced in large series, the enterprise can choose to use an order-driven approach for the ATO/MTO productions. This will probably create more production orders, but an order-driven approach is often easier and faster to execute in an ERP system and can help to increase the control of the assembly/production. The reason for this is that an order-driven planning method does not require a master planning run in many ERP systems, since the production orders are made directly to the sales order line without going into the master plan to create planned production order first.

An order-based planning method is also used to trigger the production order for the assembly if the facility uses a production configurator in the ERP system in combination with an ATO strategy. Such configure-to-order (CTO) production is often associated with a large amount of variants that are made in small series, and therefore is an order-driven approach that is often the most effective for making unique assembly orders for each sales order.

In ETO environment end products are usually unique for each customer order, and therefore, an order-driven approach is usually the only option for triggering the replenishment. The ETO strategy often requires that several productions and purchase orders are triggered from the sales order through an order-driven approach.

This is especially valid for so called "long-lead items" that must be ordered from the vendors as soon as a customer order arrives.

Using the core modules for manufacturing supply chains and configuring the planning methods for supporting ETO products only make sense in mass production environment. If the facility manufacture large engineering projects in low volumes, they are probably better off with using a project module in their ERP system to control their supply chains.

The ERP system can be set up to support several or all strategies in one production facility, and sometimes for the same items as well. For instance, a facility that produces ETO offshore installations may sell some of the components of these installations as separate products and therefore can use an MTO manufacturing strategy for this part of the business. The setup and configuration of these strategies are done by individually adjusting the planning method parameter according to the specific circumstances on each item and warehouse in the ERP systems.

The flexibility and possibilities of setup of the planning policies and other planning parameters may vary from one ERP system to another. But, as good as all ERP packages for manufacturing supply chains supports the planning methods in this book. These planning methods can often be configured in almost endless ways with creative use of the ERP software.

However, often it is not the additional depth of the planning functionality of the ERP system that has the greatest impact on the facility's supply chain performance. The strategic setting of the decoupling point for different product groups, the enterprises ability to physically shorten the lead times for making a bigger part of their supply chain running from sales order without reducing the delivery time toward the customers, and how good they can produce forecasts in cooperation with outside parties like customers are examples of things that have often better effect on the ERP system's manufacturing supply chain performance than implementing an ERP package with more planning functionality and possibilities.

OPTISTEAM

The three different production lines of pumps mentioned in the previous section follow different manufacturing strategies. The special pumps follow an ETO strategy, standard pumps use MTO, while the stock pumps are MTS products.

These three product lines use the same production equipment and goes in large degree through the same processes throughout the manufacturing supply chain in the Trondheim production facility. The way OptiStream can apply and manage the different strategies is how they deal with their information systems and especially how they have set the planning methods in their ERP application.

They are constantly reviewing the customer and market to set what pumps are going to be managed in what way. For instance, a stocked pump that is selling less than before should rather be MTO to reduce the cost for holding this on the finish goods stock. OptiStream can then be converted into a standard pump by adjusting the planning method in the ERP system.

They feel that they have limited possibilities on adjusting the planning methods on the purchasing part since they use a mix in strategies. Most purchased products are both used in production for all product lines and simultaneously sold as a spare part. Since they are consumed from a lot of sources, it makes it difficult to use material plan in the master plan as a forecast and/or create a good forecast on each purchased product themselves. Therefore, OptiStream has set up the min/max values in Microsoft Dynamics 365 Supply Chain Management to generate the planned purchase orders in the system.

They are rather working with their vendors to reduce the lead time on certain products. Reducing the replenishment lead time do open for reducing the safety stock levels in Microsoft Dynamics 365 Supply Chain Management, without risking any stockout. In this way they are constantly working with reducing the items lead times and throughput time of each item, that again propagates in a potential for exploiting Microsoft Dynamics 365 Supply Chain Management better for improved manufacturing supply chains performance.

8.5 Key Terms

- Facility
- Planning method
- Forecastability
- Manufacturing strategy
- Make-to-stock
- Assemble-to-order
- Make-to-order
- Configure-to-order
- Engineer-to-order

8.6 Chapter Summary

This chapter explored how an ERP system is used to support a manufacturing supply chain within a single facility. The setting of the planning methods on each item and warehouse can affect the behavior of the manufacturing supply chains within the facilities. The setting of the planning method may rely on many factors; three of them are the items decoupling point in the manufacturing supply chain, the relation between the replenishment order and the requiring order, and the items "forecastability". The setting of the planning method can help dictating the manufacturing strategy of a facility.

Chapter 9

Using ERP Systems in Manufacturing Supply Chains

Learning Objectives

After reading this chapter, you will be able to:

- Distinguish between two basic strategies for using ERP systems in a manufacturing enterprise with several companies and facilities
- Have a rough idea on what main types of ERP systems can be used to support a multicompany manufacturing enterprise
- Understand how ERP systems can be configured to support a manufacturing supply chain that goes across different facilities and/or companies in a manufacturing enterprise

9.1 Basic ERP Strategies for Manufacturing Supply Chains

Until now this book has mainly focused toward using ERP systems in a single-company and facility, but larger enterprises do often consist of several facilities and companies where manufacturing supply chains are flowing between the different units.

Comprehensive ERP packages have functionality for supporting several facilities and companies through a single database and installation of the software. Such a solution may hold an enterprise's complete manufacturing supply chain including all facilities in all companies into a single application and database. This allows the companies and their connected facilities within the enterprise to interact as an integrated unit through the same ERP application.

ERP strategies are a complex area with many factors to consider. But when it comes to linking the manufacturing supply chain strategy throughout several companies there are two simple strategies that an enterprise at minimum must consider before starting to implement an ERP application across companies. Either they can use a "multiple ERP" strategy where each separate company (or business unit) is using a separate ERP package. Alternatively, they can choose a "OneERP" strategy where all companies in the group are using the same installation of the ERP system.

The principles of these different strategies are shown in Figure 9.1.

9.1.1 Why Choose a "Multiple-ERP" Strategy for Supporting the Manufacturing Supply Chain

The main reason manufacturing enterprises are running a multiple-ERP strategy can be related to cost issues. Maybe their companies already have some well-functioning ERP solutions, and implementing a new OneERP solution to support the complete manufacturing supply chain will be a highly resource intensive and costly operation. When implementing "OneERP" solution, the employees must not only adjust how their work processes within their company toward the guidelines of the groups and the possibilities of the ERP application, but they also need to adjust their work processes toward other companies in the group are using the system.

Another disadvantage of using OneERP solution is connected to the loss of flexibility and ability to change work processes in the manufacturing supply chain after the ERP solution is implemented. Running a separate ERP application will make it easier to alter anything in business, since the company only needs to account for their specific business processes and specific use of the ERP application. Some enterprises, therefore, choose to not implement a single OneERP solution and rather use separate ERP solutions to keep their manufacturing supply chains more open for change.

However, it may be other, more business related, reasons for why an enterprise should choose to use multiple implementations of ERP systems. Below we have listed three typical scenarios with examples where an enterprise with several companies did choose "multiple-ERP" strategy for part of their business:

- Financial Ownership of the business units – It may be most sensible to use a separate ERP system for each unit if the main purpose for the group is to build and acquire companies in order to develop these for a resale.
  - For example, a northern European private equity is the main share owner in 17 different enterprises. Each of these businesses has been acquired to develop individually for resale or taking public at a later

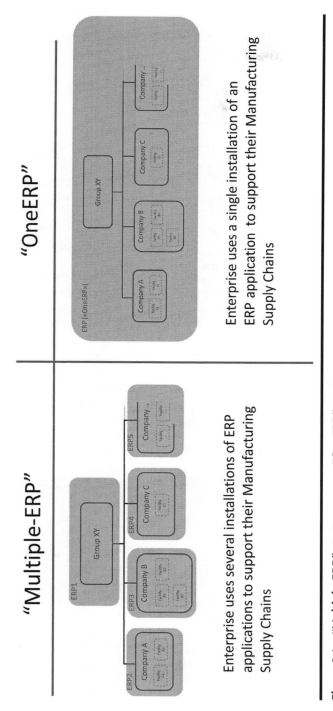

Figure 9.1 "Multiple-ERP" strategy versus "OneERP" strategy.

point in time. These businesses are spanning from everything from a manufacturer of fishery equipment, to retail groups, and fitness chains. Putting all these businesses in a common OneERP solution makes less sense. It will be very difficult to configure a single ERP solution to cover the different requirements of the various businesses, and each company must move to a new ERP when the ownership changes after they are sold or gone public.

■ Little or no intercompany trade between the units – If there is no or little trade between the parts in a manufacturing group, it may be right to use separate ERP systems for each unit.
  – For example, a Swedish provider of power and communication networks owns a Norwegian subsidiary that focuses on manufacturing and servicing of offshore equipment. This company is not doing any trade with the rest of the group. Therefore, they let this subsidiary choose and maintain their own ERP system according to their specific supply chain requirements.

■ Business units with unique requirements – If any business unit has different requirement for the ERP support, it may be a good idea to use a separate ERP applications for the individual parts.
  – For example, a larger Norwegian manufacturer and distributor of consumer goods consists of five business divisions. They have chosen a single ERP platform for most of their enterprise, except for one division. In this division the manufacturing units are smaller than the rest of the group and the OneERP solution that is considered too complex for their needs. Therefore, they implemented another, less comprehensive ERP solution to support this part of the business.

These are only few examples, and our experience says cases must be considered individually, and there is no strict rules of when an enterprise should choose to use multiple ERP installations. As a rule of thumb one can say that larger enterprise with many companies can favor of using multiple-ERP strategy if their business is loosely connected and with little or no intercompany trade between these.

9.1.2 Why Choose a OneERP Strategy

As previously mentioned, a OneERP solution is usually more costly and complex to implement than using separate ERP applications. But here are exceptions from this rule. If the enterprise has many similar companies that are going into the solution, the cost of rolling out the same OneERP solution in a multitude of companies can be lower than implementing several smaller ERP packages. The way most of the larger enterprises are implementing a OneERP solution is that they first configure a "template company" where they are defining a core solution and entering enterprise-wide master data that should be used by all companies in the group. This template is then used as a base for rollouts of the ERP applications for each company in the group. Using a template company for the rollouts only needs adjustment in the group templates to the special need for each company as well as adding some company specific data. If done correctly such preconfigured rollouts can be more efficient than implementing a tailored ERP solution for each company.

In addition, a single OneERP application can be easy to maintain and cost efficient for larger manufacturing enterprises, if a manufacturing group's internal IT department handles a multitude of ERP solution, technologies, and databases simultaneously.

So, for certain enterprises IT costs may be a driver for implementing a OneERP solution. But there are reasons rooted in the overall business strategies and their impact in the manufacturing supply chain area that may also drive such a decision. Following are some real-life examples of enterprises that chose to implement a "OneERP" solution:

■ Enabling a global manufacturing supply chain – A OneERP solution is often used where there is a global industrialization strategy behind the manufacturing group. A common information platform is therefore needed to coordinate the manufacturing supply chains throughout the globe.
  – In the middle of the 1990s, a venture capital firm started to acquire independent companies within the security product area throughout the world. Their goal was to make a leading global actor in manufacturing and deliver safety systems within safe storage, cash management, and entrance control. Today they have eight manufacturing facilities and sales offices in 25 countries around the world. The initial round of acquisitions resulted in that they initiated an integration program to get all companies under the same brand. A key activity in this process was to implement a OneERP solution to coordinate the supply chains between units in the group, so that they could sell and deliver products around the world independently from where they were produced.
■ Manufacturing supply chain standardization, optimization, and coordination – A OneERP implementations can be driven by the need for standardization and implementation of "best-of-breed" processes throughout a manufacturing group. Using a single ERP system in an enterprise is also a common platform for reporting throughout companies in the group.
  – A Norwegian enterprise with 32 asphalt manufacturing facilities had a problem where some of these facilities did run well with good result, while others had mixed result. They used a common accounting system, but all supply chain activities were documented through individual paper-based systems and Microsoft Excel spreadsheet at each facility, so they had no data to compere the supply chains within the different facilities. The management wanted to streamline the supply-chain activities throughout the group and therefore initiated a OneERP project where

they invited the managers of five best run manufacturing plants to configure a best-of-breed solution of how the supply chain should be managed. This OneERP project resulted in more efficient and standardized
supply chains in the manufacturing plants and did also open for comparing different units seeking more improvement potentials.

■ Agile supply chain management to fulfill a digitalization strategy – Most
  of the business happens online, and this increases the need for integrated
  information planning to shorten the information routes throughout the
  manufacturing supply chains. A OneERP solution can help integrating the
  manufacturing supply chain to increase its agility.

  – A furniture producer is selling products through retail chains around
    the world. They are in the process of changing their business model to
    also include direct sales to the end customer from their factory via online
    ecommerce sites. A new OneERP platform is a part of this effort to ensure
    a seamless information flow throughout the manufacturing supply chain
    from the factory floor to the doorstep of the end customer.

Roughly speaking, one can say that a larger enterprise with many companies often
choose OneERP strategy if there is tight business structure with high level of intercompany trade between the units. OneERP strategy is often selected in areas where
the enterprise wants to industrialize and consolidate their manufacturing supply
chain so that many units can cooperate as one.

OPTISTREAM

Some years ago, OptiStream consisted of the facility only in Trondheim.
They did sell and deliver their products to end customers sited in the
middle and north of Norway, whereas they used agents and resellers for
reaching customers elsewhere in Norway and the rest of the world.

The management at OptiStream knew that they delivered world-leading
technology in their segment, but despite their effort they could not increase
their sales and their market share. They knew that this specific segment of
the industry required a lot of personal contact with key industrial purchasers and these buyers required local presents. Therefore, they acquired two
companies in their largest growth markets, one was reseller of industrial
pumps in Oslo and the other was small-scale manufacturer and reseller of
similar pumps in Houston, TX, USA.

Their plan behind these acquisitions was to distribute their technologi-
cally superior pumps to their main markets more efficiently. To achieve
this, they needed an integrated information system and decided that they
would implement a OneERP solution in the group to streamline their manufacturing supply chains.

9.2 Key Factors When Choosing ERP Application for Supporting a Manufacturing Supply Chain

As explained in the previous chapter, most ERP systems have similar basic functionality when it comes to supporting manufacturing supply chain within company with a single facility. However, more fundamental differences between different ERP packages can be found when seeking a OneERP solution to support the supply chain in a multi-facility and/or multicompany organization.

Some ERP applications have built-in support for managing several companies and facilities in a single database and installation of the system. Other ERP systems support only a single company for installation of the software, where the data for each company will be set in an own, separate database. The simplest ERP packages for manufacturing supply chains do only support managing warehouses within this single company as well. This means that there is no support for having multiple facilities in the system.

Not surprisingly, the systems that have good support for using several companies in the same installations are normally ERP packages targeted for larger enterprises, while ERP systems that only support a single company are usually targeted to smaller manufacturing organizations. Table 9.1 sums up some key differences that may affect the supply chain performance between ERP packages targeted toward smaller organizations and more compressive/larger ERP packages that are made for larger multicompany organizations.

The table shows the key differences of how the manufacturing supply chain is supported in ERP packages with a single versus multicompany support. This table is only indicative to illustrate some generalized ideas of differences one should expect to find in different types of ERP systems for manufacturing supply chains. There is large variation in execution in different ERP applications; so studying the current versions of the software from the various vendors is the only way to differentiate these before taking a purchasing decision.

As mentioned, one of the key features of ERP systems with support for a single company is that these often store the data for each company in a separate database and requires a new installation of the same ERP system for every new company that will be using the system. This means that they are typically targeted toward small to mid-size manufacturing organizations that have less requirements for managing multiple organizations. ERP packages made for mid- to large-size manufacturing enterprises have more often the possibility to support several companies in one database and installation.

Some single-company ERP packages have less support for defining facilities in the system as well. This means the ERP system will only use warehouses to define the manufacturing supply chain within the company. This may be a sufficient solution for a simple manufacturing organization with only one or a few geographical locations. But if the company includes many facilities that are sited far from each other, this means that the ERP solution will provide less support to plan and manage items that are flowing through the company's internal supply chains.

Table 9.1 Some Key Differences Between ERP Systems with Single versus Multicompany Support

What	ERP packages with single-company support	ERP packages with multicompany support
Targeted against	Small- to medium-sized enterprises	Medium- to large-size enterprises
Support for multiple facilities in each company	Some packages support this, while others have limited or no support	Yes
Support for sharing of master data like items, customers, and vendors across companies	Separate databases for each company usually require programming of integration, manual steps, and/or through third-party master data management solutions in order to share data across companies.	Use separate data for each company that usually have functions for seamless sharing of key master data on things like items, customer, vendors, etc. across companies.
Support for automatic trade across companies (intercompany trade)	No or limited support	Yes
Support for master planning across multiple companies	No, or through add-on software	Yes
Functions for company-wide accounting like common chart of accounts, consolidation, intercompany accounting functions, etc.	Usually managed manually or through third-party solutions	Yes
Functionality and features	Simpler applications, but usually proved good support for most core functions. Simpler and more easy to configure and maintain.	Usually deeper and wider functionality and feature, but more complex to configure, use, and maintain.

(Continued)

Table 9.1 *(Continued)* **Some Key Differences Between ERP Systems with Single versus Multicompany Support**

What	ERP packages with single-company support	ERP packages with multicompany support
Cost	Normally lower software and implementation costs since this is less complex software. For larger enterprisers the total cost may be higher since they must purchase, implement, and manage several installations of the same application.	Higher implementation costs for smaller enterprises, but economics of scale may apply for larger enterprises by having several companies in the same ERP solution
Fit best for enterprises with...	..one or a few companies and/or a larger enterprise using a multiple-ERP strategy	...high requirement for functionality, and/or several companies with tight enterprise structure using a OneERP strategy

The possibility for sharing of master data between companies is another significant factor that separates the different types of ERP applications. Since the multicompany ERP packages support all companies within the same database, they may also ease the sharing of master data. This means that it may be possible to automate the setup and management of key master data on customers, vendors, and items across the individual companies in the manufacturing supply chain.

ERP packages with multicompany support may also have possibilities to seamlessly automate trade between companies without any need for configuring data exchange between databases. This can be as simple as sharing business information like on-hand level warehouses or the ERP system may have possibilities to automatically create and update an intercompany sales orders and corresponding purchase orders between companies.

The same goes for master planning. The master planning functions are restricted to the company in the database in a single-company ERP package, while a larger ERP packages can calculate the master plan across all companies in the database in the same master planning run. Such intercompany master planning allows the ERP system to take all intercompany trade and requirement into account when creating new planned orders for each company and creates new planned intercompany sales and purchase orders between different companies in the group when this is required.

Using a larger ERP package to support several companies in the same solution will also open possibilities in other areas that are not directly related to the manufacturing supply chain as well like in finance where company-wide accounting may be automated and simplified.

ERP packages with single-company support are usually made for smaller enterprises and therefore have less features and functions, but the core functions for manufacturing supply chains are usually in place; so most manufacturing companies can manage even with a smaller ERP package. This lack of complexity is making the smaller ERP packages less costly to implement and maintain for a single company. But for larger enterprises with a lot of companies in the group, it can be less costly to rollout and maintain a large ERP package in all companies that have individual implantations of a simpler ERP package in each company in the group.

This means that a smaller ERP package makes most sense to use in a smaller manufacturing enterprise with one or a few companies, or alternatively to support an individual company in a larger group using a multiple-ERP strategy. But for creating a multicompany OneERP solution a comprehensive ERP application is needed where all companies can be added in the same database and applications are often the best choice. ERP systems targeted toward a larger enterprise can also be used in a smaller manufacturing enterprise if the organization sees the benefit they get from the increased possibilities and functionalities, is worth the cost and effort to implement and maintain such a software package.

OPTISTEAM

When OptiStream acquired the two companies in Oslo, Norway and Houston, US, all of them run on different ERP systems. None of these ERP applications had the possibility to run several companies without doing several implementations for the system and database. OptiStream wanted to use OneERP system to transform these three companies into the same integrated manufacturing supply chain. Therefore, they choose to implement Microsoft Dynamics 365 Supply Chain Management that are Microsoft ERP systems for larger enterprises that could run several companies and facilities in the same software installation. They considered other larger ERP packages as well, many of which were just as good and even better in some areas for OptiStream use, but they ended up with Microsoft Dynamics 365 Supply Chain Management since this was most similar to their old system; so they believed that this would reduce the cost and complexity of an implementation.

9.3 The ERP System's Role in a Cross Facility and/or Company Manufacturing Supply Chain

The configuration of an ERP system to support a manufacturing supply chain in a single facility was covered in the previous chapter. Knowing that ERP systems can be used to support several facilities and companies, we can expand our previous analogy of how an ERP system supports a manufacturing supply chain with the following assumptions:

- The transfer orders and the transfer order process were described in the chapter of inventory management. Transfer orders carry replenishment information between warehouses sited in different facilities in the same company in the manufacturing supply chain.
- Sales and purchase order is used to communicate replenishment information in all trades between companies in a manufacturing supply chain. This can be trade between two companies that are subsidiaries in the same enterprise (so called "intercompany trade"), or it can be trade between two companies that are not under the same ownership/manufacturing group as well.
- The master planning process has the potential to control and coordinate the replenishment information between facilities. Normally, the master plan covers all facilities that are sited under the same company, but some ERP systems support master planning across companies as long as all companies are within the same OneERP solution.

This means that the ERP system can use transfer orders, and alternatively sales and purchase orders to connect warehouses across facilities and companies. Table 9.2 summarizes the ERP functionality used to connect the facilities for creating an enterprise-wide manufacturing supply chain.

The table sums up the types of orders an ERP system uses to connect the warehouses in a manufacturing supply chain, and some of their most important characteristics.

We have added warehouse transfers in the overview as well, since some of the ERP packages do not have support for transfer orders between facilities in the manufacturing supply chain. In such cases it is normal to use warehouse transfers to cover transfers between warehouses located in different facilities in a company. But as the table indicates warehouse transfers usually do not account for things like managing external transportation between warehouses in facilities that are located far from each other. Warehouse transfers are, therefore, optimally used where there is no external transportation involved, like running a forklift with items between two physically close sited warehouses. These warehouse transfers in ERP systems usually do not affect the cost price of the affected items and the

Table 9.2 ERP Functionality for Establishing a Manufacturing Supply Chain Across Facilities And Companies

Distribution between	ERP-system use	Includes transportation	Affects item's cost price	Affects company's revenue	Part of master plan
Warehouses within the same facility	Warehouse transfers	No	No	No	No[a]
Warehouses in different facilities within the same company	Transfer orders	Yes	Yes	No	Yes
Warehouses in different companies	(Intercompany) sales and purchase orders	Yes	Yes	Yes	Yes

[a] Some ERP systems support planned warehouse transfers through the master planning functionality, but warehouse transfers are normally not considered as part of an enterprise's overall master plan.

company's revenue. Even if some ERP systems can generate suggested warehouse transfers through a master planning run, they are normally not considered as a part of the enterprise's master plan.

Transfer orders are used in transfers between facilities or warehouses located far between each other within the same company. As mentioned, the main advantage for using transfer orders is that these can support external transportation, like linkage to shipment functionalities on the sending facility, printing of transportation documentation, management of receipt functions on the receiving facility, tracking of items under transportation, and so on. Since there is transportation and handling cost involved, the transfer orders can affect the cost price of the items but does not affect the company's revenue since they are only used for company's internal transfers. If the ERP system supports transfer orders, the planned transfer orders are usually a part of the master plan on the same level as planned production or planned purchase orders.

The last function that is found in ERP system to support manufacturing supply chains across units and manufacturing group is intercompany purchase and sales orders. These group internal purchases and sales are in principle the same as purchase and sales toward external parties since they must handle the trade between two independent legal companies. However, larger ERP systems have support for automating the creation, management, and reporting of the intercompany orders between companies in the system. There may be some other supply chain functionalities across companies using the same installation of an ERP system as well, like sharing of basic data and possibilities for doing the master plan across companies.

Hence, this shows that a manufacturing group can use ERP solutions to support the complete manufacturing supply chain for all companies. Figure 9.2 shows a simple example of a OneERP solution where the manufacturing supply chain goes between companies and facilities.

The figure illustrates a simple OneERP solution supporting two companies: "Company X" and "Company Y". "Company X" consists of only a single production facility ("Facility Xa"), while "Company Y" has both a production facility ("Facility Ya") and a distribution facility ("Facility Yb"). The distribution facility uses the ERP system in the same manner as the production facility, but without applying the production module.

For information exchange between the companies they are using purchase and sales orders. (This must be done due to legal reporting for trade between companies.) While the transfer between the facilities in "company Y" is done through transfer orders.

Since this is a "OneERP" solution, the master plan can take the whole manufacturing supply chain into account (we presume that the ERP system supports cross-company master planning). The master plan can therefore calculate a single, interconnected, master plan for the whole manufacturing supply chain. This master plan can then generate planned transfer, production, purchase as well as intercompany sales order to meet the enterprise's commitments toward customer and trading partners.

OPTISTREAM

After buying the resellers in Oslo, Norway and Houston, TX, US, OptiStream had to improve the performance and efficiency of manufacturing supply chain toward markets to achieve the growth that they were looking for. The decision of implementing a OneERP solution was a main enabler in this strategy.

In order to do this, they did some actions. The company in Oslo was incorporated as a part of the production company in Trondheim. There are many reasons for why they did this, but from an ERP system perspective, this allowed them to establish the Oslo-office and its warehouse as a facility in the same company as the production facility in Trondheim. This allowed both the Trondheim plan and the Oslo plan to work as a single unit in the ERP system and to share the same master data, orders, master plans, general ledger, and other functions in the system. The warehouse in the Oslo facility was incorporated as the other warehouses in Trondheim, using transfer order to support the flow of items in their supply chain across Norway.

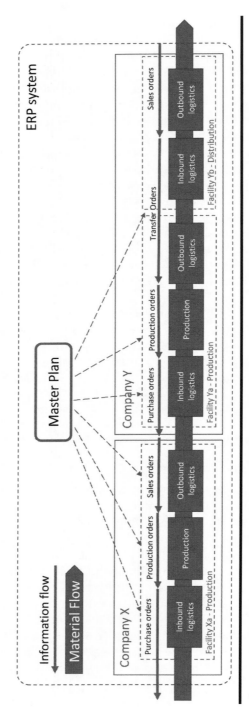

Figure 9.2   The information flow of the ERP system versus the physical flow within a simple manufacturing supply chain.

The Houston facility is in another country, and due to legal restriction OptiStream has no other choice but to establish the US part of the business as a separate company. However, since this company is sited in the same ERP systems as their Norwegian parts, Microsoft Dynamics 365 Supply Chain Management solution has some functions that were used to ease and streamline the supply chain between these subsidiaries. For instance, a common product master was opened for certain items and item information could be shared across companies making it much easier to manage and maintain the item information across company borders. On-hand information can be shared across companies, enabling the US part to check what is in stock in Norway for increased customer service, for example, checking item availability for delivery across company boarders.

Microsoft Dynamics 365 Supply Chain Management allows automated intercompany orders. This means that the staff in Houston can create sales orders on items that are in store in Norway, hence, automatically creating an intercompany purchase order in the US company will automatically create an corresponding sales order in Norway. Furthermore, this ERP application has a cross-company master planning function that allows the master plan to account for both the Norwegian and US company when calculating the supply chain requirements that will improve the manufacturing supply chain coordination significantly. This and other improvements have the potential to make the overall supply chain performance much more efficient than using separate ERP solutions.

In addition to the two operational companies, OptiStream established a holding company in Microsoft Dynamics 365 Supply Chain Management. This allowed them to share and consolidate key financial data seamlessly across the group.

9.4 Setting up an ERP-Enabled Multicompany Manufacturing Supply Chain

The setup of an ERP solution to support a manufacturing supply chain within a multicompany enterprise relies on many interconnected factors, starting with the enterprise's overall strategy. With this we mean if the enterprise has a growth strategy to become an large industrial group, alternatively, if they are more financial driven and want develop companies individually for limited time for reselling or taking public, and so on. The enterprise's strategy gives directions on the ERP strategy, the company structure, and its target markets. These factors again influence how the ERP system should be used to support the manufacturing supply chains.

In the previous chapters we discussed how the ERP systems can be used to support different manufacturing strategies on different product lines in a manufacturing facility. These guidelines for configuring the planning method within a single facility can also be applied when setting up a multicompany solution with manufacturing supply chains that goes across facilities and companies. The setup of each item or item groups in the ERP must be seen in reflection to the targeted market segments their manufacturing supply chain shall support.

Knowing this, the planning methods for replenishment can be found. The difference for setting up a manufacturing supply chain across companies compared to a single facility is to look at the manufacturing supply chain across the facilities and/or companies and then decide the decoupling point and the forecastability and the other factors for setting the item's planning methods in warehouses.

For example, a facility that is manufacturing customized products should apply an CTO or MTO strategy, while another facility that is focusing on standard products in high volumes should consider an MTS strategy. The main challenge in an integrated multicompany supply chain is that these planning methods must play together; a holistic view is required to configure the planning across facilities in a way that ensure efficient flows in the entire supply chain. This allows the enterprise to use the ERP system as a tool for enabling different manufacturing strategies in their manufacturing supply chains across facilities and companies to fulfill their overall business plans.

OPTISTREAM

The production facility in Trondheim is supplying the sales warehouse in Oslo. OptiStream is using the same master plan for both the Trondheim and the Oslo facility. The sales warehouse in Oslo is setup with a few stocked pumps so that they can deliver the most important products to their local customers in a short notice. These items set to use a reorder point (min/max) as a planning policy in the sales warehouse in Oslo. If one of the items in Oslo is getting below its minimum value, the master plan creates a planned transfer from the general warehouse in Trondheim in order to make sure that the stock is being replenished.

If they get an order from a customer in Oslo on a stocked pump that is not stored in the sales warehouse in Oslo, they can create a "direct delivery" from the general warehouse in Trondheim. Since OptiStream Trondheim and OptiStream Oslo are facilities in the same company in Microsoft Dynamics 365 Supply Chain Management, setting the delivering facility and warehouse is as simple as altering the sales order line as illustrated in Figure 9.3. (Facility is termed "site" in Microsoft Dynamics 365 Supply Chain Management.).

The same goes for all standard and special pumps (MTO/ETO products) as well. When a sales order is received in Oslo, the sales order line is set

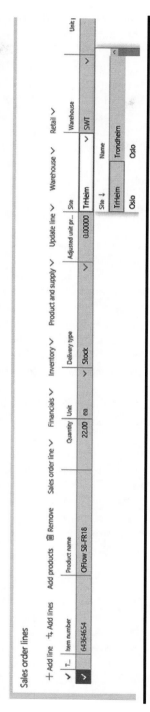

Figure 9.3 Setting facility and warehouse on sales order line in Microsoft Dynamics 365 Supply Chain Management.

on to be delivered from the sales warehouse in Trondheim, and a production order is generated in the same facility to fulfill the commitment.

For the US part it is a bit more complicated. This part of the enterprise setup is a separate company, and therefore, cannot be used to transfer orders to replenish stocked pumps in the sales warehouse in United States since there must be a legal sale and purchase between these independent companies. The lead time is longer due to product labeling and custom rules, and all items through must reach the warehouse in Huston, TX for custom handling and relabeling before going to the customer. Therefore, a large spectrum of stocked pumps is held in the Huston warehouse to keep the lead time down for the US customers. In addition, some of the items that are defined as MTO products in Norway ("standard pumps") are produced in advance and stored in the US warehouse to be able to deliver these products faster.

The warehouse in Houston is set up as min/max controlled, but master planning is triggering intercompany purchase orders to the production facility in Trondheim when replenishment is needed. Microsoft Dynamics 365 Supply Chain Management has quite extensive intercompany supply chain functions that automatically create a sales order in the Trondheim facility when a new purchase order is made in Houston. The replenishment is thereafter either picked from stock or produced from a production order generated from this intercompany enabled sales order line. The setup of the supply chain at OptiStream is summarized in Figure 9.4.

The figure outlines the manufacturing supply chains at OptiStream. OptiStream has three facilities serving different markets. Pumps to customers in middle and north of Norway are sold and sent directly from the production facility in Trondheim. The Oslo office is serving the Norwegian customers in the east and south of the country, where they have established a manufacturing supply chain that goes via the Oslo warehouse for some products and direct from the Trondheim facility on others. While all the pumps that are going to customers in the North American market are transferred via their warehouse in Houston, TX.

9.5 Configuring ERP for Increased Manufacturing Supply Chain Performance

How well an ERP system is supporting a manufacturing supply chain, is often a question of how good the ERP system is setup to support the targeted market. For example, optimizing the reorder point parameters in the ERP system is of less use, when the inventory could be eliminated by using an order-driven planning method on the item. Knowing this, we will propose some general rules on

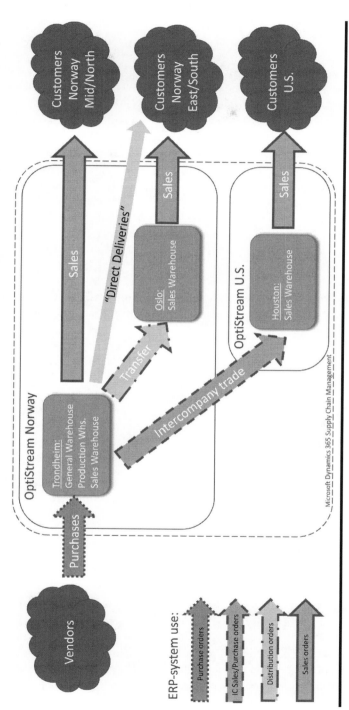

Figure 9.4   The OneERP-enabled manufacturing supply chain setup at OptiStream ASA.

how manufacturing supply chain performance can be improved through application of an ERP system:

- Choose an ERP strategy that fits the enterprise's overall strategy.
  - At minimum, decide between a multiple-ERP versus a OneERP strategy, or if these should be combined in parts of the enterprise.
- Establish an enterprise-wide ERP strategy that is aligned with the enterprise's overall supply chain strategy and its targeted marked.
  - Configure the planning methods and other master data in ERP solution so that the replenishment of each item in each warehouse reflects market the manufacturing supply chains are a part of and should serve.
- Concentrate first on exploiting the core of the ERP systems in manufacturing supply chains, namely managing the purchase, production, transfer, and sales processes in relation to the master planning routines.
  - Start implementing more functions and modules of the ERP system after the basics of the manufacturing supply chain are implemented and functioning well.
  - Seek to simplify the solution and building flexibility in critical places in the manufacturing supply chain by using add-on software where applicable.

9.6 Key Terms

- ERP strategy
- Multiple-ERP strategy
- OneERP strategy
- Transfer order
- Intercompany sales
- Intercompany purchase order

9.7 Chapter Summary

This chapter has shown that an enterprise consisting of several companies can either use a multiple-ERP strategy or a OneERP strategy. Multiple-ERP strategies may be used in enterprises with loosely couplet enterprise structure, while OneERP strategy may typically be used in enterprises where there is high relevance between the companies.

ERP systems for manufacturing can be separated between systems with single-company support targeted for smaller organizations and systems for larger enterprises with multicompany support. Single-company ERP systems for smaller organization can be used in large manufacturing organizations using a multiple-ERP strategy, while ERP systems for larger enterprises are often a choice for OneERP solution.

Setting up an ERP system for a manufacturing supply chains that goes across companies and facilities and in a group is not unlike setting up an ERP facility for a single facility, where the replenishment is dictated through the setting of the planning method on each item and warehouse combination. The difference is that transfer orders should be used between warehouses in different facilities in the same company, while intercompany sales and purchase orders must be used between companies.

The enterprise's overall strategy and the targeted market for the product/items must be considered when setting up an ERP-enabled multicompany manufacturing supply chain. Each manufacturing supply chain is a reflection of the market it should serve, and the configuration of the ERP system must therefore reflect this market correspondingly.

Index

For Product Safety Concerns and Information please contact our EU
representative GPSR@taylorandfrancis.com Taylor & Francis Verlag GmbH,
Kaufingerstraße 24, 80331 München, Germany

Printed and bound by CPI Group (UK) Ltd, Croydon, CR0 4YY
10/05/2025
01866287-0001